HISTORIC SCOTTSDALE
A Life from the Land

By Joan Fudala

Published for the McDowell Sonoran Land Trust

Historical Publishing Network
A division of Lammert Publications, Inc.
San Antonio, Texas

The McDowell Mountains.

PHOTO COURTESY OF TONY NELSSEN © 2000

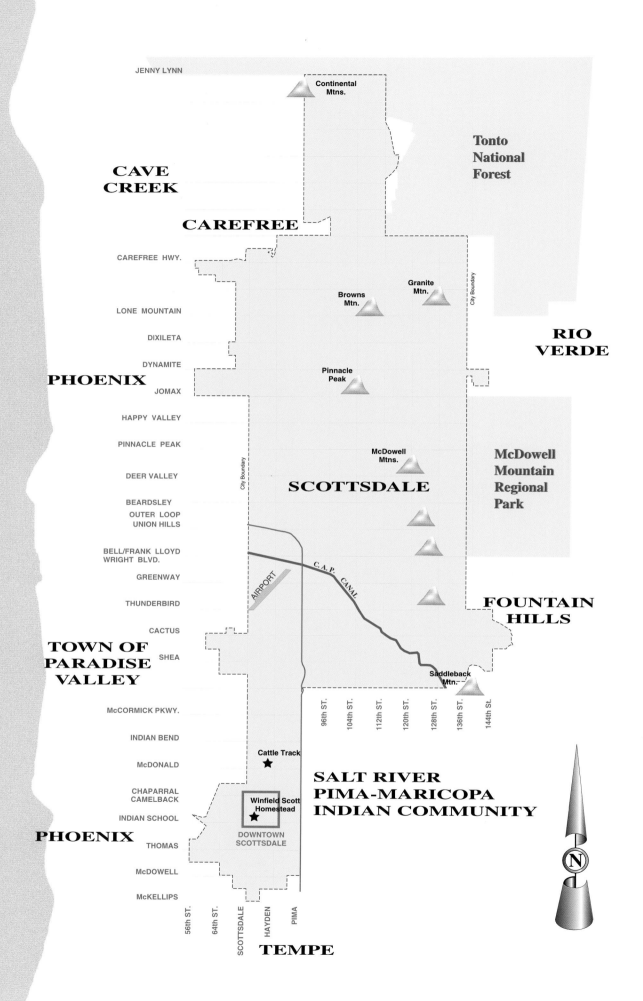

CAVE
CREEK

CAREFREE

Tonto
National
Forest

JENNY LYNN

Continental
Mtns.

CAREFREE HWY.

Browns
Mtn.

Granite
Mtn.

City Boundary

LONE MOUNTAIN

RIO
VERDE

DIXILETA

DYNAMITE

PHOENIX

JOMAX

Pinnacle
Peak

HAPPY VALLEY

PINNACLE PEAK

DEER VALLEY

McDowell
Mtns.

McDowell
Mountain
Regional
Park

SCOTTSDALE

City Boundary

BEARDSLEY
OUTER LOOP
UNION HILLS

BELL/FRANK LLOYD
WRIGHT BLVD.

C.A.P. CANAL

GREENWAY

AIRPORT

THUNDERBIRD

FOUNTAIN
HILLS

CACTUS

TOWN OF
PARADISE
VALLEY

SHEA

Saddleback
Mtn.

McCORMICK PKWY.

96th ST.
104th ST.
112th ST.
120th ST.
128th ST.
136th ST.
144th ST.

INDIAN BEND

McDONALD

Cattle Track
★

SALT RIVER
PIMA-MARICOPA
INDIAN COMMUNITY

CHAPARRAL
CAMELBACK

Winfield Scott
Homestead
★

INDIAN SCHOOL

PHOENIX

DOWNTOWN
SCOTTSDALE

THOMAS

McDOWELL

McKELLIPS

56th ST.
64th ST.
SCOTTSDALE
HAYDEN
PIMA

N

TEMPE

CONTENTS

*Gabe Brooks built Powder Horn Ranch
in 1917 for himself and his family
in the remote desert northeast
of Scottsdale on what is now
East Cactus Road.*
PHOTO COURTESY OF EMMAJEANE BROOKS HARRIS

ISBN: 1-893619-12-5

Library of Congress Card Catalog Number: 00-111864

Historic Scottsdale: A Life from the Land

author:	Joan Fudala
contributing writers for "sharing the heritage":	David M. Eskes
	Lois McFarland

Historical Publishing Network

president:	Ron Lammert
vice president & project coordinator:	Barry Black
project manager:	Wynn Buck
director of operations:	Charles A. Newton, III
administration:	Angela Lake
	Donna Mata
	Dee Steidle
graphic production:	Colin Hart
	John Barr

PRINTED IN SINGAPORE

✧

Avis Read's Stable Gallery was a popular gathering place for artists, residents, and visitors during the 1950s and 1960s. It was located in the Cattle Track area east of Scottsdale Road, north of McDonald Drive.

PHOTO COURTESY OF THE CITY OF SCOTTSDALE

PROLOGUE

History can be arrogant.

The arrogance lies in someone deciding when "history" starts—or ends—and what should be included. I'm not sure how to avoid that perception of arrogance, so when *does* one begin a history about the area now known as Scottsdale, Arizona, circa 2001?

With deepest respect to previous approaches, this history will begin, proceed and end with the most tangible and immortal aspect of Scottsdale—the land. For, as one examines the diverse eras and epochs of our area, every species, every culture, every event and development has been inextricably tied to the Sonoran Desert landscape and eco-system. Although much of this book focuses on the land, it by no means overlooks the people who have made our community a hometown. Author Barry Lopez, in *Arctic Dreams*, states it far better than I: "To look at the land was never to forget the people it contained."

Tens of thousands of people and events make up the fabric of Scottsdale's prehistoric and historic times. Any written history is bound to leave someone or something out; surely this one will. People and events have been chosen for this particular snapshot as representing significant or characteristic milestones in Scottsdale's history. Regrettably, much of what we would consider historical records now were not preserved, perhaps the "victim" of being a young community in a young state—always moving forward, forgetting to look back. If I had a personal wish as you read this book, it would be to ask you to preserve your own family history and photographs, as well as the histories of your business and community organizations, then donate copies to the local archive of your choice. You can create a legacy for your grandchildren and help current and future generations understand Scottsdale's rich heritage.

Scottsdale as a municipality celebrates its fiftieth anniversary of incorporation June 25, 2001. In relative terms, some may view this as a minor milestone for land that has been here 1.8 billion years. However, the McDowell Sonoran Land Trust, in sponsoring this historic look at Scottsdale, hopes that readers will use the fiftieth anniversary milestone to renew their interest in and personal stewardship of our magnificent land, a land which gives us life.

Joan Fudala
Scottsdale resident since 1991

Joe Mowry, Opal, Ruth and Will Ford—like countless Scottsdalians before and since—enriched their lives by relating to the land.

PHOTO COURTESY OF THE SCOTTSDALE HISTORICAL SOCIETY AND J.T. BROWN

THE LAND BEFORE SCOTTSDALE

Land. Sometimes gracious, at times overpowering, always grand…land gives and sustains life in the area we now call Scottsdale. For centuries, plants, animals and humans have depended on, expended and defended this land and its natural attributes. The history of this land began long before people arrived; it began at bedrock, when the land was formed.

From its boulder-stacked mountains in the north and across the foothills to the flat lands in the central and south, Scottsdale's 185 square miles offer a spectacular array of geological features. The most interesting geology is clearly exposed; the hot, dry climate has discouraged vegetation from covering these historic roots.

Scottsdale's location is referenced in various ways: the American Southwest, Sonoran Desert, Central Arizona, Maricopa County, Salt River Valley, Valley of the Sun and within the metropolitan Phoenix area. In geologic terms, Scottsdale is located in the area referred to as Paradise Valley (not to be confused with the Town of Paradise Valley, incorporated in 1961) in the Southern Basin and Range Province of Arizona. Scottsdale's flat land, or basin area, is bordered by the McDowell Mountain range to the east; the Continental Mountain range to the north; the Phoenix Mountain range to the west and the Papago Buttes to the southwest. In some respects Scottsdale is a valley within a valley, its ranges forming natural boundaries between neighboring communities in the larger Phoenix metropolitan area.

According to geologists at Arizona State University, Scottsdale's bedrock—including the McDowell Mountains—was formed approximately 1.8 billion years ago during the Precambrian Era. In comparison, the age of the Earth itself is estimated at 4.5 billion years old. Following continental crust formation (1.65 to 1.8 billion years ago), this entire area would have been well above sea level, several miles higher than the current elevation, and probably mountainous and eroding. The oldest relics in Scottsdale—schist and gneiss rocks in the McDowell Mountains—were produced during this era.

After about a billion years, mountainous Arizona had eroded down to plains. During the Paleozoic Era (200 to 540 million years ago) ocean waters transgressed the area, likely supporting marine and amphibious life. Although there is much evidence of the rocks from the Younger Precambrian and Paleozoic Eras in Northern Arizona at the Grand Canyon, there are no vestiges of these rocks in Scottsdale.

Central Arizona's sedimentary and volcanic rocks began to form during the Mesozoic Era, or between seventy and two hundred million years ago, when tectonic and volcanic activity occurred. Climate and environment during this Era supported amphibian and dinosaur life; evidence of Central Arizona's Jurassic Period dinosaurs has been found as close as the City of Mesa, southeast of Scottsdale. The Mesozoic Era in Central Arizona culminated with the Laramide Orogeny, a mountain-building event forty-five to seventy-five million years ago, during which time Arizona's copper deposits were formed. Uplift, followed by erosion, during the Laramide period erased any record of Paleozoic sediments that may have existed in Central Arizona.

Scottsdale's current topography was created during the Cenozoic Era, which began seventy million years ago. The area was dusted by tuff (volcanic ash) from explosive volcanoes, likely the Superstition Mountains to the southeast of Scottsdale, which exploded about eighteen million years ago. The Scottsdale area itself had volcanic activity, the remnants of which can be clearly seen at either end of the McDowell Sonoran Preserve (thousands of acres preserved in the late 1990s by the citizens and City of Scottsdale, which includes the McDowell Mountains and adjacent desert land in the northern part of the city). The volcanic remains of Browns Mountain to the north and Saddleback Mountain to the southeast are easily recognizable by their black tops, which are comprised of basalt and tuff, or lava rock.

It is believed that during the Basin and Range Disturbance ten to fifteen million years ago, the Paradise Valley area "dropped down," leaving the McDowells as a separate mountain range. Rocks washed down from the surrounding ranges into the valley, creating the alluvial fans of the *bajada*

(pronounced ba-HA-da, an area where multiple alluvial fans merge). Fossilized evidence of animal life present in the Scottsdale area in the Late Pleistocene Epoch (11,200 years ago)— mammoth, primitive horses, tortoise and possibly ground sloth—was unearthed during the construction of the Indian Bend Wash Greenbelt Flood Control Project in the 1970s.

The Scottsdale area gained its semi-arid climate fifteen million years ago when California's Sierra Madre and Sierra Nevada mountain ranges were formed, blocking moist Pacific Ocean air from reaching Arizona and the Sonora region of Mexico. Increased aridity in the late Miocene Epoch approximately eight million years ago led to conditions unique in the world that created the Sonoran Desert, a 100,000 square mile area encompassing Southern Arizona, Southeastern California, Sonora Mexico and Baja Mexico.

The McDowell Mountains are the signature geologic feature of the area around Scottsdale today. Their statuesque and beautiful form is built of volcanically- and metamorphically-produced rocks such as Taliesin quartzite, metamorphosed rhyolite, dacite and metamorphosed basalt (black lava), as well as rocks resulting from the erosion of volcanic rock, such as quartz-mica schist and metamorphosed quartz sandstone. There was also much intrusion of granite, which, when subjected to chemical weathering over millions of years, has produced picturesque boulder features such as Pinnacle Peak, Tom's Thumb, Troon Mountain and the Boulders. The McDowells also split the region into the Paradise Valley to the west (containing Scottsdale) and the Verde Valley to the east.

The Papago Buttes are also a signature and historic landmark bordering the Scottsdale area. They are the remains of a fault block, which likely formed after the Middle Miocene

LAND AND LOCATION STATISTICS

Scottsdale is located in the Northern Hemisphere, North America, United States, Arizona, Maricopa County, Basin and Range region, and is part of the Sonoran Desert.

Longitude & Latitude: 111.93' W, 33.50' N (at Scottsdale Airport)

Elevation
- Highest point: a peak in the Continental Mountains at Scottsdale's northern border, 4,789.6 ft. above sea level
- Lowest point: a point in the bottom of the Indian Bend Wash near McKellips Road, at Scottsdale's southern border, 1,277 ft. above sea level

Size
185.4 square miles within the Scottsdale municipal boundary (as of 2000)

Climate
- Annual average maximum temperature is 85.9 F degrees. Average maximum high in July is 105.5 F degrees; average maximum high in January is 67.0 F degrees. Low humidity, with summer averages of 11-30 percent and winter averages of 33-66 percent
- Average precipitation: 9.32 inches per year, creating a semi-arid climate
- Rainy seasons: typically December-February and July–September. With two rainy seasons, the Sonoran Desert is more lush than any other desert in the world.

Time
Arizona is in the Rocky Mountain time zone and does not observe Daylight Savings Time.

Epoch, fifteen to twenty million years ago. Spherical rock shelters in the Buttes, like Hole in the Rock north of the Phoenix Zoo, have been popular picnic and exploring sites for centuries. Called "taffoni," they were formed when wind and water weathered the rock. Oxidized iron (hematite) in the matrix of the sediment gives the Papago Buttes their reddish color.

Camelback Mountain on Scottsdale's western border with Phoenix and the Town of Paradise Valley is also the eroded remains of a fault block that tilted perhaps twenty-five million years ago. The camel's head and Echo Canyon, like the Papago Buttes, are characterized by sedimentary rock and cavernous weathering. Like the McDowell Mountains, the camel's hump is much older Precambrian granite and schist.

Two types of soil surfaces are common in Scottsdale between the mountain ranges: alluvial fans and pediments. Water carries soil and rock from the mountains to create alluvial fans that extend to the valley floor. Pediments result from desert erosion and are actually flat-lying bedrock at or near the ground surface. Bedrock covered with a thin (five to ten feet deep) veneer of alluvium is clearly visible

north and west of the McDowells, all the way north to the towns of Carefree and Cave Creek. North and east of an area in northern Scottsdale known as Reata Pass (a stop on the 1800s military road, now a restaurant location) is a striking example of a pediment surface, characterized by outcrops, or knobs, of rocks jutting out of the desert floor. Much of the rock throughout Scottsdale is coated with desert varnish, a mineral-rich adhesive dust; without this dark surface, petroglyphs etched into the rocks by prehistoric people would not be so striking in appearance.

Scottsdale's soil has generally evolved from erosion and alluvial deposits. Although the soil on the steep, rocky mountain slopes is thin, it has supported plant and animal life for

✦

Above: Chemical weathering of coarse-grained granite bedrock in a semi-arid environment caused the spectacularly shaped rocks in landmarks such as Pinnacle Peak.
PHOTO COURTESY OF THE AUTHOR

Left: It was the scenic beauty of the area that drew homesteaders like lawyer K.T. Palmer to Pinnacle Peak in 1933. He is shown at his homestead at the northern base of the peak in 1954 with family friend Katharine Arnold (left) and his wife Betty (right).
PHOTO COURTESY OF DEL JEANNE PALMER WEST

CHAPTER I

11

millennia. Deeper, well-drained soil in Scottsdale's basin area has been even more conducive to sustaining plant, animal and human life.

Water has been the key in exploiting the soil. One result of mixing soil and water, however, has caused headaches for the prehistoric Hohokam people and their canal building as well as modern farmers and builders—caliche (pronounced ka-LEE-chee). Over time, the combination of arid climate, seasonal rain and soil with a high level of calcium carbonate has produced this hard, rock-like substance in which sand and gravel have been cemented into a hard-tack sub-surface layer that impedes water penetration, root growth and excavation. Caliche also expands and contracts with varying water amounts, causing manmade surfaces such as foundations, swimming pools and sidewalks built above it to crack.

Natural sources of water have been scarce throughout the eight million years in which the Scottsdale area has been a semi-arid desert. Early plant and animal life depended on seasonal runoff from the mountains, the sporadic presence of mountain springs, or an ability to conserve water. The prehistoric Hohokam people harnessed water by diverting the Salt River through a series of brush dams and canals. They also used springs in the McDowells; remains of their encampments were discovered adjacent to Boulder Pass (at the north end of the McDowells) and Browns Mountain. Since the late 1800s when modern, permanent settlement began in Scottsdale, we have resurrected and improved the Hohokam canal system to divert Salt and Verde river waters and have drilled deep wells into the aquifers to pump groundwater to the surface. In the last twenty years, Scottsdale's growing population has also tapped the Colorado River, nearly three hundred miles

✧

Above: Although it was not officially named "Camelsback" until a U.S. survey of the area was published in 1906, its dromedary-like form began to take shape some 25 million years ago. The camel's head and Echo Canyon, like the Papago Buttes, have sedimentary rock and cavernous weathering. Like the McDowell Mountains the camel's hump is much older Precambrian granite and schist. This early 1900s view looks north to Camelback Mountain across grape orchards.

PHOTO COURTESY OF SRP HERITAGE

Left: North and east of Reata Pass (a historic way station, now the site of a Western-theme restaurant near Pinnacle Peak) is a striking example of a pediment surface, characterized by outcrops, or knobs, of rocks jutting out of the desert floor. This particular feature, called Balanced Rock, is near Granite Mountain; note its size relative to the hiker.

**PHOTO COURTESY OF
MCDOWELL SONORAN LAND TRUST**

CHAPTER I

away. The Central Arizona Project canal and reservoir system brings millions of acre-feet of water annually to Scottsdale. Scottsdale has also begun water reclamation, returning used but treated water to recharge underground natural aquifers.

Minerals were never as precious to Scottsdale as water. During the past two centuries prospectors and speculators have hoped to strike it rich but the land around Scottsdale did not fulfill their dreams. In the early 1900s, a claimant built the Little Dixie Mine on the southeast slope of the McDowells after traces of copper were discovered; no significant commercial use resulted. The Paradise Valley Gold Mine in the McDowells did not pan out, either, although some gold was mined in the late 1800s in the Continental Mountains at Scottsdale's north-

ernmost tip. In 1948, the Glenn Oil Company—backed by numerous hopeful investors—drilled for natural gas near Scottsdale and Bell Roads, but without the success they hoped.

Many current-day Scottsdale residents arriving from the Upper Midwest and the Northwest are accustomed to seeing land formations carved by glaciers and to hunting for fossils in creek beds. These two geologic phenomena are absent in this area. Scottsdale did experience the Ice Age beginning four million years ago, however; the closest glacier was in Flagstaff, Arizona, where temperatures at mountain elevations supported glacial ice formations. Marine-life fossils are scarcer in Scottsdale than elsewhere in the U.S. due to many eras of uplift, erosion and compression in the past 1.8 billion years. If fossils are

✧

Over the centuries, people and plants have relied on the land for life. In recent years, Scottsdale residents have become more aware of the human impact on native plants and animals and have taken a number of steps to help preserve and protect the area's natural assets.

PHOTO COURTESY OF TONY NELSSEN © 2000

found, they are likely from later, larger animals, or may be the result of trade between prehistoric people crossing through this area.

Since humans first passed through the land we now know as Scottsdale, people have imported their favorite plants and animals. At the start of the twenty-first century, it is difficult to know what flora and fauna is, or was, indigenous to Scottsdale's Sonoran Desert environment.

Although plants of many varieties have grown on the land for millions of years, eons of erosion have erased fossil records. The desert trees and shrubs of the thornscrub plant community are thought to date back to the Miocene, some fifteen to twenty million years ago; cacti and succulents are presumed to date back to the Eocene, at least thirty-six million years ago.

The current desert environment formed nine thousand years ago, and most of our modern native plant species appeared about 4,500 years ago. Scottsdale's desert pavement was sparsely vegetated with shrub and cacti since natural water sources were scarce and seasonal rain unpredictable. In the surrounding mountains with slightly cooler temperatures and natural springs, vegetation was more lush.

The creosote bush, common throughout Scottsdale, is among the oldest plants still living on Earth, dating back 11,700 years. The stately saguaro cactus has been evolving for eleven thousand years, including eight thousand years in Southern Arizona. Other indigenous plants with a long history in Scottsdale are ironwood, palo verde, mesquite and acacia trees; yuccas; teddy bear cholla; barrel cactus; ocotillo and bur-sage.

Scottsdale's climate has become hotter and drier in the last thousand years; those plants

that have been able to adapt have survived. During those thousand years, people have had an increasing impact on native plants. For example, it is believed that the prehistoric Hohokam may have over-harvested agave, leading to its decline in the area. In the past one hundred fifty years, man has rerouted natural water sources, developed large parts of the desert, introduced non-native plants and used harmful pesticides, all of which have affected plant life. Botanists today are concerned that large areas of plant habitat are disappearing due to development.

In order to attempt to protect precious native plants unique to the region, especially large cacti and trees, the City of Scottsdale enacted the Native Plant Ordinance in 1981. Further strengthened in 1989 and 2000, the ordinance requires all new construction that affects native plants to submit details of how protected plants will be treated by the project; permits are required to relocate or remove protected plants. Protected cacti include saguaro, barrel, ocotillo and soaptree yucca; trees include whitethorn and catclaw acacia, crucifixion thorn, desert hackberry, foothills palo verde, desert willow, juniper, ironwood, cottonwood, mesquite, scrub oak, sugar sumac and Arizona rosewood. While helpful, the Native Plant Ordinance does not guarantee protection. For example, the ironwood tree takes years to grow to the height the ordinance protects.

A variety of wildlife has feasted on Scottsdale's plant life for thousands of years. Records of evolution here are hard to come by, however. With clues from a few fossil remains, historians surmise that "megafauna," or large mammals, roamed this land at least eleven thousand years ago. The earliest human inhabitants in Central Arizona would have seen and hunted mammoth, mastodons, giant beavers, grizzly bears, prehistoric camels, wild horses, tapirs and large bison. Why are these animals gone? Leading theories blame over-kill by early man, as well as climate change (as the Sonoran Desert became hotter and drier, many of the animals' plant food sources died out).

Large animals shared Scottsdale's land with a variety of reptiles (ancestors of the Gila

monster date back some twenty-three to thirty-six million years), amphibians (the desert
toad species is at least eleven thousand years
old), insects (scorpions have been around
350-400 million years), small mammals (bat-
like creatures have been around fifty million
years) and birds.

As with plants, wildlife in Scottsdale has
varied with the terrain; species found on the
desert floor differ from those in the mountains. Rarely seen today, coatimundi, bighorn

sheep and pronghorn antelope once lived in
Scottsdale's mountains. A century ago the
thick-billed parrot was common in Central
Arizona. Due to its bright red and green colors, it was an easy target for hunters and is
now all but gone. Since 1980, the Arizona
Game and Fish Department has attempted to
restore the parrot with captive breeding programs at places like the Phoenix Zoo.
Researchers are also trying to restore other
bird life to the area, such as peregrine falcons

to Camelback Mountain, whose population declined in the 1950s and 1960s.

After centuries of benign neglect, Scottsdale residents and City officials have become more concerned about the fragility of the community's Sonoran Desert ecosystem. Since the early 1970s, we have paid more attention to groundwater depletion, protecting native plants, air and water quality and preserving thousands of acres of the McDowell Mountains and adjacent desert land from development. Citizen-initiated organizations like the McDowell Sonoran Land Trust are working with government agencies and local colleges and universities to protect and actually restore natural plant and animal habitat. Underlying their efforts is a key question: for nearly ten thousand years, plants, animals and people have lived in this semi-arid land by adapting; now, can the land withstand our adaptations?

VOICES FROM THE PAST:
6000 BC TO 1888 AD

People have lived in this area for an estimated eight thousand years. As today, Scottsdale's prehistoric people presumably came from similar locations—the Northwest, the Midwest, Mexico and Central America. The earliest known people came to this land seasonally, to hunt and forage when plants and animals and the weather were optimal, similar to the pattern of today's seasonal residents, known fondly as "snowbirds."

It is believed that people came to North America at least fourteen thousand years ago, moving down the western United States after crossing the Bering Straits from Asia into Alaska. The earliest occupants left scant record for us to reconstruct and understand their culture. Much of Scottsdale has still not been archaeologically explored. Although remains have been found elsewhere in the Southwest, there is no known evidence that the earliest people, the Paleo-Indians (12,000 to 8000 BC), came to Scottsdale in their quest to hunt wild animals like bison, mammoth, camels and horses at the end of the Ice Age.

In fact, it has only been in the past thirty to forty years that researchers in Scottsdale have discovered evidence of the Archaic time period (8000 BC to 200 AD). Fortunately, much more is known about the River and Upland Hohokam period (300 BC to 1450 AD) in the Scottsdale area. Recent archaeological explorations at sites of new commercial or residential developments—now required by state laws and the City of Scottsdale Archaeological Resources Ordinance—have given us a glimpse of the Protohistoric period (one hundred to six hundred years ago, or 1400-1900 AD). During this later period, researchers believe, the Yavapai people used the McDowell Mountains as a hunting ground, the same land which had previously been home to the Upland Hohokam people and, before that, a temporary home to Archaic hunters and gatherers.

Artifacts found at sites in northern Scottsdale suggest that people in the Archaic period used rock shelters as temporary or seasonal hunting camps. Projectile points made for hunting game by the Archaic people have been found in rock shelters near the former Browns Ranch north of the McDowells, at Pinnacle Peak, near the DC Ranch planned community, along Mayo Boulevard and other areas. Other stone tools indicate that seeds and wild plants were processed during seasonal trips to the area. It is also believed that during the latter part of the Archaic period, traders brought corn from Mexico to Central Arizona, a human cultural evolution from foraging for food to the start of farming.

The Hohokam people were sophisticated canal builders and farmers. [Hohokam is pronounced "Hoo-hoogam" and roughly translated as "those who have gone" in the Akimel Au-Authm, or Pima, language.] The earliest Anglo-American settlers in the Salt River Valley—Civil War veterans such as Jack Swilling—discovered remnants of the Hohokam canal system, which diverted water from the then-flowing Salt River into their nearby croplands and villages.

Hohokam occupied much of the southern part of Scottsdale in farming villages. Their canal system extended west from the Salt River across what is now the Salt River Pima-Maricopa Indian Community, across Pima Road to Hayden Road, and as far north as approximately Indian School Road. When homes and business were built in this area from 1888 through the 1960s and 1970s, little to no archaeological investigation was undertaken. As the Pima Freeway was built during the 1980s and 1990s, however, archaeologists conducted extensive excavations, adding to the knowledge of River Hohokam life, which had been previously studied at sites elsewhere in the Salt River Valley.

Adapting to the land around Scottsdale for more than 1,500 years, Scottsdale's River Hohokam were a settled culture with permanent homes located adjacent to farmland. They began to build canals along the Salt River probably by 800 AD, diverting river water year-round through ditches and brush dams. They used stone hoes to dig an estimated five hundred miles of canals, designed at just the right gradient to keep the water flowing. They lived in villages of clustered brush structures and

Right: Artifacts found at sites in northern Scottsdale suggest Archaic people used rock shelters as temporary or seasonal hunting camps. Projectile points (like the two shown here) used in hunting game have been found in archaeological sites at Browns Ranch, Pinnacle Peak, DC Ranch, Mayo Boulevard and other areas.

PHOTO COURTESY OF GREG WOODALL

Below: A by-product of development in Scottsdale is increased knowledge of prehistoric people who traveled through or lived on the land. Much of the southern, or "original" part of Scottsdale remains unexplored, however, laws now require archaeological surveys be conducted before undisturbed land is developed. Private firms team with Arizona State University faculty and students and community volunteers to carefully excavate archaeological sites throughout Scottsdale. One of the largest sites discovered has been Pinnacle Peak Village, formerly known as the Herberger site, first studied in 1963, then extensively studied in 1987-88.

PHOTO COURTESY OF GREG WOODALL

grew a variety of crops (corn, beans, cotton and squash). In addition to farming, they also hunted small and large game, and processed food from wild plants and cacti. Life was not all work; they created beautiful pottery and jewelry, conducted ceremonies and enjoyed sports (there is evidence of ball courts at numerous sites). They were also trading partners with other Hohokam cultures to the south and north, and with the indigenous people of Mexico, obtaining luxury items such as copper bells and seashells. Pueblo Grande Museum in Phoenix has preserved a Hohokam village and ceremonial site that is open for public viewing.

The Upland Hohokam people were less settled than the River Hohokam, who were tied to their crops. Although they did live in villages, such as the extensive Pinnacle Peak Village site studied since the 1960s at the northern base of the McDowells, the Upland Hohokam were

more mobile. Lacking a nearby river for irrigation, they depended on mountain springs and seasonal runoff for limited farming of crops such as corn. They gathered native plants for food—saguaro fruit, mesquite and palo verde seeds and agave—and hunted small and large game in the mountains (rabbits, rodents, mule deer and bighorn sheep). They lived in pit homes with walls and roofs of mud-caked brush. Evidence at the Pinnacle Peak Village site as well as the Browns Ranch and Dixie Mine sites shows that the Upland Hohokam also pursued other activities—making and trading for jewelry and stone objects, and creating rock art, or petroglyphs.

What happened to the Hohokam? One theory is that major flooding of the Salt and Gila Rivers in the mid-1300s destroyed their brush dams and canals. Several decades of drought followed these catastrophic floods, making subsistence farming impossible and causing them to migrate and change their culture.

Alternatively, some archaeologists and historians believe disease brought to the New World by Europeans spread among the North American indigenous people, wiping out many unprotected populations. We don't really know why Hohokam evidence is absent after about 1450 AD; the Akimel Au-Authm (also known as the Pima) and Tohono O'odham (also known as the Papago), however, are likely descendants of the Hohokam.

Following the Hohokam, the Yavapai lived in the McDowell Mountains, taking up many of the former village and rock shelter sites previously used by Hohokam and Archaic cultures. It is believed that they came from the mountains north of the Scottsdale area and lived along the Verde River only during cooler months. They were hunters and gatherers while they camped in the northern reaches of Scottsdale. The Yavapai were still traveling to the northern areas of this land when the Spaniards and, later, the U.S. Army arrived.

The Hohokam people inhabited the land now known as the Salt River Valley and Scottsdale from approximately 300 BC to 1450 AD. The Hohokam people living in villages nearest the Salt River were sophisticated canal builders and farmers. Those living in the McDowell Mountains and far away from the flowing river depended more on native plants and wild game, although they did cultivate small crops near mountain springs.

ART COURTESY OF SRP HERITAGE

CHAPTER II

23

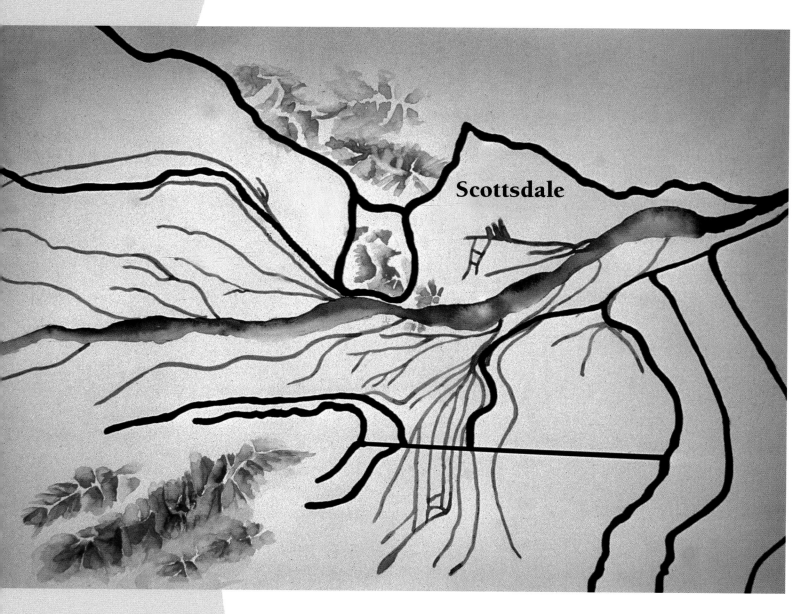

Scottsdale

The peaceful Yavapai served as scouts for the Army, and in 1903, the former Army outpost Fort McDowell was turned over to the Yavapai as a reservation, now called the Fort McDowell Mohave-Apache Indian Community.

After Columbus "discovered" the New World in 1492 for Spain, many Spanish explorers and Catholic missionaries traveled westward through Mexico and up into Arizona. Fray (Father) Marcos de Niza entered Maricopa County in the early 1500s, though it is unlikely he came as far north as Scottsdale. In 1540, the famous explorer Coronado claimed all lands of what is now the Southwestern United States for Spain, so regardless of whether Spaniards actually visited the land that is now Scottsdale, the area was under Spanish influence from the mid-1500s to the early 1800s. Following Mexico's independence from Spain in 1821, all of Arizona was a part of Mexico. The U.S. acquired Central and Northern Arizona (north of the Gila River) with the Treaty of Guadalupe Hidalgo, which ended the Mexican-American War in 1848, and in 1853 the U.S. acquired Southern Arizona through the Gadsden Purchase.

Although we have no detailed record of the period between the 1500s and the mid-1800s, we know that the Akimel Au-Authm, who believe they are descendants of the Hohokam, were in the Scottsdale area. They, too, used irrigation systems to water their crops of corn, beans, squash and melons. They also grew cotton, which the women wove into cloth, and were accomplished basket weavers.

The first Anglo-Americans to venture west into Central Arizona were the mountain men in the 1820s—folklore figures like Kit Carson and James Ohio Pattie. They were primarily hunters and trappers, and considered the Sonoran beaver pelt a valuable commodity, as beaver hats were the fashion rage in the eastern U.S. and Europe. It is unknown if the mountain adventurers entered the boundaries of what became Scottsdale, but the pelts and stories they took back East from the Salt and Gila Rivers created a rugged mystique about Arizona that endures.

Next came the soldiers and miners. The U.S. Army sent troops to Prescott, Tucson, Fort Apache in the White Mountains and other encampments in Arizona. The army was here to protect the newly acquired land and its small but growing number of residents and businesses from attack by indigenous people who had been living here for centuries and were defending their land. Prospectors headed to the California Gold Rush of 1848 also discovered Central Arizona; some never made it to California, others turned back to Arizona after going bust in the Golden State. The hardy miners tried their hand at discovering mineral riches in Arizona mountains, finding some success in nearby Cave Creek and eventually moving east into the Continental Mountains at what is now Scottsdale's northernmost border. Although not a huge bonanza, Gold Hill produced the most ore. Local mining tapered off by 1900.

The Civil War had several impacts on the area that would become Scottsdale two decades later. First, after Arizona was briefly claimed by the Confederacy in 1862,

Opposite and below: Between approximately 800 and 1450 AD the Hohokam built nearly 500 miles of canals, siphoning Salt River water to their farmlands. Hand-dug with stone hoes, the irrigation ditches may have provided water to a population of as many as 50,000 people. After being abandoned by the Hohokam in the fifteenth century, the canals fell to ruin until 1867, when ex-Confederate soldier Jack Swilling recognized their potential. Through his Swilling Irrigation and Canal Company, many of the canals were re-dug, and by 1868 were irrigating the first modern crops in what is now Phoenix. In the map on the facing page, black lines represent today's canals; gray lines depict Hohokam canals. In the map below, light blue lines denote today's canals.

MAPS COURTESY OF SRP HERITAGE

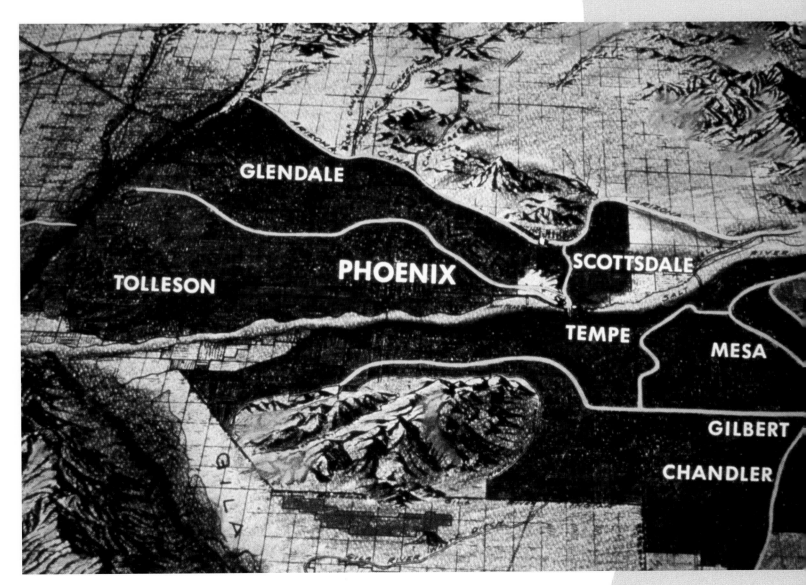

CHAPTER II

25

President Lincoln made it an official U.S. territory in 1863. Second, after the Civil War ended in 1865, Camp McDowell opened east of the McDowell Mountains near present-day Fountain Hills, bringing army troops and civilian suppliers across northern Scottsdale enroute to the desert fort from Camp Whipple in Prescott. Evidence of the army road remains near Reata Pass, Granite Mountain and Browns Ranch. Civil War veterans, seeing

✦

Above: The Upland Hohokam in the McDowell Mountains lived in pit homes with walls and roofs of mud-caked brush. Little was known of their lifestyle until a large village was discovered at the north end of the McDowells in the early 1960s and excavated in 1987-88.

PHOTO COURTESY OF JERRY AND FLORENCE NELSON

Right: The Hohokam living in and near Scottsdale created a wide variety of pottery, figures and jewelry from natural substances. Buried in "trash mounds" or in their abandoned homes and rock shelters for centuries, much has been discovered in the last half of the twentieth century as Scottsdale's land has been developed. It is Pre-Columbian art at its finest.

PHOTO COURTESY OF JERRY AND FLORENCE NELSON

HISTORIC SCOTTSDALE

the Salt River Valley and its potential to provide crops and livestock to Camp McDowell (later called Fort McDowell), put down roots. Jack Swilling formed the Swilling Irrigating and Canal Company and revitalized the ancient canal system, as the new town of Phoenix was rising up from Hohokam ashes. Finally, with the country at peace, Western exploration restarted in earnest, bringing more adventurers and fortune-seekers to the Salt River Valley.

Aided by the federal Homestead and Desert Land acts and the railroad's arrival in Central Arizona, within fifteen years of the end of the Civil War, the Salt River Valley was home to the boomtowns of Phoenix (1866), Tempe (1871) and Mesa (1878).

About that time, the U.S. government also established Indian reservations throughout the states and territories; on June 14, 1879, President Rutherford B. Hayes created the Salt River Pima-Maricopa Indian Community adjacent to what would become Scottsdale nine years later. The original Executive Order creating the Salt River Pima-Maricopa Indian Community encompassed a much larger territory—that of the new towns of Phoenix, Mesa and Tempe. Anglo-American settlers protested

that they had already laid claim to the land, established homes and opened businesses, so the Executive Order was amended to reflect only the present 52,600 acres of land now occupied by the Salt River Pima-Maricopa Indian Community.

As more people moved to the Salt River Valley, they devised ways of taming the harsh environment of the Sonoran Desert to create a

comfortable life for themselves and their families. Midwest railroad excavator William J. Murphy, lured to the Salt River Valley by early civic leaders, built the Arizona Canal between 1883 and 1885. The Arizona Canal was the first to follow a route other than those of earlier Hohokam canals. Murphy's canal had a tremendous impact on future growth by helping to assure a water supply to nearby farms. Limited electrical service came to Phoenix in 1886 with the founding of the Phoenix Illuminating Gas & Electric Company (a forerunner of Arizona Public Service). The Southern Pacific Railroad instituted branch line service to Phoenix on July 4, 1887, with the arrival of the Maricopa, Phoenix and Salt River Railroad. Later, in 1895, the Santa Fe Railroad linked the Valley to Northern

✧

Above: These projectile points, found by archaeologists in the northern area of Scottsdale, were likely used to hunt game during seasonal visits by the Yavapai people.
PHOTO COURTESY OF GREG WOODALL

Right: After the Civil War ended in 1865, Camp McDowell (later named Fort McDowell) opened, bringing army troops and civilian suppliers across northern Scottsdale enroute to the desert fort from Camp Whipple in Prescott, Arizona. Evidence of the army road is near Reata Pass, Granite Mountain and Browns Ranch. The fort, the mountain range, a major east-west street in the area and many other landmarks and facilities bearing the name McDowell were named for Major General Irvin McDowell, the commanding general at the San Francisco, California, headquarters that governed the U.S. Army posts in Arizona. Ironically, General McDowell may have visited his namesake fort only once or twice, but his name is well commemorated.
PHOTO FROM THE COLLECTION
OF JEREMY ROWE, MESA, ARIZONA

HISTORIC SCOTTSDALE
28

Arizona. The railroads made supplies such as lumber for construction obtainable, spurring further commercial and residential growth.

During a visit to Phoenix at the invitation of City officials in February 1888, U.S. Army Chaplain Winfield Scott saw the vast agricultural riches and potential of the Salt River Valley. His skills as a promoter were well known; that's why he'd been asked to visit the Valley. Early Valley civic leaders hoped he would spread the word about the opportunities in the Salt River Valley during his travels. Scott was so impressed that he invested in the land for himself.

On July 2, 1888, under the provisions of the federal Desert Land Act of 1877, Scott and his wife Helen made a down payment on 640 acres at Section 23, Township 2 North, Range 4 East, the Gila and Salt River Base and Meridian, Maricopa County, Arizona. The Scotts paid $2.50 an acre for the parcel, and it was a wise action. The nearly-completed Arizona Canal crossed Scott's property on the northwest corner, ensuring access to water for irrigating future crops. The canal would surely attract other settlers, too. Today, the humble beginnings of world-renowned Scottsdale can hardly be imagined at the site of the former Scott homestead, which was located between Indian School, Scottsdale, Chaparral and Hayden Roads.

Before he occupied the land, Chaplain Scott visited the Chief of the Salt River Pima-Maricopa Indian Community to ask his permission to settle nearby. This began a life-long friendship, based on mutual respect between the Scotts and the people of the Salt River Pima-Maricopa Indian Community.

Because he was still on active duty in the Army, Scott returned to his post at Angel Island near San Francisco, but sent his brother George Washington Scott to occupy the land and begin planting citrus and other crops. George Scott thus became the first Anglo-American resident of what would be named Scottsdale a few years later.

Homesteaders Make a Town: 1888 - 1920

Timing is everything, and so is location; in both regards, Winfield Scott was "spot on." When the chaplain's homestead papers were filed in the summer of 1888, conditions were perfect for starting a new settlement in the Salt River Valley. William J. Murphy had nearly completed the Arizona Canal that ran through the northwest corner of Scott's section. The Southern Pacific Railroad's branch line service into Phoenix was just one year old, bringing in much needed supplies and more settlers. Phoenix and Tempe had mercantiles and other necessities to support the growing population. It was still life on the frontier, and opportunities for hardworking individuals seemed endless.

George Scott, Winfield's brother, got right to work, clearing the land of greasewood brush, or creosote, and other desert growth, then planting the citrus trees that the chaplain was certain would prosper in this climate. Winfield meanwhile obtained a new posting and moved from the San Francisco area to Fort Huachuca, Arizona. He took frequent leaves to help his brother work the new ranch. They also hired farmers from the Salt River Pima-Maricopa Indian Community, long-experienced in cultivating the desert, to help them tend the fields.

Their citrus and other crops, though requiring much hard work and irrigation water, were successful from the beginning. Winfield, the quintessential promoter, took baskets of each new harvest—oranges, peanuts, raisins, peaches—to the *Phoenix Herald* newspaper offices. He also spoke about the opportunities in the Salt River Valley during his frequent travels throughout the U.S. on Army and personal business.

Within a few years, Scott had neighbors. The Utleys of Rhode Island, the Blounts of Illinois, the Haydens of Missouri, the Elliotts of Kansas City, the Underhills of New York, the Titus family, the Kings, the Taits, the Ruhls, the Wards and others bought land near Scott's ranch and began the arduous task of starting a new life in the Sonoran Desert. These settlers, despite coming from far-flung hometowns, had much in common. By and large, the new settlement was attracting educated, hardworking, Christian families who had an enthusiasm for cultivating the land. Many came because a family member's poor health required a dry, warm climate for convalescence. Together they became a close-knit community, sharing their bounty and hardships and creating a wholesome, family-oriented, temperate environment.

Albert G. Utley purchased a section of land just south of Scott's and planned to make it a 40-acre townsite, subdivided for homes, businesses and other necessities. He filed a townsite plan with Maricopa County, naming the town Orangedale to salute the area's significant new industry. He promptly changed the name on the townsite filing, however, to honor Winfield Scott for Scott's role in selecting and creating a superb setting for the community. The name "Scotts-Dale" was first officially used in 1894.

The first homes in Scottsdale were tent houses. Lumber was a precious commodity that had to be brought in by train; the few local trees were not suitable and there was no lumber mill. To supplement their tent homes, the early settlers learned from their neighbors on the Salt River Pima-Maricopa Indian Community how to construct ramadas out of brush and poles. After getting their crops in and becoming more established, early Scottsdale families started to replace their canvas and boards with more permanent homes of adobe.

Much of their living was in the open air, which including sleeping out under the stars during the summer months, often wrapping themselves in wet sheets to experience evaporative cooling at its most basic level. With electrical service in Scottsdale still thirty years away, they depended on coal oil lamps for lighting and wood-burning stoves for cooking and occasional heating. They placed "desert coolers" in the shade of their ramadas. These burlap-covered crates, evaporatively cooled by water dripping constantly, kept the butter fresh. They also hung burlap-covered ollas full

✧

In 1910 George and Mary Alice Cavalliere opened a blacksmith shop in the farming community of Scottsdale. They had wanted to locate in the heart of town, but the townsfolk, wary of the noise and smell of a blacksmith shop, asked them to move to the outskirts—then Second Street and Brown Avenue. Their first shop, made of tin, was a hub of activity—horse-shoeing, repair of farm equipment, even the site of frequent after hours boxing matches. In 1920 they rebuilt the shop in more permanent adobe.

ARTWORK COURTESY OF THE SCOTTSDALE CHAMBER OF COMMERCE, WHICH RECEIVED THE ORIGINAL ART AS A GIFT FROM THE ARTIST WESLEY SEGNER

of water that stayed cool for drinking through the same evaporative effect.

Winfield Scott retired from the army in 1893, devoting his full attention to developing new crops at his ranch and promoting the new community as a great place to live, farm and recuperate. He and his wife Helen also became leaders in the Valley's growing community of faith, starting the Arizona Baptist Foundation. Scott and canal-builder William J. Murphy are credited with launching the citrus industry in the Valley; by 1900 irrigated citrus groves occupied thousands of acres.

Scott and his fellow Scottsdale farmers were successful in growing a wide range of crops: barley, oats, wheat and alfalfa; grapes, figs, plums, pears, nectarines, peaches; potatoes and sweet potatoes; peanuts and almonds; oranges, limes, lemons and grapefruit. Scottsdale raisins were said to rival any available in the marketplace. In addition to crops, the early settlers around the Scottsdale

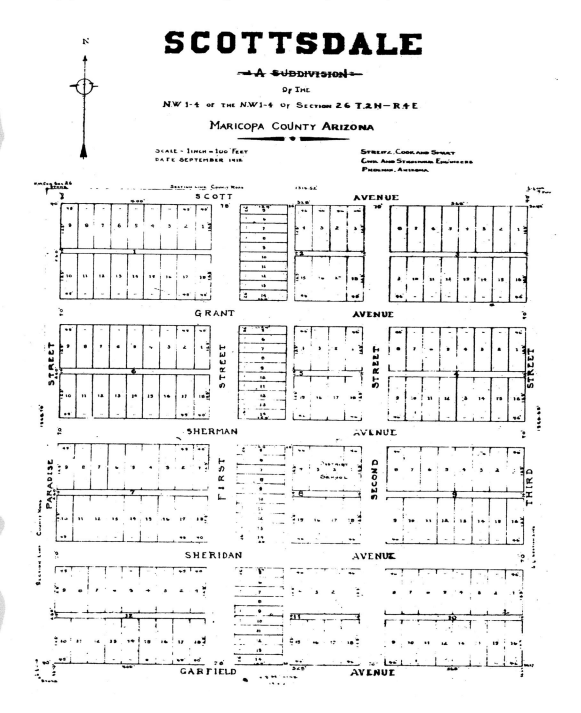

townsite raised dairy cows, chickens and other animals, at first for their own use, then expanding their herds and flocks for commercial farming.

It was during this time in the late 1800s that a few brave homesteaders ventured north of the fledgling townsite to establish cattle ranches in the foothills of the McDowell Mountains. With no irrigation that far north and a scarce number of mountain springs, water was a limiting factor in early cattle ranching "up north." Grazing land, however, seemed endless. Frank Frazier was one of the earliest homesteaders on record; his land patent was located on the western foothills of the McDowells (near the present day location of DC Ranch), where a natural spring now bearing his name provided some water. When he married Mattie Hill in 1898, the townsfolk of Scottsdale came up to serenade the newly-

weds with guitars and mandolins. The Ochoas were another early ranching family in the northern foothills of the McDowells.

Even farther removed from Scottsdale's initial townsite, in an area now located at the city's northernmost border, prospectors and businessmen were trying their hand at mining. Nearby Cave Creek had been the site of several successful mines since the 1870s, and the quest for mineral riches moved east into the foothills of the Continental Mountains. Mining claims in the Gold Hill Mining Cluster produced colorful names like Blue Boy, White Eagle, New Hope, Legal Tender, Raven and Davis. They did not turn Scottsdale into a mining center like Wickenburg, Bisbee or Jerome, but the settlements and mining camps were characteristic of the late nineteenth century/early twentieth century mining boom which occurred throughout the Arizona Territory and the western United States.

By 1896, there were enough families with children in and around the new Scottsdale townsite to warrant a school of their own. Winfield Scott, John Tait and Frank Titus petitioned the Maricopa County School Superintendent, and District 48 was created, the first official recognition for the new town called "Scotts-Dale." Once approved, the town gathered for a school-raising, erecting a wooden building in one day to serve as classroom, ecumenical place of worship and community gathering place. Mrs. Alza Blount was the first teacher; Scott frequently lectured on

Left: Advertisements like this one, which ran in the January 1914 issue of Arizona—the New State Magazine, urged people to move west to Scottsdale, saying "Come where the earth will produce greater crops; where 5 acres will make you independent." At $100 to $250 an acre, Scottsdale's land attracted many new farm families.

Below: Clara Coldwell, shown here with a group of friends, and her husband Charles were typical of Scottsdale's early farm families. They moved from Minnesota to Scottsdale in 1906 and homesteaded 40 acres for a dairy farm on the southwest corner of McDowell and Scottsdale Roads, later location of Papago Plaza. Charles' sister, Sarah Coldwell Thomas, had already put down roots in Scottsdale in 1899.

PHOTO COURTESY OF DR. JOE CARSON SMITH

his Civil War experiences. In ten years, Scottsdale outgrew its first schoolhouse, and a permanent, state-of-the-art brick school was built in 1909. The entire community turned out for the new school's dedication, held on Winfield Scott's 73rd birthday, February 26, 1910.

Scottsdale residents had to journey by horse and buggy into Phoenix or Tempe for supplies and mail services until 1897 when J. L. Davis opened a general store and post office at what is now the southwest corner of Brown Avenue and Main Street. This was the town's first retail establishment; the new post office also officially put Scottsdale "on the map."

That same year the Howard Underhills built a home at the northwest corner of what is now Indian School and Scottsdale Roads, complete with extra rooms to rent to winter guests. Called Oasis Villa, the Underhill home gave birth to both the tourism and health care industries in Scottsdale. The Scotts had welcomed visitors to their tent house from the beginning; "friends of friends" were always staying in their home or on their property. In fact, most Scottsdale pioneers took in sick family members for long, recuperative visits, or let family and friends from colder climates pitch a tent on their property for the winter.

By 1910, tourism grew a bit more upscale when Ralph Murphy, son of canal-builder William Murphy, opened the Ingleside Club at Indian School Road and 56th Street near the Arizona Falls. Guests would often stay for the entire winter season, enjoying desert adventures, elegant picnics at Echo Canyon on Camelback Mountain and croquet on the lawn. Ingleside also boasted Scottsdale's first golf course—nine holes on mostly oiled-down dirt.

One of the inn's guest families, Indiana Governor Thomas Marshall (later to become United States vice president to Woodrow Wilson) had a Scottsdale tie. His wife was the former Lois Kimsey, daughter of William and Elizabeth Kimsey, who moved here in 1915. The Marshalls liked the area, and built a home across the street from Lois' parents on Indian School Road.

Making a living in the desert required lots of sweat equity and ingenuity. But it was not all drudgery. This collegial group of early residents celebrated every holiday in a big way. Families gathered in the Scott's grove of shade trees to observe Washington's Birthday and Fourth of July. On Thanksgiving 1899 all of Scottsdale's residents took a picnic to Hole in the Rock in the Papago Buttes.

Winfield Scott himself played Santa at the community Christmas celebration in the schoolhouse. The Underhills organized youth activities such as the Scottsdale Riding Club and the Christian Endeavor Society.

Scottsdale residents were interested in the arts and culture, and welcomed artists to their new community. Walter and Helen Smith, who arrived in 1903 and were married by

Chaplain Scott in his shady grove, were musicians. Marjorie Thomas, a talented artist, arrived in 1909 from New England and opened the first art studio in Scottsdale.

Scottsdalians gathered weekly for non-denominational church services in the schoolhouse. In friendship with their neighbors the Salt River Pima-Maricopa Indian Community, J. L. Davis and George Blount helped build a Christian church on the reservation; that congregation, now the Salt River United Presbyterian Church, celebrated its 100th anniversary in September 2000. All of these events were alcohol free; Scottsdale residents were so strongly opposed to drinking that they voted for Prohibition as early as 1897 and formed the Arizona Territory's first Anti-Saloon League. Many activities of the Women's Christian Temperance Union took place in Scottsdale.

In the late 1800s and early 1900s water was the key to quality of life as well as the economy in Scottsdale and the Salt River Valley. The Arizona Canal was the main source of irrigation water for Scottsdale, and a whole economic "power structure" evolved from the expanding water system. *Zanjeros* (hired water minders and gatekeepers) controlled and guarded the gates leading from canals to individual farm and ranch lands and managed water flow among the customers of a designated area. A key water job near Scottsdale was the zanjero position at the new Arizona Cross-Cut Canal, which came with a house for the operator's family and the area's only telephone.

In order to more effectively pursue large scale water reclamation and irrigation projects, the Salt River Valley Water Users Association (SRVWUA) organized in February 1903, the first of its kind in the nation. Federal help obtained through the Reclamation Act of 1902 allowed construction to begin on the Granite Reef Dam (east of Scottsdale on the Salt River) and the Theodore Roosevelt Dam, (northeast of Scottsdale in the Tonto Valley). When completed in 1908 and 1911, these dams and their reservoirs provided a year-round water supply to the growing

agricultural economy of the Valley and Scottsdale. Farmers did not have to depend on brush dams to divert the waters of the Salt River, a great improvement, since these temporary dams had been frequently wiped out during floods caused by heavy winter or summer rains. In addition to government and quasi-government programs implemented to provide irrigation water, several private efforts were also initiated during this period. One of the most publicized was the Verde Canal, which promised investors it would irrigate the Paradise Valley north of Scottsdale with water flowing through its canal from the Verde River. It was partially built, but never operated. Vestiges of its route are still visible north of WestWorld, east of Pima Road.

Canal and dam construction projects brought many newcomers to the Valley and Scottsdale. George and Mary Alice Cavalliere came from Santa Barbara, California, when his

✧

More farms and more people put more demands on the Valley's water supply by 1900. In 1903 the Salt River Valley Water Users Association formed to manage and maintain canals, and later dams, that had been purchased or constructed by the federal government as part of its Western reclamation programs. This photo shows the continuing work done to maintain and enlarge the Arizona Canal, which cut through Scottsdale. Canal work created jobs, which attracted many new individuals and families to Scottsdale.
PHOTO COURTESY OF SRP HERITAGE

Right: The new Arizona Cross-cut Canal was built in 1912 by the Salt River Valley Water Users Association. It branched off from the Arizona Canal near 64th Street and crossed Papago Park before dropping into pipes to the Crosscut Hydro-electric Generating Station south of Washington Street. Construction of the Crosscut Canal paved the way for the generation of electric power on the canals without negatively impacting the flow of vital irrigation water. Electricity (at a mere 25 cycles) finally came to Scottsdale in 1919, with the Scottsdale Light and Power Company buying power from the Water Users Association station at Arizona Falls.

PHOTO COURTESY OF THE SCOTTSDALE PUBLIC LIBRARY

Below: Using their land as collateral, farmers who had formed the Salt River Valley Water Users Association in 1903 got a loan from the federal government to construct the Roosevelt Dam. The dam honored President Theodore Roosevelt, with whom Arizonans had served proudly in the Rough Riders of the Spanish-American War. Roosevelt, indicated in the photo by the white arrow, dedicated the dam himself in elaborate ceremonies in 1911. Towering 284 feet high and 723 feet across, at the time it was the world's tallest masonry dam, and likely still is. Combined with Granite Reef Dam, finished in 1908, the Roosevelt Dam assured a more constant and reliable water supply for farmers in the Salt River Valley, including Scottsdale.

PHOTO COURTESY OF SRP HERITAGE

brother, a Phoenix blacksmith, told him the Arizona Canal needed blacksmiths. After the canal project was complete, they moved their canal-side mobile "sled home" to Scottsdale, and opened up a blacksmith shop at Second Street and Brown Avenue in 1910. The shop was popular; farmers brought in their equipment for repair, boxing matches were held there for entertainment at night, and in later years "Cavie" created works of art from iron on his forge to adorn resorts and homes. In 1920 the Cavallieres replaced their tin shop with one built of adobe; the Cavalliere family was still producing ornamental iron in the same building nine decades later.

With a more secure water supply and a booming agricultural economy, a new crop became more important in Scottsdale and the Valley—cotton. Around 1914, Scottsdale farmers began planting cotton, and again were successful with good harvests. Each year more of Scottsdale's land was devoted to raising cotton. During World War I, when supplies of cotton from other nations were subject to embargo, the demand for the Valley's long staple—or Pima—cotton increased.

Scottsdale lost its founder and consummate promoter in October 1910 when Winfield Scott died at the age of 73. By the time of his death, he had seen his oasis in the desert blossom and take hold. The population of the townsite alone was well over one hundred, and

in adjacent areas, several hundred more. The town had a good school, successful farms and ranches, a strong community spirit and the beginnings of tourist and health care trades.

Although Scott was the foremost community patriarch in its early years, he was not alone in providing community leadership or economic direction. Among the new arrivals to Scottsdale of 1904 was the E.O. Brown family of Janesville, Wisconsin, which was to play a significant role in continuing the development of business and quality of life in the desert farm town. Shortly

✧

Above, left: Children visiting DC Ranch could anticipate many adventures, from riding horses to swimming in the cattle tank. Here, Merle (Mrs. E.E.) Brown cools off with her four children and their friend.

PHOTO COURTESY OF THE ALVIN "COTTON" BROWN FAMILY

Above, right: Cattle were driven from the Phoenix railroad freight yards right through the town of Scottsdale to DC Ranch. In the spring, the cattle were rounded up and brought back through Scottsdale enroute to the Tovrea Stockyards, located east of what is now Phoenix Sky Harbor Airport.

PHOTO COURTESY OF THE ALVIN "COTTON" BROWN FAMILY

Below, left: By the early 1950s, the cattle industry in Scottsdale was in decline. George Thomas drove the last herd of cattle down Scottsdale Road in 1952, signaling the end to a colorful authentic cowboy era.

PHOTO COURTESY OF JEAN THOMAS SCOTT AND THE SCOTTSDALE HISTORICAL SOCIETY

Below, right: "Chicken Henry" was the legendary DC Ranch roundup cook. According to E.O. Brown, grandson of ranch founder E.O. Brown and frequent participant in roundups, the thought of Henry's beef jerky gravy still makes his mouth water many decades later.

PHOTO COURTESY OF E.O. BROWN

after arriving in Scottsdale, Brown partnered with his sister-in-law Sarah Ellen Coldwell Thomas in operating the general store started by J. L. Davis. He also began raising cotton and sponsored families from Mexico who wanted to work in the Arizona Territory and raise their families. Brown helped found Scottsdale's first electric company (with William Kimsey and Charles Miller) in 1918, built the first cotton gin in 1920 and owned and operated the Scottsdale Water Company. When his first wife Mary Jane died, he married Mary Graves, who continued to operate the Graves Guest Ranch for visitors and convalescents.

Brown also began accumulating land north of Scottsdale. He and partners established a cattle ranch in 1916 that eventually spread from Bell Road on the south, to Lone Mountain Road on the north, Pima Road on the west and the McDowells on the east, encompassing 44,000 acres (only 23,000 acres, however, were actually deeded to the ranch). The ranch was known as DC Ranch (Desert Camp, or Dad's Camp). They bought cattle from Mexico, which came up by rail into Phoenix. Whether bringing new cattle from the train depot, or taking cattle to the Tovrea stockyards (east of what is now Phoenix Sky Harbor Airport) for slaughter, Brown's cattle drives created Scottsdale's cowboy legends.

Brown's nephew, and later partner, George Thomas ran the ranch; Thomas and his wife Vada lived on land they homesteaded within the ranch area. Harvey Noriega was the ranch caretaker; some say he was the inspiration for Scottsdale's official city seal, created by Gene Brown Pennington, which depicts a cowboy on a bucking horse. "Chicken Henry," a cowboy of African-American heritage, was the legendary camp cook. The route between the Phoenix rail-

Top: Cowboys and ranch hands came from all over the U.S. and Mexico. Many lived in the bunkhouse on the ranch.
PHOTO COURTESY OF E.O. BROWN

Middle, left: DC Ranch (for Desert Camp or Dad's Camp), also known as Browns Ranch, represents one of the largest and longest-operated cattle ranches in what is now Scottsdale. Established in 1916 by E.O. Brown and partners, the ranch continued to operate into the 1950s run by his eldest son, E.E. Brown, with partners George Thomas and Kemper Marley. At its largest, the ranch encompassed some 44,000 acres below the western foothills of the McDowell Mountains, from Bell Road north to Lone Mountain Road (Brown and partners actually held deeds to only 23,000 of the acres).
PHOTO COURTESY OF THE ALVIN "COTTON" BROWN FAMILY

Middle, right: Cattlemen and cowboys branded steers after they arrived at DC Ranch from the Phoenix rail yards.
PHOTO COURTESY OF THE ALVIN "COTTON" BROWN FAMILY

Bottom: Kentuckians Edward and Mary Graves moved to Scottsdale in 1908 and bought the Oasis Villa, the town's first commercial guest house, from the Underhill family. The Graves renamed it Graves Guest Ranch, and accommodated winter visitors as well as those with tuberculosis and other respiratory ailments. Frank Yore, a dairy farmer from the Chicago area with a breathing disorder, was one of many who came to the Graves Guest Ranch in 1919 to receive care and enjoy the warm, dry air.
PHOTO COURTESY OF RICHARD JOHNSON (GRANDSON OF FRANK YORE)

Right: Cotton became Scottsdale's main crop between 1914 and 1920. Farmers had to cart their cotton bales to gins in Tempe or Phoenix until 1920 when E.O. Brown started the Scottsdale Ginning Company on the southeast corner of Scottsdale Road and Second Street. Another gin opened on Pima Road about 1930. After World War II cotton farms were replaced by subdivisions to house the population boom, and the gin was no longer needed. It remained a downtown Scottsdale landmark (mostly used for storage) until it burned down in the early 1980s.

PHOTO COURTESY OF THE SCOTTSDALE PUBLIC LIBRARY

Below: In a note home to relatives, Chicagoan Frank Yore described John Rose's pool hall as "some place. A hotel, dance hall, show house [for] vaudeville, barber shop and cigar store" which he had "been in a few times." Rose opened his first Scottsdale pool hall in 1914; in 1923 he replaced the frame structure with one of glazed white bricks at the northeast corner of Main Street and Brown Avenue. Rose sold the pool hall, which also showed silent movies, to the Jew Chew Song family in 1928. They operated it as a grocery story for over 30 years before converting into the Mexican Import store, still operated by the family in 2001.

PHOTO COURTESY OF RICHARD JOHNSON (GRANDSON OF FRANK YORE)

road yard and the ranch took at least two days; the Browns also owned property near Pima Road and Shea Boulevard that served as a way station and campsite. Many Scottsdale men and their young sons participated in the annual drives, augmenting the professional cowhands. When E.O. died, his eldest son, E.E. Brown and George Thomas ran the ranch, joined by cattleman Kemper Marley.

The ranch ceased operations in the 1950s with the decline in the area's cattle industry.

As Scottsdale evolved from a remote frontier outpost to a small but established farm community between 1888 and 1920, it was affected by events and developments happening around it—the Spanish-American War, automobile travel, the quest for statehood, World War I and Prohibition.

Examples of Scottsdale's reaction to world or statewide events during this period are many. During the Spanish-American War in 1898, Scottsdale schoolchildren raised money to send as relief to the suffering citizens of Cuba (and retired Chaplain Winfield Scott tried, in vain, to be reinstated to active duty). When automobiles came to Scottsdale, E.O. Brown was one of the first to have a car; those who had cars used them not only for travel but also to help run their threshing machines. Arizona statehood was a goal of Winfield Scott when he represented Scottsdale in the Territorial Legislature; he died just eighteen months before Arizona became the 48th state on February 14, 1912. During World War I Scottsdale sent some of her young men to fight—such as farmer Jackie Smith, who served in the U.S. Marine Corps— and those who stayed home helped supply cotton and beef for the war effort. Tragically, the flu epidemic of 1918 swept through Arizona; nationally, it killed more people than World War I did. While Prohibition affected much of the rest of the country, Scottsdale had been "dry" since its founding and changed little. Bootleggers, however, found the remote desert near Scottsdale an ideal place to operate.

Arizona's economy has often been described in terms of the "Five C's"—cotton, citrus, copper, cattle and climate. In Scottsdale's formative years—1888 to 1920— the town's economy and lifestyle can be characterized by "Seven C's"—climate, citrus, cotton, cattle, canals, Christians and community.

CHAPTER III

43

ART, TOURISTS AND WATER COME TO TOWN: 1920-1945

While the rest of the nation was reverberating in the Roaring Twenties, Scottsdale seemed content to remain a calm, quiet farming community, making a living from the land. By 1920, the half-mile townsite population had grown to three hundred; nearly two thousand lived on adjacent land that is part of Scottsdale today. With World War I over and the nation's economy experiencing a post-war boom, Scottsdale's agriculture-based economy was doing well, too. Each year added a new dimension to the community, providing an interesting blend of people, culture and commerce.

Scottsdale's days as a frontier outpost—when residents journeyed to Phoenix or Tempe for supplies and entertainment—were ending; the town was becoming more self-sufficient with a variety of new businesses and services. Everyday hardships in Scottsdale were eased by the introduction of electrical service in 1919, more sources of irrigation and household water, a variety of businesses and services opening in town and increased automobile use. Adobe, brick or wood-frame buildings had replaced almost all the tent homes. Houses now had electrical appliances and even ice after Brown's Mercantile opened the town's first ice plant in 1920. The availability of ice didn't stop the summer exodus to cooler climates, however; women and children often escaped to Prescott, Arizona, or San Diego, California, and many businesses closed completely during the hottest months.

The success of Scottsdale's pioneer families enticed more and more newcomers to farm and ranch the productive land north, south and east of Scottsdale's original townsite, and to enjoy the warm, dry climate. Cotton became king among agricultural produce. Demand for cotton created demand for more field workers, and less-restrictive immigration policies with Mexico allowed farm owners to sponsor families to come to Scottsdale to work. Among these immigrating families was the Tomás Corrals, who arrived in 1919. Sponsored by E.O. Brown, the Corrals started out working in his cotton fields; Tomás became a *zanjero*, controlling the flow of irrigation to Brown's crops. The Corrals quickly became leaders in the growing community of people from Mexico, many of whom settled in the area that is now Scottsdale's Civic Center Mall. The Corrals started an adobe brick-making business in a field near their home; the Scottsdale Center for the Arts now sits atop the former adobe pit site. In 1928 the family built a facility which later became Los Olivos restaurant on Second Street, still popular today.

The growing number of farms and ranches depended on the town for support. In 1920, E.O. Brown opened a cotton gin on the southeast corner of Second Street and Scottsdale Road. The following year he also helped found the Scottsdale Farmers Bank next door to his general store, giving the town its first financial institution. Between 1918 and 1928, Scottsdale added several service stations and a car dealership, a number of cafes, a second pool hall, a barber shop, at least three more mercantiles, numerous small grocers, a hatchery, a second blacksmith shop and a soft drink emporium which also housed the stage (bus) office. Perhaps due to the restrictions of Prohibition, one pool hall operator, Johnny Rose, sold out. Scottsdale's first Chinese family—Jew Chew Song, his wife and children—bought the former pool hall on the northeast corner of Main Street and Brown Avenue in 1928 and reopened it as a grocery. It became a popular shopping place, especially for Scottsdale's Hispanic community and people from the Salt River Pima-Maricopa Indian Community. The family continued to operate it as a grocery for over three decades, then converted it into Mexican Imports, which the family still ran in 2001.

The town had grown enough to need some organization and infrastructure. In 1922 Maricopa County established a voting precinct and justice court in Scottsdale. William Kimsey was appointed Justice of the Peace; Al Frederick became the long-serving Constable. To foster civic improvements for residents and businesses alike, the first Scottsdale Chamber of Commerce was formed in the early 1920s, operating out of a room in the Farmers Bank. Scottsdale got its first stand-alone post office in 1928 at the northwest corner of Brown Avenue and Main Street. A daily gathering

✦

Scottsdale artist Lotan Lotan captured the essence of one of the Scottsdale area's best-known cattlemen, E.E. "Brownie" Brown, son of E.O. Brown. Here, he is shown on his horse at Browns Ranch, also known as the Upper Ranch, which was located east of Pima Road and north of Dynamite Road in what is now northern Scottsdale. Browns Mountain and the land area which housed the ranch are permanently protected as public open space as part of the McDowell Sonoran Preserve.

ART COURTESY OF LYNDA PERSON

Right: Scottsdale became more self-sufficient in the 1920s and 1930s, adding new stores and services, from mercantiles, to gas stations, to an ice plant, to cafes. This aerial view, circa 1936, shows Brown's Mercantile in the lower left-hand corner, which was located at the southwest corner of Brown Avenue and Main Street.

PHOTO COURTESY OF PAUL AND CORA MESSINGER

Below: Gabe Brooks' "punch and judy" water drilling rig was a familiar site in the Scottsdale area. Many private water companies provided water to homes and businesses near groundwater wells. Homesteads and farms some distance from town had to have their own wells drilled.

PHOTO COURTESY OF THE ELLIS FAMILY

place at the time, it has been occupied by Porter's Western Wear since the 1950s.

The growing population also demanded more schools. In 1923, Scottsdale High School opened on land donated by Charles Miller, which was originally a part of the Winfield Scott homestead on Indian School Road. Miller's son William and daughter Murle were two of the three graduates in the Class of 1923. Needing additional classroom space, the school district built a new grammar school on the southwest corner of Second Street and Marshall Way in 1928. Originally called the Scottsdale Grammar School, it was later renamed the Loloma School and is now home to the Scottsdale Artists School. The 1910-vintage "little red schoolhouse" on Main Street became an entry-level elementary school for Hispanic children, where they could learn English as well as the traditional subjects of the primary grades. The area's first private schools also opened during this time. George A. Judson built the Judson School for Boys in 1928 in the sparsely populated desert of Paradise Valley northwest of Scottsdale. In 1933 R.T. Evans opened the private Jokake School for Girls on Camelback Road.

Farms, ranches, homes and businesses in Scottsdale and other Valley communities needed increasing amounts of water. Newcomers were facing the realities of living in a semi-arid climate. Private water companies sprang up to drill groundwater wells for both domestic consumption and irrigation.

Left: By the early 1920s Scottsdale needed its own high school; Charles Miller donated part of his land on Indian School Road east of Scottsdale Road for construction of the new school. His son and daughter, William and Murle, were in the first graduating class of 1923. Over the years, the school was used as a community center, drawing in the population for plays, concerts and public hearings. The school closed in 1983 and was torn down in 1991-92. The Scottsdale High mascot was the beaver because beavers lived in the canal near the school site.

PHOTO COURTESY OF SCOTTSDALE HISTORICAL SOCIETY

Bottom: Scottsdale Postmaster J. Lee Conrad (standing) and rural letter carrier Carleton Lutes (looking out postal window) operated out of Scottsdale's first stand-alone post office, built in 1928 on the northwest corner of Brown Avenue and Main Street. In the 1950s Porter's Western Wear took over the building, where it was still operating in the year 2001.

PHOTOS COURTESY OF THE ALVIN "COTTON" BROWN FAMILY AND THE AUTHOR

The Salt River Valley Water Users Association (SRVWUA) continued to expand, building more dams and reservoirs. In 1922, the Water Users Association sponsored members of the Yaqui Indian tribe from northern Mexico to immigrate to the Valley in order to dredge the Arizona Canal. The SRVWUA provided a work camp for the Yaqui workers and their families in the area southwest of Scottsdale now known as the Paiute neighborhood. The Yaquis named their new settlement *Penjamo.*

There they continued to conduct their seasonal and religious ceremonies, such as the Yaqui Easter observance.

The state government, recognizing that the demand for water would constantly require new sources, entered into negotiations with other states in the West to determine each state's water access rights to the mighty Colorado River. In 1922, the federal Colorado

River Compact divided the states into upper and lower basins and developed tentative water allocations. Arizona protested California's proposed share of the water, a matter that deadlocked the compact until Governor Sidney Osborn finally signed an amended agreement for Arizona in 1944. In the meantime the federal government, as part of its Colorado River water reclamation effort, began construction on Boulder Dam in 1933.

During the 1920s the nation's prosperity benefited tourism in Arizona. Families wanted to take vacations in their new cars. Wealthy Easterners, Midwesterners and Hollywood celebrities enjoyed spending winters in the scenic, warm and exotic desert. The advent of motion pictures and the popularity of authors like Zane Grey created a keen national interest in the rugged cowboy life and heightened their curiosity about Native American culture. Tourists were also drawn to the wide-open spaces and the awe-inspiring beauty of the land. The Grand Canyon, which had been dedicated as a national park in 1919, was an additional attraction. It was now easier to get to the Phoenix area: the Southern Pacific Railroad added Phoenix to its main line in 1926, linking the Valley with El Paso, Texas and Los Angeles, California, and Sky Harbor Airport in Phoenix opened for air travel in September 1929.

To accommodate winter visitors, Mildred Bartholow and her sister Imogene Ireland turned the former Blount house—which previ-

ously had been a cheese factory and the Roy George residence—into The Adobe House guest ranch at the approximate location of the City Court Building today. Lottie Sidell opened her cottages on the north side of East Main Street, for visitors and convalescents. Sylvia Evans and Lucy Cuthbert turned their Jokake Tea Room into the Jokake Inn, which continued to host celebrities and wealthy guests into the 1960s. The Graves Guest Ranch and Ingleside Inn were constantly full of winter guests.

Arizona was a haven for tuberculosis, asthma and bronchitis sufferers and much of Scottsdale's visitor business in the 1920s still focused on helping people recover from respiratory ailments. World War I veterans who had been exposed to poisonous gases in the trenches also came here for relief. Sanitariums sprung up around the Valley catering to "lungers." Many who thought they had come here to die ended up living many decades and becoming community leaders.

Scottsdale had just what the doctors of the day ordered. According to the February 1912 edition of *Arizona, the New State Magazine*, TB patients needed "rest, nourishment, care and pure air"; it advised, however, "don't take anyone in with a cough." Health camp operators and a few small sanitariums located in residents' homes took in the ailing, though; Scottsdale itself had no hospital until 1962.

Wall Street's Black Friday—October 29, 1929—caused instant desperation in East

Coast cities and triggered the nation's Great Depression. The Depression took longer to reach Arizona and Scottsdale, but it certainly did. Most Scottsdale families depended on the land for their livelihood; farming and ranching continued, but with great difficulty. As markets for produce and livestock from Arizona and Scottsdale dried up in other parts of the nation, many local farms and ranches went out of business or down-sized. Scottsdale Farmers Bank closed during the 1933 "bank holiday," never to reopen as a bank (in 2001 the building on Main Street was home to the Rusty Spur Saloon). The first chamber of commerce, located inside the bank, also closed. The state and town populations declined. Immigration from Mexico

Above: In the 1920s, Mildred Bartholow and her sister Imogene Ireland turned one of Scottsdale's first permanent homes into The Adobe House guest ranch (near what is now the intersection of 75th Street and 2nd Street). It had been built in the late 1890s by the Blount family, then had been used as a cheese factory, and as the residence of playwright Roy George.
PHOTOS COURTESY OF RICHARD JOHNSON

Below: In the 1930s, Lottie Sidell opened cottages on the north side of Main Street (between Scottsdale Road and Brown Avenue) for visitors and convalescents.
PHOTO COURTESY OF LABEULA STEINER MOWRY

CHAPTER IV

49

Below: The Corral family led the construction effort for Scottsdale's first Catholic Church in 1933, Our Lady of Perpetual Help. The beautifully-crafted adobe structure at the intersection of First Street and Brown Avenue, is now home to the Scottsdale Symphony Orchestra. Wesley Segner, one of the founders of the Arizona Craftsmen Center and first president of the Scottsdale Chamber of Commerce, did this watercolor in the 1950s.

ARTWORK COURTESY OF THE SCOTTSDALE CHAMBER OF COMMERCE, WHO RECEIVED THE ORIGINAL ART AS A GIFT FROM WESLEY SEGNER

Above: The Works Progress Administration, a New Deal program of the federal government to spur the economy during the Great Depression, provided funds to build additions onto both the Scottsdale Grammar (Loloma) School (shown here) and Scottsdale High School. These construction projects created jobs for local residents and provided much-needed additional school space for the growing population. The Scottsdale Grammar School was originally built in 1928 and used as a Scottsdale School District school into the 1980s. It is now home to the Scottsdale Artists School, and is located at the southwest corner of Second Street and Marshall Way.

PHOTO COURTESY OF THE SCOTTSDALE PUBLIC LIBRARY

HISTORIC SCOTTSDALE

stopped; scarce jobs went to U.S. citizens. Migrant workers came to the Valley from the Southern U.S. to pick cotton, which was still a relatively strong industry. Displaced individuals lived in makeshift shantytowns on the empty desert and tried to subsist on the land.

The federal government's New Deal programs helped revive the area with some money, relief and jobs that brought in new people. The Works Progress Administration provided funds to build additions onto both the Scottsdale Grammar (Loloma) School and Scottsdale High School. These construction projects also created jobs, as did the federal government's Civilian Conservation Corps (CCC). The CCC made much-needed improvements to the Arizona Canal which the financially strapped SRVWUA had been unable to do. The corps also built roads and structures in state and national parks in Arizona that would attract future tourists as they sought to savor the scenic beauty around the state. The Federal Writers Project wrote the first comprehensive guidebook to Arizona, promoting the state as a desirable visitor destination. The Federal Artists Project sent painter Philip Curtis, carver Phillips Sanderson and painter Lew Davis to Arizona to create art in public facilities; they became part of a growing art community in the area.

CHAPTER IV

World-renowned architect Frank Lloyd Wright, greatly impressed by the power and beauty of the McDowell Mountains north of the small farming town of Scottsdale, established his winter home and school of architecture here in 1937. Calling it Taliesin West (his summer home and school of architecture in Wisconsin were named Taliesin), he taught his apprentices the concepts of organic architecture, designing buildings in harmony with their environments. As part of their introduction to organic architecture, the apprentices lived in tent homes they constructed in the remote desert surrounding Taliesin West. Here Wright is shown (left) enjoying a tea party with Mrs. Wright (center) and Aunt Sophie (right) in the desert tent home of apprentice David Dodge.

For those families most in need, the federal government provided a small allotment of meat and other staples, known as "the dole," which was distributed each week at the Scottsdale Justice Court building, then located on Main Street west of Scottsdale Road.

Despite the Depression, Scottsdale's business district expanded. During this decade, the Boswell Ginning Company and Willmoth Appliance opened, as did the Valley Super Service Station. Earl Shipp bought out his former employer, Byer's Market, and renamed it Earl's Market, which he continued to operate as a downtown grocery for many decades. The

tough times of the Depression continued to unite the small town of Scottsdale into one big family. People shared whatever they had with their neighbors. Clubs—the Garden Club, American Legion, the American Legion Auxiliary, PTA, Women's Club, Boy Scouts, Girl Scouts, Red Cross—met regularly and organized ice cream socials and potluck barbecues (often roasting a steer from E.E. "Brownie" Brown's ranch). The entire community turned out for plays at Scottsdale High School. There were men's and women's sports teams; softball was a particular favorite. The Scottsdale Blues played teams throughout the

Valley. Kids swam in the irrigation ditches and played marbles right in the middle of the street with no danger of car traffic. Fathers and sons hunted in the slough east of Scottsdale (the Indian Bend Wash), and went out in the desert to shoot quail from horseback or from the backs of cars and trucks. In the worst of times, Scottsdale residents tried to make it the best of times.

Churches and their organizations flourished. Although Chaplain Scott wished the community to worship together ecumenically, by the time of his death in 1910, individual congregations had begun to emerge. The Presbyterians organized in 1910, the Baptists

in 1912 and the Methodists in 1924. The Corral family led the construction of Scottsdale's first Catholic Church in 1933, Our Lady of Perpetual Help. The beautifully crafted adobe structure, known as the Old Mission Church at the intersection of First Street and Brown Avenue, is now home to the Scottsdale Symphony Orchestra.

Scottsdale looked quite different in the 1930s. Its main thoroughfare, Paradise Street (later named Scottsdale Road), was lined on both sides with tall, leafy trees, creating a cool, green tunnel. Many residents drove cars or trucks, but others rode horses to town and school. Streets were unpaved, creating clouds of dust with the slightest breeze or movement. The ultimate customer service at Earl's Market was having the dust wiped off your purchases before they were bagged. Perhaps the most welcome sight during the 1930s was the swamp cooler, which appeared on more and more rooftops. A technologically-advanced version of the wet-burlap-over-a-crate desert cooler, this electric-powered evaporative cooler made life in the desert heat infinitely more bearable.

North of the town site, several new projects began during the 1930s that would have lasting impact on Scottsdale. Despite the Depression, tourism promotion continued; in the 1930s, promoters coined the term "Valley of the Sun" to replace the less-descriptive Salt River Valley. Catering to well-heeled winter vis-

✧

Above: On a Sunday drive with his children in 1933, the beauty of the area surrounding Pinnacle Peak, 18 miles north of the Scottsdale townsite, captivated Phoenix lawyer K.T. Palmer. He filed a claim to homestead 640 acres on the north base of Pinnacle Peak, which required that he and his family actually live there in order to validate the claim. He colorfully documented living in the desert without running water, electricity or phone in his 1971 book, For Land's Sake. *He later became a real estate developer, with offices at Pima Plaza in downtown Scottsdale. With partner Tom Darlington, Palmer founded the Town of Carefree, north of Scottsdale.*

PHOTO COURTESY OF DEL JEANNE PALMER WEST

Left: Children living in the desert, like Alan and Del Jeanne Palmer, had to learn to share the land with its flora and fauna. In this 1934 photo, Del Jeanne is gingerly holding a red racer snake, while Alan is bravely squatting near a diamondback rattlesnake. The Palmers were one of only a handful of residents in the remote Pinnacle Peak area north of the unincorporated town of Scottsdale in the 1930s.

PHOTO COURTESY OF DEL JEANNE PALMER WEST

CHAPTER IV

53

✧

itors, John C. Lincoln and Jack Stewart opened the Camelback Inn in 1936, and immediately began marketing the area throughout the U.S. The Grubers turned part of Judson School into El Chorro Lodge to accommodate winter guests. The Kiami Lodge opened on the northwest corner of Scottsdale Road and Vista Drive in 1937, complementing the existing visitor accommodations in Scottsdale. In the area of McDonald Drive east of Scottsdale Road, enterprising builder and designer George Ellis built a dozen homes of adobe and redwood he salvaged from an abandoned canal. Artists, including Philip Curtis and Phillips Sanderson moved in, and the area became an art colony, now known as Cattle Track. Ellis' wife Rachel and daughter Janie continued to welcome artists to the Cattle Track area, and made significant contributions to the cultural life of

Scottsdale. In the Pinnacle Peak area in the 1940s, Ellis also built a stunning ranch house for Lois Maury called Crescent Moon. It was torn down in the late 1990s to make way for the Four Seasons Resort.

Scottsdale's reputation as an art center got a real boost when world famous architect Frank Lloyd Wright, a long-time winter visitor, established a winter home in the foothills of the McDowells. Wright was particularly drawn to the power and beauty of Scottsdale's Sonoran Desert and the McDowell Mountains. He and his apprentice architects created Taliesin West, a home and architectural school that is organically integrated into its desert surroundings. Wright became a popular figure each winter season in Scottsdale, participating in community activities, designing homes and resorts, and bringing added atten-

tion and glamour to the area. His influence lives on—not only with Taliesin West as an architectural school and a significant tourism attraction, but in the environmentally-aesthetic buildings he and his architects have designed in Scottsdale and the Valley.

In 1933, Phoenix lawyer K.T. Palmer homesteaded 640 acres on the north face of Pinnacle Peak Mountain, eighteen miles north of Scottsdale. He and his young family joined several other hardy souls already there, and recognized the potential the area could have—if only there could be water and electricity! E.E. "Brownie" Brown, with George Thomas and Kemper Marley, continued to operate the thousands of acres known as DC Ranch in north Paradise Valley, driving their cattle south to the Tovrea stockyards in Phoenix. Although there were a few other homesteaders and residents in the area (the Yuskos, Richardsons, Christiansens, Phillips, Demerbiex, Fraziers and others), water was extremely limited, and so also were the immediate opportunities for settlement.

When war broke out in Europe in 1940, demand for American goods and services put an end to the nation's economic depression. Arizona and its land were primed for helping with the war effort. After Pearl Harbor, the U.S. military and its allies needed training bases in areas that had good weather, and the Valley was the perfect spot.

Land north of Scottsdale—on the northeast corner of today's Scottsdale and Thunderbird Roads—was selected as a primary pilot training

base. Operated by the civilian-owned Southwest Airways on contract with the Army Air Force, Thunderbird II Airfield was a sister field to Thunderbird Airfield in Glendale, Falcon Field in Mesa and Sky Harbor Airport in Phoenix. Between 1942 and 1944, Scottsdale's Thunderbird II Airfield trained 5,500 Army Air Force aviation cadets and provided jobs for men and women from Scottsdale. Businessman and future mayor Malcolm White was a flight instructor. Dorothy Cavalliere Ketchum Roberts was a parachute rigger. Lucy Lutes was one of the first women certified as an aircraft mechanic; her daughter Virgie Lutes Brown was a switchboard operator. Men from the Salt River Pima-Maricopa Indian Community worked in the aircraft maintenance department. Airfield manager John Swope, married to movie actress Dorothy McGuire, lived in one of George Ellis' adobes in Cattle Track; after the war he became a renowned photographer for *Time* and *Life* magazines.

The Scottsdale area's other "military installation" was the prisoner-of-war camp at Papago

✧

Above: Many of Scottsdale's youth were drafted or volunteered to serve in the Armed Forces during World War II. Two men from Scottsdale's Yaqui village, Alberto Osuna (left) and Manuel Campoy, (right) are shown here in uniform with Martin Pina (standing, center) and Antonia Leyvas (seated).

PHOTO COURTESY OF NELLIE MUÑOZ

Left: Scottsdale businessman Malcolm White was among the cadre of civilian flight instructors at Thunderbird II Airfield during World War II. Flying Stearman bi-plane aircraft, White and his fellow instructors provided primary flight training to over 5,500 U.S. Army Air Force aviation cadets during 1942-1944. In 1951 following Scottsdale's incorporation as a town, the Maricopa County Board of Supervisors appointed White the town's first mayor.

PHOTO COURTESY OF MRS. MALCOLM WHITE

Park. Opened in 1943, it held hundreds of Italian POWs, then German U-boat officers and crewmen. Guarded POW work details often picked cotton and worked in the canals near the camp. On December 23, 1944, twenty-five German POWs escaped through a 178-foot tunnel, which they dug from their bathhouse to the Arizona Cross-Cut Canal. Their escape route took them through farmland that is now the Hy-View and Tonalea neighborhoods in Scottsdale. By the end of January 1945, all of the escapees had surrendered or been caught. After the war, at least one of the POWs returned to live in Scottsdale.

Housing was scarce for the influx of war workers. To alleviate the shortage in Scottsdale, the federal government provided funds to build a housing project, Thunderbird Homes, for war workers and dependents of military personnel serving elsewhere. Located at the northwest corner of Second Street and Marshall Way, its recreation room was a popular meeting place during and after the war for community groups such as the American Legion and Veterans of Foreign Wars (VFW) Auxiliaries. The project was torn down in

1960; several of its buildings were moved to the Reata Pass and Greasewood Flats outdoor restaurants in the Pinnacle Peak area. The Loloma Transit Station now occupies the site of Thunderbird Homes.

While war workers and military trainees were streaming into Scottsdale and the Valley, Scottsdale's youth were drafted or volunteered to serve in the Armed Forces. Gold star flags hung in many Scottsdale homes. Labeula Mowry often had the sad task of delivering telegrams to families of missing or killed in action.

Among the many Scottsdale residents who gave their lives in World War II were Stanley Crews (the Scottsdale VFW honors his name), and Travis Sipe and Clayton Peterson (the Scottsdale American Legion Post honors their names). To support the war effort, and their men and women in service, Scottsdale residents collected grease and scrap, volunteered at Red Cross canteens, planted Victory Gardens, used their ration stamps at Earl's Market and Kimsey's garage and were praised for their per capita purchase of war bonds.

Several families who moved to Scottsdale during the war years would provide a new crop of leaders for the town. The Messingers and the Schraders both bought land on Indian School Road and started dairy farms. Bill Messinger served on the Scottsdale School Board and created a strategy for future school growth (his "no child ever learns anything riding a school bus" philosophy led to a plan to build schools within one mile of each other). His son Phil served as an early Town attorney; his son Paul served on the Scottsdale Town Council and in the Arizona legislature, and opened Messinger Mortuary with his wife Cora in 1958. Schrader's son, William P. Schrader, served as Scottsdale's mayor (1962-1964) and as president of Salt River Project. Retired chemist Merle Cheney and Chicagoan Fowler McCormick (grandson of International Harvester's Cyrus McCormick) bought land north of Scottsdale and established horse and cattle ranches. Along with Ed Tweed, who moved to Scottsdale in 1949, the McCormicks and Cheneys started Scottsdale's world-renowned Arabian horse industry.

Despite the hard times of the Great Depression and World War II, the small farming community of Scottsdale remained a close-knit, wholesome community with an entrepreneurial spirit and the determination to be a good place to live and raise a family. During this period, Scottsdale's breathtaking scenery had helped to attract artists and tourists, adding a new dimension to the town. New technologies such as electricity and evaporative coolers helped residents cope with the realities of living in the semi-arid desert. Scottsdale's land continued to provide opportunity to those who were willing to work hard in cultivating its potential.

✧

The William Messinger farm operated at the corner of Miller and Indian School Roads from 1942 to 1958 when the farm buildings were removed and Messinger's Mortuary was built, where it operates today. In the early 1950s, Our Lady of Perpetual Help Catholic Church purchased 10 of the Messinger's 20 acres on Miller Road to build its campus.

PHOTO COURTESY OF PAUL AND CORA MESSINGER

POST-WAR GROWTH MAKES A CITY: 1945-1970

Victory dancing in the streets had hardly stopped when people began to stream into Arizona after World War II. Scottsdale had the ingredients that would catapult this dusty, familial farm town into a glamorous southwestern destination. Some say it was the sudden, new availability of gasoline, cars, and train and air travel for a war-starved nation. Others say it was the GIs and war workers who had come to the Valley, liked what they saw (wide open spaces and no snow!) and decided to stay. Maybe it was the newly available air conditioning that tempered the desert heat. Or maybe it was the creative imaging by merchants and artists in the late 1940s of Scottsdale as the "West's Most Western Town." Likely it was a combination of all these factors that began to change Scottsdale's lifestyle and land use more than any other time in her 1.8-billion-year history.

One of the first groups to get organized after the war was the artists who had been gathering in Scottsdale since the late 1920s and early 1930s. Some were back from war duty; others had come earlier for the inspiration of the desert's scenic beauty, and stayed. Most had heard that Scottsdale, although a small town, appreciated art and culture and welcomed creative talent of all kinds. Wartime AiResearch manager, now real estate entrepreneur Tom Darlington, purchased the old Brown's Mercantile at Brown and Main, and converted it into a working studio for artists and crafts people. Called the Arizona Craftsmen, the studio housed silversmiths Wes and Joyce Segner, leather-crafter Lloyd Kiva, woodcarver Phillips Sanderson, calligrapher and photographer Leonard Yuschik, painter Lew Davis and sculptress Mathilde Schaefer. With a brochure and a few well-placed ads, the craftsmen began attracting winter visitors, who liked to watch their desert souvenirs take shape. Former First Lady Eleanor Roosevelt was among their customers; she stopped in while visiting her grown children who lived here. Regrettably, the Arizona Craftsmen center burned down in 1950, but with the help of local patrons like Anne McCormick, was immediately rebuilt on Fifth Avenue, launching that part of town as a new shopping and dining area.

The area resort industry, which had been dormant during the travel-limiting war years, now re-awoke with many new players. Adding to the allure of the Camelback and Jokake Inns (the Ingleside Inn had closed and reopened as the Brownmoor School for Girls in 1945), the Paradise Inn (now the site of the Phoenician Resort) and the Casa Blanca Inn were built in 1944 and 1945 for upscale clientele. Numerous guest ranches opened throughout Scottsdale and Paradise Valley between 1945 and 1950, providing room, board and Western adventure for families and couples escaping the cold and ice "back East." After a few visits, many of these winter visitors decided to move here permanently, including New York advertising mogul Robert Rubicam and his wife Bettina, Midwest department store owner Bob Herberger and his artistic wife Kax, industrialist Daniel Gainey, author Clarence Buddington Kelland, and others. They immediately became involved in business and community projects and helped create the re-born community's cultural and civic infrastructure.

Scottsdale's potential for increased visitor business seemed great; the merchants, resort owners and artists realized, however, that without some infrastructure, such as paved streets, street lights, a fire department, a zoning ordinance and business licensing, the potential might never be reached. In 1947, they formed a new Scottsdale Chamber of Commerce to help guide the town toward its newfound opportunities. The chamber adopted the slogan "West's Most Western Town" to use in brochures, ads and promotions. It encouraged merchants to build or rebuild with Western-motif storefront architecture. The group organized Street Pavers Balls to raise money to oil the dirt streets and keep the dust down. And, as interest grew for formal incorporation, the chamber held frequent public hearings at the Scottsdale High School to hear the pros and cons of becoming an official town. In many respects, the chamber performed the functions of a municipal government during its first years, raising money for civic improvements, providing some regulation of new businesses,

conducting public hearings and implementing community welfare programs.

The chamber's first president Wes Segner and Dr. Phil Schneider were two leading proponents of incorporation. Businessman Malcolm White and several long-time Scottsdale residents were wary of it, preferring to wait and see if it was really necessary. After

two years of hearings, and many pro and con letters published in the new weekly newspaper, the *Scottsdale Progress*, a chamber committee circulated petitions among eligible property owners to put the question of incorporation to a vote. Many residents and business owners were concerned that Phoenix might try to annex the town, which they felt would lead to a loss of Scottsdale's special character, small town atmosphere and control over its destiny. So many signatures filled the petitions that the Maricopa County Board of Supervisors declared Scottsdale incorporated as of June 25, 1951, without the need for an election. The County then appointed Malcolm White as the first town mayor, and Mort Kimsey, Bill Miller, E.G. "Scotty" Scott and Jack Sweeney as the first members of the town council.

The new Town of Scottsdale covered less than one square mile and had 2,032 residents. Its borders were roughly Miller Road to the east, Camelback Road/the Arizona Canal to the north, Orange Road (now 70th Street/ Goldwater Boulevard) to the west and Osborn Road to the south. After an interval of sixty years, the new townsite was remarkably similar to that drawn up by town pioneers Albert Utley and Winfield Scott in 1894.

Within the first six months of incorporation, Scottsdale enjoyed a small amount of revenue from its share of county and state taxes. Bills were paid by the town clerk out of a cigar box. The town council met in each other's homes and businesses until space was rented from the Rural Fire Company (a private fire company started in Scottsdale by Lou Witzeman in 1948) in their new building at Second Street and Brown Avenue in 1952. The new town also had its first police officer and criminal code, a contract with the Rural Fire Company, an ordinance that covered zoning procedures, a plan to pave streets, an ordinance to control peddlers and itinerant vendors and signs at the town limits.

Scottsdale was the fun place to be in the Fifties. Visitors as well as residents enjoyed the Western ambiance, art, activities and adventures of Scottsdale. They held cookouts in the desert, staged the annual Sunshine Festival parade (later renamed the Parada Del Sol by the Scottsdale Jaycees in 1953), held the first annual Arabian Horse Show in 1955, turned out by the hundreds for artist Ted DeGrazia's first Scottsdale exhibit at Buck Saunders' Trading Post and enjoyed the annual Miracle of the Roses Pageant choreographed by Jesus

Corral, Paul Coze and Patricia Benton Evans. There were horse rodeos starring trick rider Dick Griffiths. The "Howdy Dudettes," Scottsdale high school girls dressed in Western gear from head to toe, greeted visitors, celebrities and convention attendees. Resorts held grand opening bashes for local residents to kick off the coming tourist season. Townsfolk and tourists gathered at places like the Pink Pony bar and restaurant, the soda fountain at Lute's Pharmacy (for mouth-watering, homemade pies!) and Los Olivos restaurant.

Left: Needing infrastructure and municipal services to accommodate Scottsdale's post-war population boom, and fearing annexation by Phoenix that would take away the town's character and independence, residents voted to incorporate in 1951. As the headline in the Scottsdale Progress proclaimed, the Maricopa County Board of Supervisors declared Scottsdale incorporated as a town on June 25, 1951.

USE OF THE FRONT PAGE COURTESY OF THE SCOTTSDALE TRIBUNE

Below: The first town council—Mayor Malcolm White and Councilmen Mort Kimsey, Bill Miller, E.G. "Scotty" Scott and Jack Sweeney—was appointed by Maricopa County in June 1951. The town's first election was held the following May. This photo shows the mayor, town council and city staff in the mid-1950s, (left to right) Doc Cavalliere, councilman; Joe Willmoth, councilman; Phil Messinger, town attorney; John Shoeman, councilman; Dorothy Cavalliere Ketchum, town clerk; Malcolm White, mayor; E.G. Scott, councilman; Mort Kimsey, councilman and Lute Wasbotten, councilman. From 1952-1955 the town rented space from the Rural Fire Department on Second Street at Brown Avenue for the town offices.

PHOTO COURTESY OF MRS. MALCOLM WHITE

The whole town turned out in January 1951 when *Harper's Bazaar* and Goldwater's Department Store staged an outdoor fashion show. *Harper's* models displayed the new "Sunset Pink" fashions while walking down a five-hundred-foot runway on Main Street, from Scottsdale Road to Brown Avenue. In fact, Scottsdale had become an important fashion center by the early 1950s, with crafts people creating one-of-a-kind, Western-theme couture in Scottsdale shops. Names like Christina Rea, Jerome, Chick Davis, Michelle's, Gene of the Desert, Lloyd Kiva, Sally Neary's and Leona Caldwell were the must-shops on Scottsdale's new Fifth Avenue and in the Old Town area. After *Life Magazine* featured the Scottsdale-designed western dress with a broomstick skirt (at the time called a "squaw dress"), the style was seen at patio and cocktail parties from coast to coast.

✦

Above: In 1952 the Scottsdale Chamber of Commerce commissioned local artist Dee Flagg to build a Western-theme sign for Scottsdale Road that would let visitors and residents know of upcoming events. Flagg came up with a cowboy that became the town's symbol. First made of Masonite ™ with a black chalkboard inside his lasso, the cowboy was later re-made of tin. It still stands on the northeast corner of Scottsdale Road and Main Street.

PHOTO COURTESY OF
THE SCOTTSDALE HISTORICAL SOCIETY

Right: The Miracle of the Roses Pageant, originally choreographed by Jesus Corral, Paul Coze, Patricia Benton Evans and others, started as an annual event in 1949 and continued until 1971. Honoring the Virgin of Guadalupe, it featured a procession that began at the Old Mission Church (Our Lady of Perpetual Help), traveled north on Brown Avenue and ended at the Scottsdale High School auditorium.

PHOTO COURTESY OF
THE SCOTTSDALE HISTORICAL SOCIETY

Farming was still the backbone of the economy at the time of Scottsdale's incorporation and into the 1950s, but its importance had peaked. Armed with well-paying jobs, new college degrees and the guarantee of a GI Bill veterans home loan, men were moving their families to Scottsdale. They needed houses, fast. Farmers sold out to home-builders like John Hall, and land that had grown cotton and grazed dairy cows now turned into subdivisions of modern, mass-produced Hallcraft Homes. The more homes built meant that more schools were needed. Bill Messinger's school board had had the foresight to set aside numerous sites for elementary schools, and the town passed school bonds to help get them constructed. By 1960, only a few crop or dairy farms still operated in

Scottsdale. George Thomas' last cattle drive down Scottsdale Road from DC Ranch in 1952 signaled the end of the cattle ranching era. The 4-H Club and Future Farmers of America lost their status as popular clubs at Scottsdale High. The only farms which continued were the Arabian horse farms and ranches, started and run initially as second careers, hobbies or investments by wealthy industrialists who had recently moved to the Scottsdale area, or by locals, like Tom Chauncey.

Through the mid-1940s, retail in Scottsdale was strictly for farming support. During the late 1940s through 1960s, art galleries, craft studios, fashion stores, Native American jewelry and art shops and Southwestern gift shops of all kinds opened to attract tourists. As the permanent resident population grew, so did the

number of shopping areas. Goldwater's Department Store became the anchor of the new Fashion Square Mall when it opened on the site of the former rodeo grounds at the northwest corner of Scottsdale and Camelback Roads in 1962. The Valley's first enclosed mall, Los Arcos, opened at the southeast corner of Scottsdale and McDowell Roads in 1969.

The business scene was changing, too, from one of strictly retail, farming and tourism. In 1949, Motorola established its first electronics manufacturing plant west of Scottsdale. The high-tech giant then added a large facility in the southern part of Scottsdale in 1957, its Military Electronics Division. This major corporate location not only created additional demand for housing; it launched Scottsdale into the space and high tech era. After decades of being known as a destination with a climate for good health and convalescence, Scottsdale finally got a hospital in 1962 when the City Hospital of Scottsdale opened. Off to a shaky start, it was taken over by the Western Baptist Hospital Association the next year and renamed Western Baptist Hospital of Scottsdale.

With a town government and staff concentrating on municipal services for the growing community, residents and businesses turned their attention to building the variety of civic and charitable organizations that have greatly enhanced Scottsdale's quality of life. The Boys Club was formed in the early 1950s. The Scottsdale Jaycees organized in 1953. The Scottsdale Baseball Club, which built a stadium on Osborn Road to house a major league baseball spring training team, turned its team-hosting responsibilities over to a new group, the Scottsdale Charros, which had organized in 1961. Residents enthusiastically supported the March of Dimes, Easter Seals and Community Chest campaigns. Churches expanded and new ones organized to accommodate the growing population. In the 1960s the first Jewish Synagogue as well as the first congregation of the Church of Latter Day Saints came to Scottsdale.

Throughout the 1950s and 1960s, Scottsdale's tourism industry grew in breadth and depth. The Safari, Valley Ho and Executive Inn resort hotels opened in downtown Scottsdale, complemented by the Paradise Valley Guest Ranch (still owned by the Silverman family but rebuilt and renamed Chaparral Suites), Ride-n-Rock Ranch, Sun Down Ranch (now Scottsdale Country Club), Yellow Boot Ranch, Sundial Ranch and other properties. A group of businessmen lobbied Major League Baseball to locate a spring training team in Scottsdale's newly built stadium; in 1955 the Baltimore Orioles were the first team to practice here, another large draw for winter visitors. More art galleries opened; many art festivals and events attracted huge crowds of locals and visitors. Lew and Mathilde Schaefer Davis opened the Desert

Farming was still strong through the 1950s in Scottsdale. This view, north to Camelback Mountain from Jack and Nora Smith's farm near McKellips and Scottsdale Roads, shows acres of cotton fields where houses soon would stand. George Ellis and his daughter Janie tend their maize field at the intersection of Scottsdale and Bell Roads north of Scottsdale; the aerial photo looking south toward Camelback Mountain from Bell Road shows how undeveloped this unincorporated area was in 1950. By the mid-1950s, farmers began selling land to homebuilders, and by the mid-1960s, farming was no longer a major industry in Scottsdale.

PHOTOS COURTESY OF DR. JOE CARSON SMITH, THE ELLIS FAMILY AND ROBERT MARKOW PHOTOGRAPHY

Art Center in Paradise Valley. Louise Lincoln Kerr held small performances at the studio adjacent to her home near Scottsdale Road and McDonald Drive (the Kerr Center later became an Arizona State University performing arts venue). Resorts began to include golf courses on their properties. Western-themed restaurants—Lulu Belle's, the Red Dog Saloon, the Pink Pony—opened in downtown Scottsdale, as well as a family favorite, the Sugar Bowl ice cream parlor.

Cattle ranching was declining in the northern reaches of what is now Scottsdale. E.E. "Brownie" Brown and Kemper Marley still operated DC Ranch, but on a smaller scale into the 1950s. Rancho Vista Bonita Guest Ranch opened in 1950 at the present site of the Pinnacle Peak General Store, giving winter visitors a taste of the remote and beautiful high desert, with awesome views of Pinnacle Peak and the McDowells out their cabin win-

dows. Pinnacle Peak Patio opened in 1957, followed by Reata Pass in 1959, providing Western dining and entertainment adventures under the stars. For a rustic taste of the Old West, visitors and residents could visit Don Pablo and his curio stand at Curry's Corner (northeast corner of Scottsdale and Pinnacle Peak Roads), complete with Native American jewelry and pottery, cowboy paraphernalia, a

CHAPTER V

65

Ed and Ruth Tweed moved from the Midwest in 1949 and started BruSally Ranch, an Arabian horse farm named for their children, Bruce and Sally. Located off Hayden Road just south of Cactus, the ranch produced many world famous Arabians. Tweed was the first president of the Arizona Arabian Association, and together with Anne and Fowler McCormick and the F.K. Wrigleys staged the first All Arabian Horse Show in Scottsdale in February 1955. Tweed is pictured here with his prized stallion Skorage in approximately 1960; his granddaughter Shelly Groom Trevor, who was the ranch's trainer for many years, is shown riding through the former gates to the ranch on Hayden Road. The ranch house is now used by the Arizona Transplant House Foundation.

PHOTOS COURTESY OF THE GROOM FAMILY
AND THE ARIZONA TRANSPLANT HOUSE FOUNDATION

collection of tea pots, and other wonders. A handful of residents ventured into this mostly desert landscape, including artists Lew Davis and his wife Mathilde Schaefer, Walter and Anne Bohl and Andy Tsinajinnie.

To keep the community apprised of all that was going on, Scottsdale got its own media outlets to complement *The Arizona Republic* and *The Phoenix Gazette*, which served the region. Although there had been several, short-lived publications in the 1930s (the *Scottsdale Bulletin* and the *Scottsdale Verde News*), in May 1948 Jim Boyd first published the *Scottsdale Progress* as a weekly newspaper. Later, during the twenty-five years that Jonathan and Maxine Marshall owned and edited the newspaper, the *Progress* became a daily paper. Over fifty years and several owners later, the paper renamed the *Scottsdale Tribune* in the 1990s, continued to serve Scottsdale. Also in 1948, Cletus Smith, Land O'Sun Printing, began publishing the weekly *Scottsdale Booster*. In 1953, Brooks Darlington's Desert Paradise Publishers began *The Arizonian* in Scottsdale (published weekly through 1969).

By 1960, Scottsdale's population had tripled to more than ten thousand full-time residents. That same year, the Town Council imposed a sales tax (3/4 of one percent), the town's first property tax (48-cents per $100 valuation) and a business license tax, all at the same July meeting. The town adopted a charter and in 1961 graduated to city status. Also

in the 1960s more than three hundred residents participated in the Scottsdale Town Enrichment Program (STEP) to establish the direction in which they wanted their city to go. One of the most significant STEP committee initiatives was an innovative partnership begun with the Army Corps of Engineers to turn the Indian Bend Wash from a flood-prone slough into a park-filled greenbelt flood control project (rather than one with a miles-long concrete channel). The wash had been an area of dairy farms, a place to hunt small game and, during heavy rains, a raging river that cut the community in two; now it would be a focal point for recreation and the city's first planned open space. STEP committees also recommended a junior college, a municipal airport and a beautifully designed and landscaped Civic Center Mall with a new City Hall and public library. Residents made such significant and creative contributions to community planning and vision that the STEP program was revived again in the 1970s and 1980s.

In order to exercise some control over city growth and how adjoining land would be used, the City of Scottsdale began annexing land in the 1950s and continued to add parcels throughout the 1960s. Annexation started south to the Tempe border and east to the Salt

River Pima-Maricopa Indian Community, absorbing farmland-turned-subdivisions. In 1961, the land to the west of Scottsdale incorporated as the Town of Paradise Valley, so Scottsdale could only grow north and northeast. Annexation plans in 1962 would take Scottsdale as far north as Deer Valley Road. Then-Mayor Bill Schrader personally took the annexation petition to major landowner Kemper Marley at the Stockyards Restaurant on a Sunday afternoon to explain its importance. Marley had preferred keeping his land as unincorporated county land, but rather than be

absorbed by Phoenix, he willingly signed Scottsdale's petition. Attempts were made at least twice to annex lands to the northwest and southwest of Scottsdale, but were stopped by Phoenix. During this period of annexations and attempted annexations, the community went through some rough and controversial times. Not everyone agreed that Scottsdale needed to be bigger to be "better;" not everyone wanted to be annexed. In this period before open meeting laws were enacted, accusations flew that land deals were being made behind closed doors.

After fifteen years as an incorporated entity, the City of Scottsdale had developed a basic infrastructure—sewer system, paved streets, police department, municipal services. In 1968, the City moved into a $2.4 million dollar Civic Center Complex in heart of downtown Scottsdale, which had been designed by renowned local architect Bennie Gonzales. By the end of the 1960s Scottsdale had also dedicated Eldorado as its first City park (located south of Thomas Road and East of Miller Road), enacted a strict sign ordinance banning billboards and controlling building signage and adopted the first general plan in the state to help determine land use.

Scottsdale wanted its own airport, and the Seventh Day Adventists, a faith organization with Arizona headquarters in Scottsdale, helped make that dream a reality. The Adventists had taken over the field and facilities of Thunderbird II training airfield, built for

duty in World War II, to operate a private high school. They, however, having more land than they needed, provided land to the City for the airport, which opened in 1967. The Adventists also hired developer and visionary George Tewksbury to see what could be done with the rest of their excess land adjacent to the airport. He developed and promoted plans for an industrial and business park where businesses could have taxiway access to the airport from their own facilities. One of the first major companies to move into the new industrial park was the Armour-Dial Technical Center in 1976. Other forward-thinking business people and developers like Bill Arthur realized the potential of the Scottsdale Industrial Airpark and began projects of their own.

As Scottsdale absorbed more and more peo-

ple and became urbanized, it also faced the social changes that other parts of the nation were experiencing. Hispanic and African Americans, as well as Native Americans, were fighting discrimination and segregation, and demonstrating for equal opportunity and treatment. Women were working outside the home in increasing numbers and also demanding equal opportunities. As more religious and ethnic groups moved into and visited Scottsdale, facilities, area resorts and country clubs had to drop their restrictive policies. In today's more culturally-sensitive environment, it is shocking to see "Gentiles only" written in resort brochures from the 1940s and 1950s. As elsewhere in the 1960s, youth protested the Vietnam War and the authority of "the establishment." And, at long last, environmental consciousness was awakening in an area that had long taken its land and resources for granted.

✧

Top, left: Concerned about maintaining scenic views and to avoid "advertising blight," Scottsdale residents and their City government enacted one of the toughest sign ordinances in the nation in the 1960s. It banned billboards; this one at the southeast corner of Hayden and McDowell Roads, and many like it, came down. By the year 2001, only one or two billboards that had been "grand-fathered" before the ordinance took effect in 1962, remained in Scottsdale's 185 square miles.

PHOTO COURTESY OF CITY OF SCOTTSDALE

Right, top to bottom:
In May 1948 Jim Boyd first published the Scottsdale Progress as a weekly newspaper. Its first office was located on Brown Avenue, next door to the Arizona Public Service office. After fifty years and several changes in ownership, the paper, renamed Scottsdale Tribune, continued to serve Scottsdale.

PHOTO COURTESY OF THE SCOTTSDALE PUBLIC LIBRARY

In the 1950s Scottsdale's business district expanded well west of Scottsdale Road, as this photo shows a busy West Main Street shopping district. Western-style architecture gave the area character; however, the introduction of non-native plants, such as palm trees, began to create an artificial image of what the Sonoran Desert was really like.

PHOTO COURTESY OF ARIZONA PUBLIC SERVICE

Within a few years after incorporation, Scottsdale had established a well trained and equipped police department. Keeping with the "West's Most Western Town" theme, the officers wore cowboy hats. After operating out of the basement of the Little Red Schoolhouse when it served as the Town Hall, the Scottsdale Police Department built its own facility next door to the schoolhouse. That building was torn down as part of the Civic Center Mall construction, and the police department relocated to a facility on 75th Street. This 1960s photo shows the back of the police facility, next door to the schoolhouse.

PHOTO COURTESY OF MARION WARCHOT

SCOTTSDALE: IT'S A BOOMTOWN: 1970-2000

By the 1970s, there was one thing you could definitely say about Scottsdale: it wasn't a farming community anymore. Just exactly what is was, or should be, would become the subject of much debate. After more than two millennia of sustaining life by farming and hunting the land, people who lived in the area were now using the land for acres of houses, an increasing number of service and light industries and as a scenic lure for tourists from around the world. It was difficult to stay far enough ahead of growth to define: This is what we want Scottsdale to be when we grow up. To pessimists, Scottsdale was having an identity crisis; to optimists, the city was developing a well-rounded personality.

Scottsdale's population in 1970 stood at 67,800, living on 62.2 square miles. The City had purchased its first computer in the 1960s, and upgraded to a larger one (yes, just one) in 1975. The City also began to address the special needs of its citizens by opening the Vista Del Camino social services center in 1973 (located east of Miller Road on Roosevelt) and the Civic Center Senior Center in 1976. One of the most innovative programs begun by the City was mechanized garbage collection. Using trucks nicknamed "Godzilla"—because they looked like a huge beast devouring residential garbage—Scottsdale was first in the nation with this robotic garbage pick-up system. Rural Metro, the City of Scottsdale's contracted fire protection service, also provided the community two innovations: lime green fire trucks (which are more visible in the desert environment) and residential fire sprinkler systems (required in all homes built in Scottsdale after 1986).

Citizen-driven STEP (Scottsdale Town Enrichment Program) committees continued to offer innovative solutions for Scottsdale and their earlier efforts began to take shape when Scottsdale Community College opened in 1970. Another STEP initiative, Indian Bend Wash Greenbelt Flood Control Project, began in 1971, though not in time to stem the flow of two damaging floods through the wash in 1970 and 1972, which temporarily cut the city in half and closed schools and businesses. In 1975 citizens were an integral part of the discussion concerning the Northeast Area Plan, giving shape to how the newly-annexed area east along Shea Boulevard to the border of the new Town of Fountain Hills would be developed.

In 1970, the sale of a prominent Arabian horse ranch set the direction that Scottsdale would take in approving developments and creating neighborhoods. The Kaiser Aetna Company bought the former ranch of Anne and Fowler McCormick at Indian Bend and Scottsdale Road, and built the state's first modern, planned community, McCormick Ranch. This city-within-a-city contained a variety of housing types (single family homes, condominiums and apartments), and included neighborhood retail and commercial areas, parks, trails and its own governing board of property owners. McCormick Ranch set a precedent when the developer provided some infrastructure—certain facilities and roads—that would have otherwise been funded and built by the City. Before McCormick Ranch was completed, other planned communities had begun, and continued to rise out of former ranch land or open desert, enticing the population further north and east. For example, just north of McCormick Ranch, Daniel Gainey's Arabian farm became the Gainey Ranch planned community.

Tourism had become Scottsdale's number one industry and largest employer. Visitors were so important to its economy in the 1970s and later that Scottsdale could have called itself a "company town": it loved and welcomed "company." The hospitality industry knew from surveys that visitors came from around the globe to experience Scottsdale's wide open spaces, scenic beauty, Western ambiance, arts and culture and outdoor adventures. Improved air travel and the desire to escape the "rust belt" for the "sun belt" brought young and old to Scottsdale and the Valley. Many new resorts and attractions opened and signature events were established in order to appeal to the varied interests of Scottsdale's visitors.

❖

Preservation of cultural heritage and natural assets became increasingly important to Scottsdale residents during the last part of the twentieth century. In 1999, members of Scottsdale's Yaqui community, concerned that their language and traditions might be lost for future generations, enlisted the support of artist Mario Martinez, who grew up in Scottsdale's Penjamo village, to help them create a mural depicting Penjamo and Yaqui history. In 2000, the Library of Congress honored the Yaqui mural program as part of its Local Legacies Project.

ARTWORK COURTESY OF
CONCERNED CITIZENS FOR COMMUNITY HEALTH
(MURAL BY MARIO MARTINEZ AND CARLOS FLORES)

Among the new resorts were Doubletree Hotel on Civic Center Mall (1971, now a Holiday Inn), the Scottsdale Hilton (1972), Scottsdale Conference Resort (1976), Scottsdale Registry (1977, now Radisson), Cottonwoods Resort (1980), and several others. Jim Paul opened Rawhide, a Western theme park, in the unincorporated area north of Scottsdale in 1972. The McCormick Railroad Park opened in 1975, a gift to the community from Guy Stillman and his family, the late McCormicks. Signature events begun in the 1970s included the Barrett Jackson Classic Auto Auction (1970), Tempe's Fiesta Bowl (1971) and the Scottsdale Culinary Festival (1978). These complemented the existing Parada Del Sol, spring training baseball and Arabian horse show to bring visitors. Many fine dining and theme restaurants opened, as well as art galleries and retail shops, all catering to visitors, but also offering a "resort lifestyle" to residents. To fund marketing of Scottsdale to tourists and as a meeting location, hoteliers and the Scottsdale Chamber of Commerce persuaded voters to approve a bed tax for Scottsdale; a two percent occupancy tax on hotel rooms began in 1977.

During the 1970s and 1980s, the arts continued to grow in importance. The Fine Arts Commission had already organized in 1967 and the Scottsdale Arts Center Association formed in 1974. Also in 1974, Irv Fleming

started the Scottsdale Symphony Orchestra. The Scottsdale Center for the Arts, part of the Gonzales-designed Civic Center Mall, opened in 1975, becoming a focal point for performing and visual arts. With dozens of art galleries located in the West Main and Marshall Way area, the Thursday Night Art Walk began in 1973; in 1988, the galleries formed the Scottsdale Gallery Association to market the art district on a level with other national and international art centers. Scottsdale had become a major art market in the United States. To provide continuing art education, the Scottsdale Artists School opened in 1983.

Scottsdale's "movers and shakers" welcomed new businesses, and the community embraced a "growth is good" mantra. Some long-time residents and independent merchants, however, were not convinced all growth was good, and began to question where it would lead.

By the mid-1980s the City and Scottsdale Chamber of Commerce felt that to ensure a healthy, recession-proof economy, it would be helpful to entice a more diverse range of businesses to Scottsdale. In 1984, the McManis Group did an economic development study, then helped the City and chamber formulate a strategy to attract certain types of industries to move to Scottsdale. They sought corporate and regional headquarters, research and development firms and business and professional services companies—all with high-paying jobs. With Armour-Dial's research facility in the Scottsdale Airpark since 1976, and plenty of land available in and north of the airpark, other corporate and regional headquarters, research and development facilities and high-tech companies began locating in the airpark in the late

1980s and 1990s. They included Discount Tire, Franchise Financial Corporation of America, Allied Waste, The Vanguard Group and JDA Software. By the late 1990s, the Scottsdale Airpark was among the top three employment centers in Arizona.

Scottsdale was also attracting a new level of entrepreneurial activity. Potential business

Above: By the late 1990s Scottsdale Fashion Square had evolved into the state's largest and most successful shopping center. It merged with adjacent Camelview Plaza in the early 1990s, then added Arizona's first Nordstrom and more than fifty new stores in a bridge over Camelback Road in 1998—over one million square feet of specialty shopping.

PHOTO COURTESY OF SCOTTSDALE FASHION SQUARE

Left: In 1955 the northwest corner of Scottsdale and Camelback Roads was the site of a rodeo ground that hosted many community events. In 1962, Goldwater's department store was the anchor of a new mall, Scottsdale Fashion Square, built on the site.

PHOTO COURTESY OF SCOTTSDALE FASHION SQUARE

owners chose the area for its resort lifestyle and its potential customer base. Starting in their garages or workshops, companies like Arizona Sun Products, China Mist Tea and Antigua have since expanded into national and international markets. In 1992, the Arizona Technology Incubator opened in Scottsdale, spawning a variety of cutting-edge ideas, from satellite-linked golf cart systems to biometric computer security systems.

During the 1970s and 1980s, specialty malls like The Borgata, the Seville and el Pedregal Festival Marketplace opened to serve both visitors and residents. While these specialty malls were welcomed by many, the introduction of national chain stores began to dilute Scottsdale's retail reputation—Western flavor and one-of-a-kind shops—that had been established in the late 1940s and 1950s.

Hoping to attract the most upscale of all shoppers, the Scottsdale Galleria opened with much hoopla in 1991 at the corner of Scottsdale Road and Fifth Avenue. Its marble and "dancing" fountains, restaurants and boutiques failed to attract enough customers to keep it open longer than eighteen months. It closed in 1992, and, after several attempts to open it for shopping or as a cultural venue, it was scheduled to be transformed into a high technology office complex in 2001. Just as the Galleria was failing, Scottsdale Fashion Square, however, was evolving into the state's largest and most successful shopping center. It merged with adjacent Camelview Plaza in the early 1990s, then added Arizona's first Nordstrom and more than fifty new stores in a bridge over Camelback Road in 1998.

Just as basic to Scottsdale's character as tourism and the arts, Scottsdale's reputation as a place for healthy living got a boost in the 1970s and 1980s.

Nearly failing after its modest start in 1962, the town's one hospital was taken over in 1971 by the Scottsdale Baptist Hospital's Governing Board. Operating as a not-for-profit community healthcare provider, the hospital changed its name to Scottsdale Memorial Hospital. In 1978, Scottsdale Memorial opened the Kenneth M. Piper Family Health Center on Shea Boulevard, just east of Pima Road. Six years later in 1984, Scottsdale Memorial expanded its Shea location to include Scottsdale Memorial North, Scottsdale's second full-service hospital. In 1987, Scottsdale welcomed Mayo Clinic to east Shea Boulevard, a second satellite location in the U.S. from its Rochester, Minnesota headquarters. Mayo Clinic brought additional national and international awareness on Scottsdale as a place not only for healthcare, but tourism, as patients and their families returned for visits.

In 1974, Scottsdale annexed twenty-one square miles, growing to eighty-nine square miles and extending the city east to the newly formed community of Fountain Hills on the eastern slopes of the McDowells. In 1982, the city added about 30 square miles, absorbing land north past Lone Mountain Road; in 1984, another thirty-six square miles were added, pushing the city limits north to the Continental Mountains. Scottsdale's area had now grown to 185 square miles. Although much of the newly-annexed land was wide open desert, a few enterprising landowners and developers had already been working with Maricopa County to create planned communities in the scenic area.

One of the first major developers "up north" was Jerry Nelson. He and his wife Florence, while vacationing at Camelback Inn in 1969, fell in love with the desert and bought a big chunk of land in the Pinnacle Peak area. Much like Winfield Scott and his pioneer neighbors of 1888, the Nelsons and their construction crews faced many desert hardships in the early 1970s—no phone, no water, no paved roads, and a really long drive to the grocery store. By necessity, learning to live in a desert environment created a bond between the Nelsons and their land; they became a force to help preserve important natural features as development continued. Even before the area was annexed by Scottsdale, the Nelsons worked with county and state land planners to develop guidelines for limiting hillside development and setting aside natural open space areas. Ironically, when they bought the property in 1969, the Nelsons were told that the only "development" that might prosper in the Pinnacle Peak area would be mobile home parks, similar to those in Mesa. Today, their former property contains the luxury golf communities of Pinnacle Peak Village, Troon Village and Troon North.

Although there had been golf in Scottsdale since the Ingleside Inn opened in 1910, it did not become a major industry until the 1970s. As planned communities developed, each built at least one golf course. So did the new crop of luxury resorts. When the Tournament Players Course Scottsdale opened in 1986 and lured the Phoenix Open golf tournament to its links in 1987, Scottsdale was instantly on the golf map. Golf became not only a tourism draw and a quality of life amenity for residents, but also a source of jobs and business ventures. The Scottsdale Airpark became home to golf course designers and golf equipment manufacturers. Demand for tee times exceeded the rapid pace of golf course construction. By 2001, there were more than forty golf courses with a Scottsdale address, and several more under construction.

Access to an adequate supply of water continued to be a significant challenge to the City of Scottsdale. Citizens were questioning how the community would have adequate water resources to support growth of new residential areas, golf courses, resorts, businesses and schools, and if growth should continue at this pace.

Historically, Scottsdale residents had relied primarily on groundwater sources—deep wells drilled through bedrock—run by numerous, privately-owned water companies. This patchwork of private water sources included names such as Mockingbird, Ocotillo, Indian Bend, Desert Springs, Ironwood and Carefree Ranch water companies, plus many others. These companies tried to keep up with the demand of Scottsdale's burgeoning population, but dependence on groundwater had its downsides.

Water users throughout Arizona had been pumping groundwater faster than it was being replaced naturally, creating a situation called overdraft. Groundwater overdraft can create significant problems, such as increased well drilling and pumping costs. The quality of the water can also suffer because groundwater

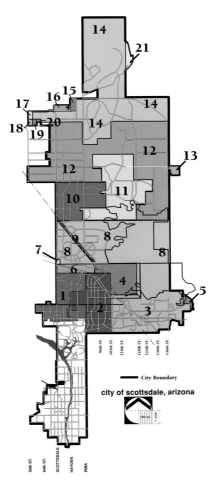

Annexation History
North of Shea Boulevard

Date of Annexation

1	11/26/62	11	1/5/82
2	2/19/63	12	10/6/83
3	5/20/75	13	5/15/90
4	4/18/72	14	7/2/84
5	5/19/86	15	10/2/84
6	8/1/78	16	8/6/84
7	8/1/78	17	8/4/86
8	3/4/63	18	6/2/97
9	1/5/82	19	6/2/97
10	1/5/82	20	8/4/86
		21	10/18/88

pumped from greater depths contains more salts and minerals. In areas of severe groundwater depletion, the earth's surface may also subside, causing cracks or fissures that can damage roads or building foundations. Recognizing that continued depletion of finite groundwater supplies threatens quality of life, the Arizona Legislature created the framework to attempt to manage the state's water supply for the future: the Arizona Groundwater Management Act, adopted in 1980.

Starting in the 1970s and continuing into the 1980s and 1990s the City of Scottsdale negotiated to buy most of the private companies supplying groundwater in order to control the quality of water and its delivery within the city. In 1985, Scottsdale also became one of the first municipal customers of the newest source of water, the Central Arizona Project (CAP). The city's original CAP allocation was 19,000 acre-feet per year; by 2000, the allocation had grown to over 60,000 acre-feet per year through negotiation with other communities and the CAP to buy additional water rights.

With passage of the Arizona Groundwater Management Act and the opening of CAP water flow by 1986, the City of Scottsdale began to concentrate on surface sources for its water. By the year 2001, Scottsdale's primary water sources were surface sources, supplied by the CAP from the Colorado River and by the Salt River Project (SRP) from the Verde River via the Arizona Canal. Scottsdale does use groundwater, pumped from thirty-four City wells, but is reducing its dependency on groundwater. Scottsdale also started a wastewater reclamation program at the City's Water Campus, which opened in 1999 west of Pima Road near Hualapai Drive. Most of the wastewater treated at the water campus plant is

used for golf course irrigation. The surplus is treated to drinking water standards and stored underground for later use.

The community's dedication to quality education—started by the early pioneers in 1896—continued through the last thirty years of the twentieth century. Scottsdale Unified School District built schools as the population continued north. The newly annexed parts of the city brought two new school districts into the picture, Paradise Valley Unified School District and Cave Creek Unified School District. By 2001, there were more than forty public schools with a Scottsdale address providing kindergarten through high school instruction. Even with this number of schools, the school districts couldn't keep up with explosive growth "up north," and schools were dealing with overcrowded conditions.

In addition to the growth in public schools, many private and charter schools opened in Scottsdale. Scottsdale Community College opened in wooden, temporary buildings on the Salt River Pima-Maricopa Indian Community in 1970. By 1999 it had added a second campus in the Scottsdale Airpark to serve the business community and the population in the northern parts of Scottsdale and Phoenix. Other institutes of higher learning helped educate people in Scottsdale: University of Phoenix, Ottawa University and the Scottsdale Culinary Institute.

Residents continued to identify needs in the community and start organizations to fill those needs. In 1985, the City and the Scottsdale School District helped establish the Scottsdale Prevention Institute to keep students and parents informed about the consequences of substance abuse. In 1986, Scottsdale Leadership formed to help groom residents for community leadership positions. In the early 1990s, parents, educators and community leaders formed LINKS, a community collaborative that shares resources in order to ensure a healthy, safe and productive community for all residents. Citizens concerned about the loss of mountain and desert lands to development established the McDowell Sonoran Land Trust in 1990. Also in the early 1990s, the Scottsdale Youth Leadership Council earned national recognition for its fundraising efforts—mostly pennies collected from other students—to create a new display honoring Martin Luther King Jr. at the Lincoln Memorial in Washington, D.C.

By 1990, Scottsdale's population reached 130,000 and showed no signs of stopping.

The world was literally converging in Scottsdale—tourists, new businesses, new residents, seasonal residents. The once sleepy farm community was experiencing the positives and negatives of becoming a big city. On the positive side, its strong and diverse economy earned the city top ratings with Wall Street agencies, kept the unemployment rate at less than three percent a year and maintained property taxes at an attractively low rate. More parks, libraries and community facilities provided additional services to residents, but were soon stretched thin to accommodate the growing population. On the nega-

tive side were concerns about air pollution, traffic jams, increased crime and the "anonymity" of many new residents in a town where once everyone knew everyone. Established residents feared the loss of the small town friendliness that they had enjoyed for years. Bells of alarm were sounding in hospitality industry circles; many said growth and the replacement of wide open spaces with red tile roofs was "killing the golden goose" of Scottsdale's economy and taking away its special character.

In 1991, following the citizen participation success of the STEP committees of earlier decades, Scottsdale conducted a community visioning process to help define what characteristics about the community were important and

needing nurturing. Four dominant themes evolved from hundreds of hours of public meetings: Sonoran Desert, arts and culture, health and research, and resort lifestyle. To put structure to this vision, citizens then participated in the CityShape 2020 process, which created a road map to follow in developing, redeveloping and preserving Scottsdale into the future.

During the 1990s, Scottsdale, more than ever before, became part of the global economy. International visitors accounted for nearly twenty percent of Scottsdale's seven million annual visitors. World-renowned resorts—such as the Scottsdale Princess, the Hyatt Regency at Gainey Ranch, the Boulders and the Four Seasons—now hosted visitors year round. International television coverage of the Scottsdale-based Phoenix Open PGA tournament showed larger audiences Scottsdale's warm and inviting environment. In 1995, the City and a number of businesses launched sites on the Internet's World Wide Web; by

✧

Above: World class luxury resorts opened in the Scottsdale area during the 1980s and 1990s, drawing the most upscale of visitors. By 2001, Scottsdale had nearly 8,600 resort and hotel rooms, hundreds of restaurants, and many attractions. However, as the population exploded and more of the former "wide-open spaces" were consumed by red tile roofs, the hospitality industry became increasingly concerned about the character of the destination. Surveys continued to show that visitors had been attracted to Scottsdale for its scenic beauty and Sonoran Desert ambiance. In the late 1990s the question became: would visitors continue to be drawn to Scottsdale as it became more urban?

Left, top and bottom: As development encroached to the foothills of the McDowells and into the desert, fighting mountain and desert wildfires became more challenging. The Troon North fire in June 1992 and the Rio fire in July 1995 demonstrated how conditions in the semi-arid desert environment could pose a danger to nearby homes.

Drivers along Scottsdale's portion of the Pima Freeway are treated to a remarkable example of Scottsdale's commitment to public art. The freeway noise suppression and retaining walls are covered with stylized Sonoran Desert plants, animals and mountains scenes created by artist Carolyn Braaksma. Former mayor and leader in the arts community (Kathryn) Sam Campana championed the freeway art program.

PHOTO COURTESY OF THE SCOTTSDALE CULTURAL COUNCIL AND COMMISSIONED THROUGH THE SCOTTSDALE PUBLIC ART PROGRAM. PROJECT DESIGN TEAM: CAROLYN BRAAKSMA, JEFF ENGLEMANN, ANDREA LEE FORMAN. PHOTOGRAPH BY LAURIE CAMPBELL.

2001 Scottsdale had become a new haven for "dot com," or Internet-based, companies whose workers wanted the lifestyle that Scottsdale and its land had to offer.

Transportation had become nearly the challenge that water had previously been for a growing population. Transportation planning, funding and construction could not keep up with the explosive commercial and residential growth in Scottsdale and the Phoenix metropolitan area; traffic jams were inducing a new phenomenon, "road rage." In 1996, Scottsdale was initially linked into a "better-late-than-never" freeway system that began to encircle the Salt River Valley in the 1980s. The Pima Freeway, or Loop 101, helps Scottsdale residents get around the area and also assists employees and customers living elsewhere get to Scottsdale. The freeway also spawned new retail and corporate development along its route on the eastern side of the Scottsdale. When complete in 2003, the Pima Freeway will provide new opportunities and challenges to Scottsdale and the Valley, socially and economically. Completion of the freeway system may expedite travel through Scottsdale and the Valley, but many fear it will only spread the sprawl of development to yet pristine areas of the desert.

Managing growth became a major focus of citizen groups and City government in the 1990s. As more of the wide-open spaces in Scottsdale's northern desert area developed and the population topped 200,000, the dialogue often became contentious and frustrating. Homeowners associations rallied to oppose high-density housing, commercial development, mega-stores and even schools. People who had moved to Scottsdale in earlier decades to pursue an equestrian lifestyle were now finding it difficult to ride their horses amid the concrete and construction. In 1995 a citizen-driven ballot measure allowed residents to vote to increase the Scottsdale sales tax to provide funds to preserve the McDowell Mountains and adjacent Sonoran Desert. A second vote in 1998 set in place a plan to preserve nearly one-third of Scottsdale's land as natural open space.

At the same time the community was trying to find reasonable solutions for developing, or not developing, new areas, it was also focusing on redeveloping mature areas. The downtown and Los Arcos areas were beginning to show signs of decay, and plans were drawn up for new mixed-use projects. In 1998 and 1999, voters approved plans for redeveloping the Los Arcos area, and demolition of the mall began in 2000. Voters, however, rejected a plan in 1999 for downtown redevelopment that focused on the area along the south bank of the Arizona Canal; several alternative plans were in the works in 2001.

Scottsdale entered its fiftieth year of incorporation in 2001 with a population of nearly 220,000. There were more than 108,000 dwelling units. The top three industries were business services, retail and tourism. Its lifestyle and economy could be described by a new set of "Cs"—climate (the constant), commerce, culture, cowboy cachet, construction, computers, citizen collaboration and concern about conserving the charisma and character of the community.

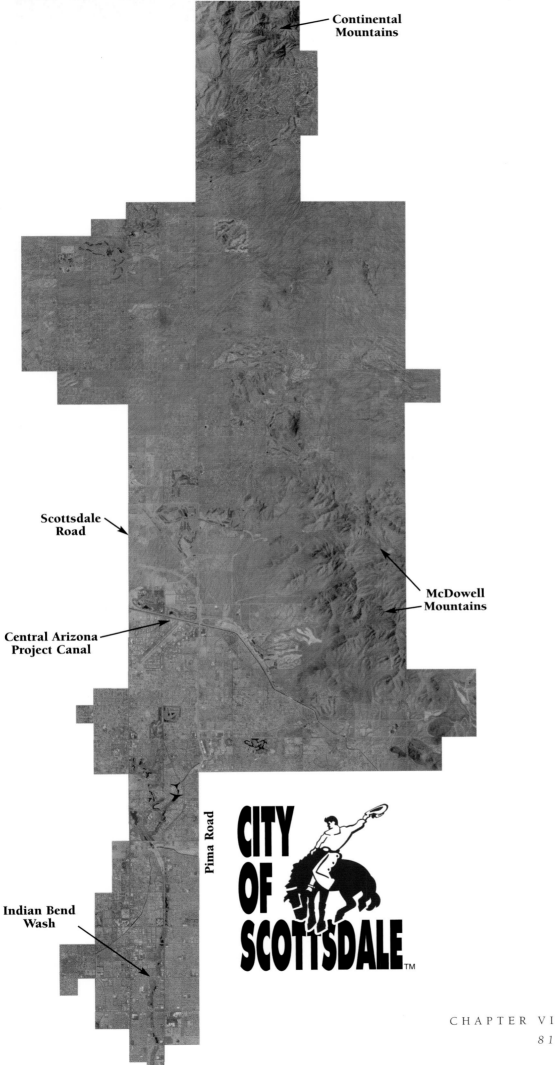

Continental Mountains

Scottsdale Road

Central Arizona Project Canal

McDowell Mountains

Pima Road

Indian Bend Wash

CITY OF SCOTTSDALE™

Scottsdale entered its 50th year of incorporation in 2001 with a population of nearly 220,000. There were more than 108,000 dwelling units. The top three industries were business services, retail and tourism. Through an aggressive preservation program started in 1990, nearly one-third of Scottsdale's land is already or planned to be preserved as open space. This aerial view, produced by the City as part of its implementation of Geographic Information System (GIS), shows Scottsdale in 1999.

GIS PHOTO COURTESY OF THE CITY OF SCOTTSDALE

Just a reminder to vote yes on Proposition 400, Tuesday, May 23.

It will preserve scenic views, wildlife habitat, and archeological sites in the McDowell Mountains now threatened by development. Funds will come from a two-tenths percent increase in the Scottsdale sales tax.

Without Proposition 400, roads and homes will scar our mountains, wildlife will vanish and hiking/riding trails will be locked behind private security gates.

Don't let roads and homes climb our mountains. Vote yes on 400.

Photo: Nathan Wardleigh.

SAVING THE LAND:
SCOTTSDALE'S PRESERVATION MANDATE

It's a place of quiet solitude, a tapestry of silence punctured by coyote howls, woodpecker knocks and breezes rustling the branches of mesquite trees. A rainbow of color treats the eye...cactus green, cardinal red, dark gray granite, yellow-spined cholla, blue sky. Shapes, angles and contours of rock challenge the imagination. Each season gives us new experiences—winter's cool, starry nights...balmy and fragrant spring breezes...hot summer days that turn into torrential downpours...the sunny, mild days of autumn. The land holds treasures of history—Hohokam petroglyphs, detritus of the dreams of miners and homesteaders, cowboy gear. This is Scottsdale's Sonoran Desert, skirting the majestic McDowell Mountains. This is what the citizens of Scottsdale are dedicated to preserving.

Over the years, thousands of people have devoted countless hours to protecting this land, most notably by creating the McDowell Sonoran Preserve—envisioned as 36,400 acres, fifty-seven square miles, of rugged mountains and adjoining Sonoran Desert preserved as natural open space. The non-profit McDowell Sonoran Land Trust (MSLT) spearheaded the preservation effort, which has been truly community-wide, in partnership with the City of Scottsdale staff and elected officials, and with the support of citizen groups, outdoor enthusiasts, state and federal officials and agencies, the Scottsdale Chamber of Commerce, the tourism industry, real estate developers, students and voters.

When did Scottsdale begin to focus on preserving its 1.8 billion-year-old land? When did the community start to change from expending the land and its resources to staunchly defending it?

History shows that people have always admired, even worshipped, these eloquent mountains and desert land. Petroglyphs left in the McDowells by the earliest inhabitants show their deep connection to nature – figures of deer, rabbits and snakes, and rocks aligned to denote the changing of seasons and the position of the sun and stars. Even these early people, however, most likely over-hunted certain species and over-harvested native plants.

In the last two centuries people used the desert and mountain lands in various ways, from farming and mining to residential and commercial development, outdoor recreation and as a scenic backdrop for tourism. Each generation has savored the natural beauty, open spaces and warm, dry climate of Scottsdale's desert, but our rush to make a life here has often damaged the environment. As novelist Wallace Stegner has written, "...we may love a place and still be dangerous to it."

Although it is difficult to pinpoint when our environmental consciousness as a community rose to the action level, many meaningful steps occurred in the last four decades of the twentieth century. In the 1960s, for example, the first Scottsdale Town Enrichment Program (STEP) forums and committees recommended bold measures to retain Scottsdale's character: a stringent ordinance to ban billboards, a multi-use park (instead of a concrete channel) to control flooding of the Indian Bend Wash, and a commitment to build parks and equestrian trails throughout the community.

While the nation was turning environmental and celebrating the first Earth Day in 1970, Scottsdale citizens and their city government began to plan land use in designs more compatible with the desert environment. The Northeast Area Plan was adopted in 1976 to guide development of the newly annexed twenty-five square miles east on Shea Boulevard to Fountain Hills, and it included many environmental guidelines regarding the McDowell Mountains. Concerned citizens encouraged Mayor Bill Jenkins and the City Council in 1977 to enact the first Hillside Ordinance, which spelled out how mountain land could or could not be developed. Meanwhile, conscientious developers like Lyle Anderson and Jerry Nelson voluntarily limited mountainside construction and included natural open space in their new Desert Highlands and Troon communities located in the yet-to-be-annexed lands north of Scottsdale. In 1986, Anderson would also do the same in the foothills of the Continental Mountains when he developed the Desert Mountain community.

The 1981 Native Plant Ordinance enacted by the Scottsdale City Council was an important step to preserve the cacti, trees and shrubs that give the area its unique character.

Again through thoughtful and forward-looking citizen involvement, both the 1981 General Plan update and the Tonto Foothills Plan (which influenced the thirty-six square miles to the north annexed in 1984) strongly emphasized the need for open space, environmental design, protection of natural features and use of natural vegetation. Implementation of these goals was not always successful, but they did mark a commitment to retaining the Sonoran Desert character.

Many groups, such as the Friends of the Desert Foothills Scenic Drive (founded in 1963) and the Greater Pinnacle Peak Homeowners Association (founded in 1976) continued to speak out about the need to permanently preserve and protect the desert and mountains as people moved farther north and east onto undeveloped land.

As community spirit was rising to preserve the desert environment, it was, however, denied the tool that had previously served other preservation-minded communities. In 1986, the state courts struck down the Hillside Ordinance as unconstitutional; the ordinance was perceived as a "taking" of the land's potential value from its owners. This opened the door to development up the very face of the McDowells and into the interior valleys of the mountain range. Private landowners and developers were poised to begin.

At this time most Scottsdale residents still lived far south of the mountains and were unaware of this very real threat to their signa-

ture scenic feature. People commonly thought that the northern mountains and deserts were part of the McDowell Mountain Regional County Park (which contains mostly desert slopes east of the actual McDowells) or the Tonto National Forest north of Scottsdale. It was community visionaries who would foresee the unprecedented and explosive growth that was about to occur "up north."

By 1990, alarmed citizens from all areas and backgrounds in the community had formed the McDowell Sonoran Land Trust. In the words of co-founder Jane Rau (a desert activist, fondly known at City Hall as "the burr under Scottsdale's saddle"), the MSLT was formed "to act as a facilitator to gain public access as well as the setting aside of the McDowells and portions of the Sonoran Desert for the enjoyment of all future generations." The new organization was determined

to act as the chief advocacy group on behalf of the voiceless but vital McDowell Mountains and the Sonoran Desert.

The MSLT attracted a wide range of residents and non-residents as members—from hikers and retirees to zoning attorneys and developers—who shared a goal of preserving the land before it was too late. The first MSLT chair, advertising executive and avid mountaineer Pete Chasar, was a resident of Phoenix. Tempe attorney Mark Knops joined local attorney Fred Davidson in donating countless hours to establish the MSLT. Co-founder Karen Bertiger was active in the business of land investment. Retired Salt River Project engineer Chet Andrews would serve as the second MSLT chair and initiate key public outreach and land stewardship programs. Joining the board in 1992 were the brother and sister

✧

The importance of preserving the McDowell Mountains and adjacent Sonoran Desert is underscored by the Arizona Game and Fish Department, which considers the area the most significant wildlife habitat in the Valley (outside the Tonto National Forest). Arizona Game and Fish has been a partner from the beginning in helping Scottsdale and its citizens plan the McDowell Sonoran Preserve. Animals shown here are among those commonly found in the McDowell Sonoran Preserve (left to right): mule deer (so named for its big ears), mountain lion (Arizona has one of the largest lion populations in the U.S.) and desert tortoise (whose burrows may be up to 30 feet long).

PHOTOS COURTESY OF ARIZONA GAME AND FISH; MULE DEER AND DESERT TORTOISE PHOTOS BY BOB MILES; MOUNTAIN LION PHOTO BY GEORGE ANDREJKO

team of archaeologist Greg Woodall and Carla (her full, legal name); they grew up in a Hallcraft home in the southern end of the city but spent their free time exploring what was then the "far away" northern desert and mountains. Greg used his extensive knowledge of this land to draw the first maps envisioning a large, natural open-space system that would stretch from the McDowell Mountains north to the Tonto National Forest. Carla was the driving force and political strategist behind the preservation movement and eventually became the executive director of the MSLT.

The MSLT organized public hearings about the benefits of preservation and conducted hikes to acquaint people with the threatened areas. In partnership with the City and Scottsdale School District officials, the MSLT created an education program, "Our McDowell Sonoran Heritage," available to fourth graders in Scottsdale, Fountain Hills, Paradise Valley and Cave Creek, providing school assemblies and desert hikes. In the first year City of Scottsdale Outdoor Recreation Specialist Yvonne Massman led more than 1,700 students into the envisioned preserve. These children then became "preserve ambassadors" to their parents, neighbors and friends. The MSLT also began raising money to buy land for a preserve.

Scottsdale citizens entered the 1990s in high gear for saving the environment, and said so during the citywide Scottsdale

Visioning Process in 1991. Embracing, enhancing and preserving the Sonoran Desert was one of four dominant themes to emerge from the Visioning process. Also in 1991, residents crafted, and the City Council passed, the less stringent but legally acceptable Environmentally Sensitive Lands Ordinance to replace the negated Hillside Ordinance—but there were still private ownership rights to consider. Zoning restrictions could only work so far; the only way to ensure permanent preservation of the mountains and adjacent desert was to buy land and place it in a permanent preserve. Development pressures created an urgent mandate for action.

People had used them for centuries, but Scottsdale's magnificent mountains and lush Sonoran Desert with abundant wildlife and unique desert flora had never been as threatened as they now were with the approaching tidal wave of homes, golf courses and business development. Since most of the land in the mountains and foothills area was privately owned and zoned for development, Scottsdale's signature landmark would be significantly marred forever. The mountain and high desert environment is what drew most residents and tourism businesses to

✧

Right: The McDowell Sonoran Preserve offers urban dwellers a place to escape the pressures of city life. This view, below Frazier Spring, looks west from Windgate Overlook. The McDowell Mountains signature Windgate Pass got its name from equestrians, who on rides through the area, saw the strong winds which exist at that elevation consistently blowing open an old ranch gate.

**PHOTO COURTESY OF
THE MCDOWELL SONORAN LAND TRUST**

Below: City of Scottsdale Outdoor Recreation Specialist Yvonne Massman and the McDowell Sonoran Land Trust co-founder Jane Rau share stories with fourth-graders about the mountains and desert as part of the "Our McDowell Sonoran Heritage" program.

**PHOTO COURTESY OF
THE MCDOWELL SONORAN LAND TRUST**

Scottsdale; those who came for other reasons promptly fell in love with these natural treasures, too. Tourism—Scottsdale's number one industry, employing nearly twenty-five percent of the population and creating over $2 billion in economic impact annually—also depended on the beauty, ambiance and adventure of the undeveloped desert areas.

Scottsdale was growing in the 1990s (from 130,069 residents in 1990 to 168,176 in 1995) and residential development was beginning to encroach on the McDowell Mountains. At least four residential and commercial developers announced plans for major developments, which included mountain-side lots. Scottsdale was nationally honored in 1993 as America's "most livable city," and land values were rising significantly, as many newcomers wanted to live in or near the mountains. Rather than take an adversarial, anti-growth approach, volunteer and City-appointed citizen groups came together to plan how to preserve the McDowell Mountains and adjacent desert.

Early in 1993 the MSLT urged Mayor Drinkwater and the City Council to form a task force to identify land important to preserve, and then to recommend ways to fund that effort. The McDowell Mountains Task Force, chaired by business leader and avid

equestrian Virginia Korte, embraced its mission, recommending a study boundary to the City and encouraging the City Council to create a citizen body—which would become the McDowell Sonoran Preserve Commission—for advice on matters regarding the preservation effort. Under the leadership of Scottsdale Community College President and long-time civic leader Dr. Art DeCabooter, the new Commission held public hearings and received valuable and encouraging input from citizens. The Commission and the MSLT formed a partnership from the very beginning (sharing many of the same members) that took the message not only to the community, but to landowners and potential developers: It is the public's will to preserve the mountains.

The official commitment to the preservation effort is exemplified by the early 1995 City staff reorganization that created a Preservation Division in the city manager's office. The purpose of this action was to raise the visibility of the preservation effort in the City organization and to focus preservation issues in a single location. Preservation Director Bob Cafarella and his two staff members would soon facilitate numerous, complex preservation land purchases.

In July 1994 the City Council, led by Mayor Drinkwater and Councilmen Mary Manross and Robert Pettycrew, adopted a 16,240-acre Recommended Study Boundary for the McDowell Sonoran Preserve. By October the City celebrated the establishment of the infant Preserve comprised of 2,860 acres of mountain land purchased previously from Maricopa County and additional slope areas donated by development companies Suncor (adjacent to Scottsdale Mountain) and Newhall Land and Farming Company (adjacent to McDowell Mountain Ranch).

Key members of the development community, once feared as threatening adversaries, were discussing how preservation would work. The heart of the McDowells was controlled by the Corrigan-Marley family and DMB Associates, and was slated for development as a planned community, DC Ranch. After long negotiations with the Preserve Commission and City officials, the head of DMB Associates, Drew Brown, promised to hold back development in much of the McDowells if the City would buy the land.

By now, there was no more time for study; the time to act had arrived.

In 1995 members of the McDowell Sonoran Land Trust and McDowell Sonoran Preserve Commission along with key business and community leaders formed a political action committee, *Save Our McDowells*. The committee promoted passage of a City ballot measure in which citizens would vote to tax themselves and the city's visitors (whose spending, at the time, accounted for approximately fifty percent of Scottsdale's sales tax revenues) through a two-tenths of one-percent sales tax for thirty years. As proceeds of the tax accumulated, they would be used to purchase the envisioned Preserve lands.

Building the broadest community support for the ballot measure—called Proposition 400—was critical. Strong support came quickly from leading hoteliers who recognized the benefit to their tourism clients. One of the freshest and most passionate voices came from middle school student Kristen Jaskie, who would join the MSLT board of directors at age thirteen and serve until leaving for college. Bill Ensign, retired City parks director, chaired the board at this pivotal time and would initiate the successful "I Got My Ten" campaign whereby supporters would each sign up ten friends to support the ballot measure. During this time trained leaders took nearly two-thousand hikers into the mountains—believing firmly that every visitor to the land would be a sure "yes" vote. Writers like Cynthia Lukas, later a City Councilwoman, penned eloquent arguments about the need for land preservation. Many other volunteers spent untold hours. After

RECOMMENDED STUDY BOUNDARY FOR THE MCDOWELL SONORAN PRESERVE

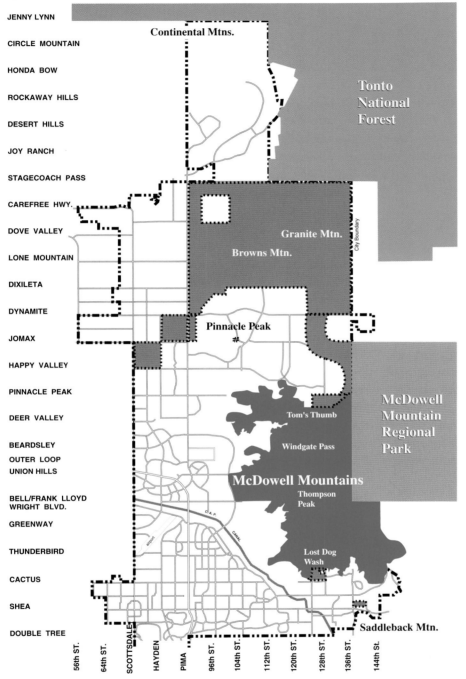

RECOMMENDED STUDY BOUNDARY FOR THE MCDOWELL SONORAN PRESERVE: 36,400 ACRES TOTAL

 16,460 Acre Original Recommended Study Boundary Used from 1995 to 1998 for Expenditures of Voter Approved Sales Tax Revenues

 19,940 Acre Expanded Recommended Study Boundary August 1998

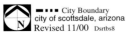
▪ ▪ ▪ ▪ City Boundary
city of scottsdale, arizona
Revised 11/00 Dsrtbs8

I GOT MY 10
VOTE 400

intense and sometimes contentious community dialogue, all these efforts paid off. In May 1995, in a time when anti-tax sentiments prevailed across our country, this measure passed by a healthy sixty-four percent.

In 1996, eighteen months later, and worried that sales tax revenues would not come in fast enough to stay ahead of development, Scottsdale again put a ballot question before the voters, this time asking for permission to sell revenue bonds which would be repaid from the preservation tax. With a healthy economy, a fast-growing retail sector and a passion to protect the McDowells, the voters again overwhelmingly supported the measure by an even greater margin, seventy-three percent favoring. This would expedite land purchases.

The City began purchasing land within the recommended boundaries of the Preserve in 1996. Unfortunately, some earlier-approved developments in the foothills of the McDowells

were already being built. While these developers did work with the City to either donate or sell some of the higher elevations for the Preserve, there will always be regret that community support for preservation efforts did not get underway in earnest much sooner.

That same year, Mayor Sam Campana and the City Council appointed a Desert Preservation Task Force, chaired by Carla. The task force recommended adding 19,940 acres to the McDowell Sonoran Preserve, creating a continuous open-space system to support desert flora and fauna and maintain historic trails. In a ballot proposition in 1998 voters overwhelmingly agreed (by seventy percent in favor) to use the mountain preservation sales tax to buy desert land also. The planned Preserve was thereby enlarged to protect nearly one-third of the City. It was, as well, connected to the Tonto National Forest in the north and the trails and open space systems of neighboring communi-

ties. This natural connectivity is critical to ensuring the biological sustainability of the land. On the same ballot was a change to the City charter, which would prohibit any future City Council from selling or leasing land in the Preserve without a vote of the people. This passed by eighty-one percent in favor. People from all walks of Scottsdale life had spoken with their hearts and wallets to say preserving open space and natural habitat was important to them.

With such strong community support—and an excellent bond rating—Scottsdale was moving fast to lock up the land for preservation. In 1998, the City purchased DC Ranch property inside the recommended Preserve boundaries, thus preserving the bulk of the McDowells. In 1999 voters approved the issuance of General Obligation bonds for preservation purchases by seventy-seven percent in favor. That same year, the City made key purchases in the southern Lost Dog Wash access area, and also bought the historic Browns Ranch in the expanded northern desert Preserve area. By 2000, over 45 percent of the envisioned 36,400 acres were set aside for preservation, paid for by sales tax monies and financed by bonds based on future tax revenues. Developers and the McDowell Sonoran Land Trust have donated additional land.

There are tough battles ahead in creating and maintaining the Preserve. Much of the remaining land envisioned for the Preserve is state trust land. State trust lands, transferred to Arizona at statehood by the federal government, by law must be auctioned to the highest bidder with the interest from the proceeds going to benefit primarily the state's school system. Representative Carolyn Allen is Scottsdale's champion at the State Legislature, pushing for reforms to aid the land preservation effort. Great challenges confront the completion of the Preserve, but a strong citizen-driven momentum exists to face them and succeed. When elected in 2000, Mayor Mary Manross pledged that Scottsdale is dedicated to achieving this goal.

Saving the McDowells has benefited the city far beyond land preservation. A spirit of partnership among many diverse entities has been formed and thrives as measures are

designed to manage the Preserve. Management of a preserve is far different from park management, and groups must find acceptable ways to balance appropriate public use with protection of the Preserve's wildness and the treasures it contains.

The project also has helped unify residents separated by geography. Scottsdale is a shoestring town over thirty miles long and generally no more than two to five miles wide, making it easy for residents to stay in their own part of the city. The Preserve project has joined Scottsdale's "new north" to its venerable "old south" in common purpose.

The preservation project has also created a dramatic shift in our attitudes about open space. It is no longer accepted that open space is what is "left over" after development occurs. Citizens, officials and forward-thinking developers insist that open space be the beautiful framework within which our community grows. It has also changed the attitudes of

those who believed that preserving land would harm the robust economy; to the contrary, it has boosted the community's economy by offering a quality of life avidly desired.

Scottsdale citizens have also enjoyed the opportunity to work with the neighboring town of Fountain Hills (located on the southeastern foothills of the McDowells) in their successful 1997 sales tax initiative to fund preservation of the southeastern side of the McDowell Mountains and add to the shared Preserve.

It is truly citizens who have built the McDowell Sonoran Preserve. The McDowell Sonoran Land Trust, comprised of hundreds of residents who love this unique land and seek to preserve it, began the process in 1990. While land acquisitions continue, so do advocacy and education programs. Scottsdale Community College and the MSLT have together created a Preserve Stewardship course to train volunteer stewards to patrol the Preserve. These two organizations were also the recipients of a grant from the Nina Mason Pulliam Charitable Trust in 2000 to establish a Center for Native and Urban Wildlife at the college which will restore habitat in damaged areas of the Preserve. Scottsdale, Fountain Hills and the MSLT also sponsor an annual McDowell Sonoran Month

during October, taking programs into schools and bringing hundreds of people into the Preserve for hikes and clean-ups.

Scottsdale's McDowell Sonoran Preserve is a model for other communities. It was among the first to recognize the importance of saving not just mountain tops, but of creating a sustainable open space system with undisturbed habitat in which desert plants and wildlife can continue to thrive and be enjoyed by future generations.

To have gone from a "crazy" idea (preserving such a large area by taxing ourselves) to a reality that is embraced by the overwhelming majority of residents—and to have accomplished so much in such a short time—is an astonishing achievement.

If the Archaic people, the Hohokam, Winfield Scott and E.O. Brown—and all the others—could see Scottsdale now, they would no doubt be amazed at what has happened here. We like to think they would also be pleased with how their dreams are being carried forth by those who are now the stewards of this land, those who see it as the structure upon which our homes—and our spirits—rest, those who realize our lives come from the land.

✦

The people came together and saved this precious land.

PHOTO COURTESY OF MCDOWELL SONORAN LAND TRUST

Right: Looking west on Christy Road, later renamed McDowell Road, from the Hedger Ranch south of Scottsdale, 1917.
PHOTO COURTESY OF SRP HERITAGE

E.O. Brown, Brown Avenue

Mayor Mort Kimsey, Kimsey Lane

Vice President Thomas Marshall, Marshall Way

SCOTTSDALE STREETS AND PLACES: A REFLECTION OF HISTORY

Brown Avenue – Honors E.O. Brown who moved to Scottsdale from Wisconsin in 1904 and owned, or was a partner in, Brown's Mercantile, the Scottsdale Ginning Company, the Scottsdale Water Company, DC and Browns Ranches and the Scottsdale Light and Power Company.

Butherus Drive – Daniel C. Butherus was the President of the Arizona Conference of the Seventh Day Adventists, which had taken over the land of the former Thunderbird II World War II pilot training base in 1953. In 1963, the Adventists deeded, at no cost, 100 acres of their land to the City of Scottsdale to establish Scottsdale Municipal Airport.

Curry's Corner – Intersection of Scottsdale and Pinnacle Peak Roads formerly known as Curry's Corner, named for J.B. Curry who operated a remote general store there. It was also the site of a curio stand operated by Don Pablo during the 1950s and 1960s.

Drinkwater Boulevard – Honors Herb Drinkwater, who served as beloved Mayor of Scottsdale from 1980 to 1996. The street was previously called Civic Center Boulevard.

Frank Lloyd Wright Boulevard – The famed architect established his winter residence and school of architecture at the southern foothills of the McDowells in 1937. He was a popular figure around Scottsdale through the 1940s.

Greenway Road – The Greenway family was closely associated with the Roosevelts. John Greenway was one of Teddy Roosevelt's Rough Riders and a Spanish-American War hero. Isabella S. Greenway was a lifelong friend of Eleanor Roosevelt, and served as U.S. Representative from Arizona 1933-36. She and her husband owned copper mines, the Arizona Inn and a cattle ranch.

Hayden Road – Named for the family of Wilford Hayden, who farmed just south and east of the original Scottsdale town site from the late 1890s through the 1950s. Most think it honors Charles T. Hayden, founder of Tempe and father of U.S. Senator Carl Hayden…now you know differently.

Indian School Road – Named for the school for Native Americans established in the early 1900s at Indian School Road and Central Avenue in Phoenix. The portion in Scottsdale was originally called Utley Avenue, then Scott Avenue since it ran adjacent to the properties of early resident Albert Utley and founder Winfield Scott.

The Wilford Hayden family (and friends), Hayden Road

Kalarama – Name of trotting horse favored by W. W. Creighton who, in the 1950s, built one of Scottsdale's first neighborhoods, Peaceful Valley (located north of Osborn Road, east of Miller Road). He gave his own family name to Creighton Court within the development.

Kierland Boulevard – Mrs. G. (Katherine "Kax") Robert Herberger's maiden name is Kierland; Kierland was developed by Herberger Enterprises and Woodbine Southwest. Developer and land investor Bob Herberger also named two streets in the vicinity of the northwest corner of Scottsdale Road and Shea Boulevard after two of their three children: Gary and Gail.

Kimsey Lane – Mort Kimsey was Scottsdale's second mayor; his father, William Kimsey came to Scottsdale in the early 1900s and was co-founder of Scottsdale's first electric company.

Lincoln Drive – Honors John C. Lincoln, an industrialist from Cleveland, Ohio who moved his family here in the early 1900s. He and Jack Stewart built the Camelback Inn in 1936.

McDowell Road – Major General Irvin McDowell was the commanding general at the San Francisco headquarters to which Fort McDowell reported during the late 1800s; many area structures bear his name, although he rarely visited Arizona. The road was previously named Christy, after Colonel William Christy, who had a 440-acre farm near the intersection of 10th Street in Phoenix.

Marshall Way – Honors the Vice President of the United States Thomas Marshall (under President Woodrow Wilson), whose wife was Lois Kimsey, daughter of William Kimsey, Scottsdale pioneer. The Marshalls had a winter home in Scottsdale on Indian School Road, just west of Scottsdale Road.

Miller Road – Charles Miller moved to Scottsdale from North Dakota in 1913 and bought the land of the town's founder, Winfield Scott, on Indian School Road. He farmed the land, helped start Scottsdale's first electric company, and donated the land on which the old Scottsdale High School was built (where Lincoln Towne Center was built in 1998).

Pima Road and Pima Freeway – Honors the Akimel Au-Authm, also known as the Pima, who live on the Salt River Pima-Maricopa Indian Community and are likely descendants of the prehistoric Hohokam people. U.S. President Rutherford B. Hayes officially established the what is now the Salt River Pima-Maricopa Indian Community in 1879, nine years before Army Chaplain Winfield Scott first settled in what is now Scottsdale.

Scottsdale Road – Named for the town of Scottsdale, established as a townsite in 1888 by Army Chaplain Winfield Scott, his wife Helen and his brother, George. The road was previously called Paradise Street since it let north into the Paradise Valley area. Before being called Paradise Street, it was named Murphy Avenue in honor of Arizona Canal builder William J. Murphy.

Thompson's Peak – One of the tallest peaks in the McDowell Mountains, it is recognizable by the antennas on its top. Regrettably, no records have been found as to how it got its name, which is seen on maps as early as 1910.

McCormick Parkway, Ranch and Railroad Park – Honors civic patrons Anne and Fowler McCormick (son of International Harvester founder Cyrus McCormick) who owned an Arabian horse and cattle ranch at Scottsdale Road and Indian Bend in the 1940s through 1960s.

Thunderbird Road – Named for the World War II pilot training airfields operated by Southwest Airways; Thunderbird I in Glendale (now Thunderbird, The American Graduate School of International Management) and Thunderbird II (now Scottsdale Airport/Seventh Day Adventists Thunderbird Academy and the Scottsdale Airpark).

Sometimes streets are named or renamed to honor businesses moving into the Scottsdale area, such as Dial Boulevard, Dillon Way, Princess Drive and Pacesetter Drive. There used to be a Hamill, named for Olympic figure skater Dorothy Hamill, during the brief time in the early 1990s when she headquartered her Ice Capades here.

Anne McCormick, McCormick Parkway

Murle & Bill Miller (children of Charles Miller) and Hunter Chesnutt (Scottsdale High Class of 1923), Miller Road

PHOTO COURTESY OF TONY NELSSEN © 2000

HISTORIC SCOTTSDALE

SHARING THE HERITAGE

historic profiles of

businesses and organizations

that have contributed to

the development and economic

base of Scottsdale and served

as sponsors of this book

SPECIAL THANKS ALSO GOES TO

APS

Ladlow's Fine Furniture

*Scottsdale
Cardiovascular Center*

✧

Ed and Ruth Tweed's BruSally Ranch was the site of many post-Arabian Horse Show parties. The ranch, east of Hayden between Shea and Cactus, produced many prized Arabians.

COMMUNITY RESOURCES

institutions which provide

essential services to Scottsdalians

RURAL/METRO FIRE DEPARTMENT

✧

The photo above, taken in the early 1950s, shows the Rural/Metro fire company fleet outside of St. Francis Church along Central Avenue. Now part of Phoenix, it was then in an unincorporated Maricopa County area covered by Rural/Metro. The 1950s photo was recreated below using 1990s Scottsdale Rural/Metro trucks. The photo was taken in the parking lot of Saguaro High School near Hayden Road and McDonald Drive in Scottsdale.

Every time a Rural/Metro fire truck pulls out of a station, it carries a half-century of tradition. Starting with a single pumper manned with four firefighters, Rural/Metro has mushroomed into a multinational corporation with more than 11,000 employees and twelve million calls for service. Annual revenues exceeded $550 million in 1999.

Despite all that, Scottsdale remains Rural/Metro's home. It was Scottsdale that awarded Rural/Metro its first contract and encouraged it to pursue technological and fiscal innovation. As a result, Rural/Metro became a national role model for privatization. At the start of the twenty-first century, its diversified services range from fire protection and ambulance transport to staffing centers for emergency training and medical calls. In the beginning, things were not so complicated; there was only the matter of water.

In 1948, Scottsdale was a sleepy little outpost at the eastern end of Camelback Road, then a two-lane strip of concrete heading straight through the desert. It boasted a handful of businesses such as Earl's Market, Cavalliere's Blacksmith shop, and the new Pink Pony restaurant. It was unincorporated and unpaved. It could be said of Scottsdale "a cattle drive ran through it." Every year ranchers would pick up a herd at the Tempe railhead and drive them north along Scottsdale Road to Pinnacle Peak, raising clouds of dust and the curiosity of Valley residents.

One of them was Lou Witzeman, a twenty-three-year-old newspaper reporter at *The Arizona Times* in nearby Phoenix. In those days, Witzeman recalled, the Valley was sparsely populated and "everyone knew each other. The canals were lined with big cottonwoods; you could sit under them and fish." Other people went boating in the canals, and some even water-skied, pulled by cars driving along

the banks. In Scottsdale, residents rode their horses into town on the weekends and tied them up to hitching posts. "Scottsdale had a laid-back country atmosphere that was a good description of the West," Witzeman said.

However, in February of that year, Witzeman saw a dark side of country living when a neighbor's house burned down. The area was unincorporated and had no fire protection. Nothing could be done. It occurred to the young journalist that here was an opportunity to launch a business that would fulfill a growing need. Witzeman scraped together $3,000 for a fire station and $900 for a down payment on a 500-gallon pumper (fire truck). Lacking tax support, he went door-to-door soliciting subscriptions for $12 a year. Then he set up shop with three colleagues at Seventh Avenue and Camelback in Phoenix.

"We sat around the first two weeks," Witzeman said. "There weren't any fires." But as the trickle of newcomers in the Valley increased to a stream, the calls started coming in. Even though Scottsdale was some distance away, the fledgling company did its best to provide fire protection. "The only source of water was the canals and what you could carry on the trucks," Witzeman said.

"Scottsdale didn't count on us doing much, but the city fathers gave us 'E' for effort." In 1951, they did much more than that: under Mayor Malcolm White, the city incorporated and awarded Rural/Metro its first contract at $3,600 a year. The timing was perfect.

The ink was hardly dry when the first great wave of migrants from the Midwest and East poured in. Many were ex-fliers from World War II who had trained at such Valley bases as Luke, Williams, and Thunderbird Field and liked the climate. Soon, the fields around Scottsdale began to sprout suburbs with modest red brick homes. "They were building houses by the thousands," Witzeman said. "As they moved in, we followed them down the street selling subscriptions to our fire service."

In 1955, Scottsdale Stadium, host to innumerable spring training games, was built. It was followed a year later by the Safari Resort, the first of many such establishments along the "corridor" that would make Scottsdale a prime tourist destination.

During those early years, Rural/Metro established a reputation for innovation that persists today. It was one of the first firefighting companies in the area to make first-aid runs, using a van outfitted with resuscitators, oxygen machines, and other life-saving apparatus. In 1954, it acquired its first ambulance. It also developed a robot fireman, a remote-control device that could transport hose into dangerous environments and lessen the risk to firefighters. The robot was tested with good results but never finished. "We didn't have the technology then," Witzeman said. Updated versions are now being used in Tokyo, attesting to their value in life-threatening situations involving explosions, toxic fumes and collapsing roofs.

✧

Above: Company founder Lou Witzeman sits in his office at the now Station 10 at Miller and Thomas Roads during the 1970s plotting station response areas in Maricopa County, a recurring job during those growth days in the county.

Below: Rural/Metro firefighters train more than 300 hours a year using propane props such as this one. This type of training gives firefighters a chance to experience the heat of a real fire.

✦

Above: Longtime Scottsdale Mayor Herb Drinkwater was an ardent supporter of the fire department. Here he climbs an aerial ladder parked near Hayden and Osborn Roads in the mid-1980s.

Below: Rural/Metro firefighters treat a car accident victim after cutting open the car to get him out. Rural/Metro firefighters all are trained emergency medical technicians and many of them are certified emergency paramedics.

Witzeman, a firm believer in free market efficiency, also departed from convention with his use of full-time firefighters in tandem with well-trained "pay-per-call" reserves. "The traditional concept is to staff for a big fire," he said, "but very few fires need a lot of people. We could maintain fifteen reserves for the cost of one full-time firefighter." As a result, Rural/Metro avoided overstaffing and waste while fully meeting its obligations. Rural/Metro still relies on a dedicated force of reserve firefighters to complement and support its brigade of full-time professionals.

In 1962, Rural/Metro ventured beyond Maricopa County for the first time with a contract to provide fire protection to residents living outside the Tucson city limits. That year saw the last cattle drive along Scottsdale Road and the construction of Scottsdale Memorial Hospital. In 1964, future Mayor Herb Drinkwater opened up a liquor store in north Scottsdale, preparatory to a civic career that would change the city forever. In 1969, Scottsdale built Los Arcos, an upscale mall that set the tone for others to follow. By decade's end, Rural/Metro had transformed itself into a major player with fire-protection contracts not only in Pima County and Yuma County, but also Knox County, Tennessee. Equally important, it had entered the ambulance transportation and security services business.

The 1970s saw the Indian Bend Green Belt approved, which, along with the development of McCormick Ranch and the passage of strict ordinances regarding billboards and building height, marked Scottsdale as an upscale community with exacting standards. Rural/Metro stayed ahead of the curve throughout this period, opting for large-diameter fire hose to improve the tactical efficiencies of fighting fires. Four-inch fire hose, which was imported by Witzeman from Germany, carried more than three times as much water as the conventional 2 ½-inch hose and proved to be more efficient and cost-effective.

During the same period, Witzeman directed that Rural/Metro apparatus be painted "safety green," a scientifically validated move designed to make the trucks easier for motorists to see. The move nonetheless ignited the wrath of red-truck traditionalists. "It was a motherhood issue," Witzeman quipped.

In 1978, Witzeman set the wheels in motion for his retirement by selling his Rural/Metro stock to employees and introducing an innovative employee stock ownership program, transforming Rural/Metro employees to "employee-owners." "He could have gotten more money [elsewhere]," said Lou Jekel, vice chairman of the Rural/Metro Board of Directors, "but he saw the stock as a reward for hundreds of employees and the work they had done."

That year Witzeman also appeared on *60 Minutes* with Mike Wallace. He was so worried about the interview that he crammed for

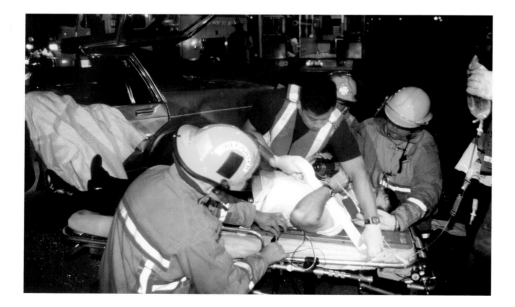

a month. In the end, he presented Rural/Metro's story well and scored points for privatization. "The phone rang off the hook," Witzeman recalled. "It gave Rural/Metro a level of acceptance that would have taken years to acquire."

Rural/Metro had its finest hour in 1985 when it led the charge for the most comprehensive sprinkler ordinance in the nation. The Scottsdale City Council passed the ordinance on June 4, 1985, requiring all new structures, including residential, to be fitted with automatic fire sprinklers. It underscored Rural/Metro's commitment to fire prevention efforts, which now command nearly fifteen percent of its fire operations budget in Scottsdale.

Rural/Metro Fire Department devotes about ten percent of its workforce to fire prevention efforts, including inspections, investigations, public education forums, and other duties designed to prevent fires from occurring. "Everything built since the ordinance is equipped with fast-response (thirty seconds) sprinklers," Witzeman said. "Ten lives have been saved." More than fifty percent of Scottsdale structures now have sprinklers.

The 1980s were years of phenomenal growth for both Scottsdale and Rural/Metro. Under Mayor Herb Drinkwater, thirty-six square miles were annexed to the city. "Herb was incredible," Jekel said of the hands-on mayor who died in 1997. "He had a red light and siren in his car, plus a police radio. He carried at least two pagers." Rural/Metro continued to meet Scottsdale's needs while expanding nationwide and diversifying its services to include a wildland fire division, alarm system monitoring services and home healthcare.

In 1993, Rural/Metro went public. It was a big step and "very scary," according to Witzeman. "We did it because it was the only way we could finance our growth." Since then, Rural/Metro continues to refine its mission as it anticipates new challenges. In an age of specialization, it has become increasingly specialized. "I think industrial fire protection and aircraft rescue and fire fighting are going to grow," said Jekel. One of Rural/Metro's major industrial fire clients, for example, is the Bethleham Steel plant in Burns Harbor, Indiana. Rural/Metro also provides fire protection to a dozen airports in the United States and Latin America. Such

areas require in-depth knowledge of the industry itself and the ability to handle challenges with surgical precision.

Rural /Metro is equally dedicated to Scottsdale's unique desert landscape. Since the creation of the McDowell Sonoran Preserve in 1995, it has worked with preservationists to develop non-intrusive ways of protecting the ecosystem. In sensitive areas of the preserve, for example, Rural/Metro avoids using fire lines to stop brush fires, emphasizes the use of aerial retardant, and limits the use of power equipment.

Truly, the old days "ain't what they used to be." "It was more fun then," Witzeman reflects. "Bigger is better in some ways but also a little colder. It's great to be young and not know that you can be whipped."

✧

Above: Fife Symington, who was Arizona governor at the time, visits the command post of the Rio wildland fire that burned more than thirty-six square miles in and around north Scottsdale. It took more than 300 firefighters nearly four days to douse the blaze that was started by lightning July 7, 1995.

Below: Rural/Metro firefighters stand behind founder Lou Witzeman in this picture taken during the late 1990s in front of Rural/Metro's corporate offices at Indian School and Granite Reef Roads in Scottsdale.

THE SCOTTSDALE TRIBUNE

Scottsdale was an emerging little town of less than 2,000 people in 1947 when the *Progress*—an eight-page weekly tabloid—began publishing in Scottsdale from a small office near Scottsdale Road and Main Street.

As the town began its growth following World War II, so did the newspaper market. Two men, Victor J. Morgan, and James G. Edmiston bought the paper from James Boyd in 1959 and turned it into the *Scottsdale Daily Progress* on February 16, 1961. The city's population had increased to 10,000.

Less than two years later, in 1963, Jonathan Marshall purchased the paper with a circulation of 4,800. By 1968 the circulation had increased to more than 9,400 and in March 1987 the paper had reached 22,500 homes and businesses.

Under Marshall, the *Progress* championed changes in the state's open meeting and public records laws so that citizens could keep better tabs on their elected representatives. He also maintained a dedicated search for justice in the fatal car bombing that killed *Arizona Republic* reporter Don Bolles in 1976.

The former publisher recalls the paper's fight with the Army Corps of Engineers over its plan to build a concrete flood-control ditch through Scottsdale much like the aqueduct in Los Angeles. The city and the *Progress* held out for a park-like setting of trails, lakes, and recreational amenities, which led to the present-day seven-mile-long lush green Indian Bend Wash Flood Control project.

In March 1987, after twenty-five years, Jonathan and Maxine Marshall sold to Cowles

Media of Minneapolis. In 1993, Cox Arizona Publications purchased the *Scottsdale Progress Tribune* and in 1997, the Canada-based Thomson Newspapers purchased the paper, re-naming it the *Scottsdale Tribune*, an edition of the *Tribune*, published in Mesa.

The *Scottsdale Tribune*, with offices at 7525 East Camelback Road, and other *Tribune* newspapers—the *East Valley Tribune*, *The Daily News-Sun*, the *Ahwatukee Foothills News*, and *The Yuma Daily Sun*—were welcomed into the Freedom Communications, Inc., family of newspapers on June 29, 2000. With corporate headquarters in Irvine, California Freedom publishes 25 daily newspapers and 37 weeklies grouped largely in the Midwest, South and West Coast. The flagship paper is the *Orange County Register* with a circulation of 360,000. The chain's combined daily circulation is 615,000.

Meanwhile, the *Tribune* continues to garner numerous awards for its dedication to being the best newspaper in Scottsdale and the East Valley. The paper won eight statewide first-place awards from the Arizona Newspapers Association in 2000 including first place in general excellence and in departmental news coverage. Staff writers at the Scottsdale paper continue to break national news such as the Howard Mechanic alias Gary Tredway and Alt-Fuel stories.

"People are interested in news, first from the town in which they live, but they also care about news from neighboring cities and from

✧

Above: A delivery girl walking her route with the help of her dog to deliver the afternoon Scottsdale Progress before conversion to an a.m. paper and motorized delivery.
COURTESY OF THE *TRIBUNE* ARCHIVES.

Below: The Scottsdale Progress *plant at 7320 East Earll Drive where the city's daily newspaper was published from 1970 to 1993. The metal sculpture sign was fabricated from parts of old linecasting machines.*
COURTESY OF THE *TRIBUNE* ARCHIVES.

around the Valley," says publisher Karen Wittmer. "Our presentation of local news is to make it the first thing readers see when they open the paper. We devote more space to local news to satisfy the demand for news that is relevant to the lives of people who live here."

In addition to focusing on local news, the *Tribune* provides national, international, business and sports coverage. The paper features a daily East Valley Living Section; Desert Nesting; a Perspective Section where in-depth commentaries on local, regional, and international issues are debated and a separate *Get Out* magazine, a weekly entertainment and recreation guide.

The *Scottsdale Tribune* is an integral part of the community and involved in nearly every aspect of community life. Through the *Tribune in Education* program, newspapers and educational materials are provided to schools throughout Scottsdale and the East Valley to help with reading, vocabulary, social studies and literature. The paper supports the arts and cultural events as well as charitable sponsorships to Scottsdale Healthcare, Scottsdale Foundation for the Handicapped, the Paiute Neighborhood Center, the Boys & Girls Clubs of Scottsdale, the Scottsdale/Paradise Valley YMCA, Scottsdale Leadership, the Community Heroes program, and the Scottsdale History Hall of Fame. Community events such as Spring Training

Baseball, Mighty Mud Mania, Rural/Metro Safety Day, the Parada del Sol Parade, and the Thunderbird Balloon Classic all receive support from the *Tribune* and its employees.

Just as *Freedom*'s founder, the late R. C. Hoiles left as his legacy values that stress "integrity, self-responsibility, respect for individual freedom, community and life-long learning," the *Tribune*'s commitment is to provide the foremost daily newspaper in the East Valley now and in the years to come.

Above: The Scottsdale Tribune, winner of the 2000 General Excellence Award among large newspapers in Arizona from the Arizona Newspaper Foundation.

Below: The Scottsdale Tribune covers news that hits close to home.

SRP

The Arizona Canal runs through the very heart of Scottsdale—a fact that not only adds to the character and charm of the city, but also symbolizes the close relationship between Scottsdale and its long-time partner, SRP (Salt River Project). Through its support of the Scottsdale Symphony Orchestra, the Scottsdale Cultural Council and Scottsdale Leadership—not to mention many other non-profit events and organizations—SRP takes pride in its commitment to Scottsdale's future. And, like the City of Scottsdale, SRP is proud to celebrate a rich and colorful past.

As one of the oldest companies in metropolitan Phoenix and one of the nation's largest public power utilities, SRP has played a pivotal role in the economic progress of Scottsdale, Phoenix, and the surrounding communities for nearly a century. Therein lies the dual-character of SRP—it is, simultaneously, a treasured relic of Arizona history and a future-focused leader in the industries of water and energy. Both roles are prized equally at SRP, where state-of-the-art performance is pursued with the same spirit of partnership, innovation, and environmental stewardship that were hallmarks of the company's founders nearly one hundred years ago.

Today, SRP is made up of two principal operating entities: The Salt River Valley Water Users' Association, and the Salt River Project Agricultural Improvement and Power District.

The Salt River Valley Water Users' Association is a private corporation and the largest water supplier in the Phoenix area, delivering nearly one million acre-feet of water annually. The Association manages a system of six reservoirs, which feed an extensive water delivery network comprising 1,265 miles of canals, laterals and smaller channels contained within its 240,000-acre service territory.

The Salt River Project Agricultural Improvement and Power District is a political subdivision of the State of Arizona and operates SRP's power business, which provides energy to more than 730,000 customers in a 2,900-square-mile service territory in Central Arizona. SRP's power business includes generation, transmission, distribution, and metering and billing services.

The roots of the SRP run deep, tracing back to the Hohokam people who inhabited the Salt River Valley at the dawn of the first millennium. Irrigating thousands of acres with water from the Salt and Verde Rivers, the Hohokam sustained a thriving community for over a thousand years, until their mysterious disappearance around 1450 A.D.

The framework of the Hohokam's original irrigation system was a source of inspiration for enterprising pioneers who, nearly four hundred years later, began to settle the newly formed Arizona Territory.

Beginning in the 1880s, the need for a dam and reservoir was identified as the key to success for the Salt River Valley. Such a dam would cost from $2 to $5 million dollars—a debt the United States prohibited the territory of Arizona from assuming.

In a heroic demonstration of putting community good before personal interests, Salt River Valley landowners pledged their homes and farms as collateral to secure loans from the federal government, forming the Salt River Valley Water Users' Association in 1903. Construction of Theodore Roosevelt Dam—the largest masonry dam ever built and the largest man-made body of water in the world at the time—was completed by 1911.

The completion of Roosevelt Dam was a turning point both for SRP and the State of Arizona as a whole. By providing dependable access to water, SRP sparked a city in the desert—a place where economic growth and development have flourished ever since.

The same spirit of partnership, innovation and environmental stewardship that defined SRP a hundred years ago continues to define it today. A pioneer on many fronts, SRP became one of the first public power entities in the country to adopt and implement a comprehensive plan for electric utility competition for all customers.

SRP also is renowned for its water management expertise, as well as its product research and development. Of particular significance are its efforts to protect and preserve Arizona's environment, having recently announced a $29 million program to fund renewable energy resources.

In addition to its leadership in resource management, SRP has long been recognized

as a leader in the community. During 2000, SRP and its employees contributed more than $3 million dollars to non-profit events and organizations, and SRP employees (together with their friends and families) logged more than 703,000 volunteer hours assisting non-profit agencies throughout the state.

SRP looks forward to providing service excellence to Arizonans and their communities for years to come. In doing so, it will reflect on achievements of the past—like the historic Arizona Canal in the heart of Scottsdale—as a model for tomorrow. The founders of SRP constructed the Arizona Canal in a pioneering spirit of environmental stewardship, innovation and partnership. So too will SRP build its future, a future that protects Arizona's natural resources, provides cutting-edge water and power technology, and honors a proud heritage of extraordinary community spirit.

✧

SRP President William P. Schrader photographed when he was mayor of Scottsdale in 1964, reviews an announcement for an upcoming western parade, Parada del Sol.
COURTESY OF THE SCOTTSDALE PUBLIC LIBRARY, SOUTHWEST COLLECTION.

McDowell Sonoran Land Trust

SAVING OUR MOUNTAINS
AND OUR DESERT
McDOWELL | SONORAN
LAND TRUST

✧

*MSLT board members—Stewardship Chair
Chet Andrews, co-founder Jane Rau, and
archaeologist Greg Woodall—celebrate
"Hands Across the McDowells" on
November 1, 1997. Hikers carried a
ceremonial "key to preservation success"
from Scottsdale over the mountain to the
town of Fountain Hills.*

COURTESY OF THE MCDOWELL SONORAN LAND TRUST.

Explosive growth was smothering Scottsdale's desert style of living. A sea of red tile roofs was engulfing the fragile Sonoran Desert, even threatening the slopes of Scottsdale's signature natural feature, the magnificent McDowell Mountains. City ordinances were unable to substantively preserve Scottsdale's desert ambiance and Southwestern character.

In 1990 a diverse group of dedicated citizens formed the non-profit McDowell Sonoran Land Trust (MSLT) to address these problems. With training and expertise from the National Land Trust Alliance, the MSLT became the leading advocacy group for the voiceless land and created one of the most successful preservation movements in the country.

The MSLT taught the citizens of Scottsdale about the benefits of preservation through public hearings and hikes into the threatened mountains. In partnership with the City and the Scottsdale School District, the MSLT created a program of school assemblies, video, and desert hikes for all fourth-graders called "Our McDowell Sonoran Heritage."

Early in 1993 the MSLT urged the Scottsdale City Council to create an official City board to identify what land to preserve and ways to fund that effort. This McDowell Mountains Task Force evolved into the McDowell Sonoran Preserve Commission, a close partner with the MSLT and sharing many of the same members.

In 1994 the city adopted a recommended study boundary for the McDowell Sonoran Preserve. Members of the MSLT and the Preserve Commission then joined business and community leaders to form a political action committee, "Save Our McDowells." This coalition led the overwhelmingly successful effort in 1995 to pass a city sales tax increase of two-tenths of one percent over thirty years to fund the purchase of lands for preservation.

In the following years, citizens voted repeatedly to support the preservation movement. In five public votes (with an average approval rate of seventy-two percent) they approved bonding to expedite land purchases; they changed the City charter to prevent future Councils from disposing of preserved land; and in 1998 they expanded the planned McDowell Sonoran Preserve to include additional desert areas. The envisioned Preserve now encompasses 36,400 acres or nearly one-third of Scottsdale's land area as natural, public open space.

The MSLT is the Preserve's chief advocate, providing citizen support that land acquisitions continue and weaving a tapestry of community involvement. Along with the City's preservation staff, MSLT volunteers are planning for Preserve management and public access. They build trails and they train "Preserve Stewards" at Scottsdale Community College (SCC). The MSLT has also partnered with SCC to create the "Center for Native and Urban Wildlife" to teach students of all ages about local ecology while restoring damaged habitat in the Preserve.

Great challenges confront the completion of the Preserve, but strong support to do so exists among Scottsdale citizens. The McDowell Sonoran Land Trust will continue to lead that support on behalf of all future generations.

Scottsdale celebrates fifty years of incorporation… honoring our past, imagining our future

Scottsdale celebrates its fiftieth anniversary of incorporation on June 25, 2001. While it's a relatively young city, Scottsdale has actually been a place of many faces—and one spirit—for more than 1,200 years. As far back as 800 A.D., the Hohokams farmed this area now known as Scottsdale and built hundreds of miles of canals to support their agricultural lifestyle.

Founded in 1888 by Winfield Scott, Scottsdale was primarily a farming and ranching community. The town had a handful of health camps/resorts and a cotton gin to supplement the economy in its early years and through the Great Depression. But soldiers returning from World War II and visitors who wanted to stay year-round quickly swelled the population in the late 1940s. People needed housing, shopping, services, and recreation.

The Scottsdale Chamber of Commerce was formed in 1947 and essentially performed the functions of a municipality during its first years. By 1949 residents and business owners began to talk about the need to incorporate as a town to get police and fire protection, street paving and lighting, garbage collection, and other services.

In January 1951, a citizens committee began circulating petitions for a vote on incorporation. If ten percent of the property owners and taxpayers signed, an election would be called. If two-thirds signed, the Maricopa County Board of Supervisors could declare Scottsdale incorporated without an election. Petitions with more than two-thirds of the required signatures were turned in on May 21. On June 25 of that year, the board declared Scottsdale an incorporated town and appointed a five-member town council to serve until an election could be held the following May. Appointed were: Mort Kimsey, Bill Miller, E. G. Scott, Jack Sweeney and Malcolm White. At its first town council meeting on July 2, White became Scottsdale's first mayor.

At that time, the new Town of Scottsdale was just one square mile with 2,000 residents. Scottsdale received "city" status in 1961 and grew to more than 11,000 residents living in about five square miles. By the year 2000, Scottsdale encompassed 185 square miles and was home to more than 215,000 residents, making it the fourth largest city in Arizona. Scottsdale lies within the Sonoran Desert at the base of the McDowell Mountains, a location that includes a dynamic Southwestern culture and love for natural beauty, support of the environ-ment, and concern for future generations. Thanks to Scottsdale citizens' commitment to preservation, more than one-third of Scottsdale's total area is planned to be set aside as "open space."

And like Scottsdale's quest to become a city of its own, essentially all of its success stories have resulted from citizen-generated ideas, energy, and enthusiasm. Whether it's mountain and desert preservation or flood control provided by the Indian Bend Wash greenbelt, Scottsdale residents' willingness to participate in the community has made Scottsdale a special place to live, work, and visit.

SCOTTSDALE CHAMBER OF COMMERCE

The pioneers who called Scottsdale home at the turn of the last century witnessed a much different landscape than the one in which we now live. Those rugged individuals could hardly have imagined the bustling, sophisticated business center and resort town that Scottsdale has become. But the night sky they gazed up into very likely looked much the same as it does now. And the stars that they wished upon most likely filled them—as they do us—with hope for a future bright with progress and prosperity.

Now as we sit on the cusp of the twenty-first century, urgency and technology have replaced the laid-back pace that Scottsdale has historically known. Local businesses, like businesses worldwide, face a breadth of challenges that we could virtually string to the moon and back.

Just as we helped shape the beginnings of a new city in 1947, the Scottsdale Chamber of Commerce continues to steer its community through the tides of change and challenge. Over the years, the scope and diversity of Scottsdale business has changed, due in large part to the concerted efforts of the City of Scottsdale and the Scottsdale Chamber.

We succeeded in nurturing a diverse and sustainable economy, which has grown far beyond the bounds of the hospitality industry. Our business community is now a haven for all manner of businesses, from software manufacturers to Fortune 500 headquartered firms, and that trend will continue.

But change ushers in its own set of obstacles. Among them: a global economy, and intense international competition. Not to mention, computerization, automation, and even robotics, and multimedia and mass communications, e-commerce, and X-generation employees, software, and hard knocks.

The ultimate goal of the Chamber is to assist businesses by delivering a suite of programs and services that will enable them to thrive in the New Economy. In the public policy arena, we are a loud and powerful voice, protecting the interests of business while protecting our quality of life. And as a driver of business growth, we are working to achieve lasting economic viability for all Scottsdale area business.

Even as we work toward our ideals, we know that our success, and the success of our community, depends upon our people—leaders, volunteers, visionaries—who generate the inspiration, dialogue and elbow grease which breathes life into ideas and gives wings to original thought. Indeed, they are the champions of the future.

Business people gathering to solve problems and create opportunities that no one can do alone is what chambers of commerce have always been. That is what the Scottsdale Chamber is today, and it is what we will continue to be as we move into the next fifty years.

Feel free to contact the Chamber at (480) 945-8481 or www.scottsdalechamber.com

Above: (From left to right) Scottsdale Chamber of Commerce 2000-2001 Chairman of the Board Curt Smith, President and CEO Phil Carlson, and 2001-2002 Chairman of the Board Linda Milhaven..

Right: The horse sculpture in Scottsdale's Perimeter Center.

SCOTTSDALE CULTURAL COUNCIL

Situated upon the lawns and fountains of the Scottsdale Civic Center, the Scottsdale Center for the Arts and the Scottsdale Museum of Contemporary Art are our community's source of arts and cultural celebration. Annually, thousands of residents, winter visitors and tourists attend performances, view exhibitions and enjoy such special events as the annual Scottsdale Arts Festival and the free weekly Sunday A'Fair concert in the park series.

The vitality of the arts also extends throughout the community, as the Scottsdale Cultural Council manages the public art program for the City of Scottsdale, lauded recently for the art installation along the Pima Freeway, which debuted in 2000.

The arts in Scottsdale flourish thanks to an innovative public/private partnership, founded in 1987, between the City of Scottsdale and the private, non-profit Scottsdale Cultural Council which leverages the City's investment with

earned revenue (ticket and retail sales) and contributed revenue (membership, sponsorship, and donation). Today, the City provides less than twenty-five percent of the Cultural Council's operating budget.

"We serve a vibrant community that is passionate about its art," notes President and CEO Frank Jacobson of the Scottsdale Cultural Council. "Our history and our future intertwine beautifully in a singular mission to make the arts an integral part of the Scottsdale experience."

✧

Public Art Project: Pima Freeway, Scottsdale, Arizona. Carolyn Braaksma, artist, The Path Most Traveled, 1999, concrete. Jeff Engelmann, landscape architect; Andrea Lee Forman, architect. COURTESY OF TARAH RIDER BERRY.

SCOTTSDALE AIRPARK NEWS

When *Scottsdale Airpark News* (*SAN*) debuted in 1981, it boasted four pages with one map, two articles, four advertisements, and three letters of welcome. Three hundred copies were printed.

Today, what was once a newsletter has grown into a four-color monthly business news magazine boasting more than 150 pages and a readership exceeding 135,000. *SAN's* pages, which are filled with pertinent news and features, reflect its mission of informing readers about business activities and community events in the Airpark and north Scottsdale area.

If there is an editorial constant, it is the map of Scottsdale Airpark and the Airpark directory that appear in every monthly issue. They are the grains of sand that agitated the oyster into making the pearl.

In its infancy, Scottsdale Airpark was a lot of land with dumps of scattered buildings. Visitors had difficulty finding their way around and would drop into the Leach Corporation, a publishing company just off Scottsdale Road, for directions.

As traffic grew, disrupting business, owner Kent Leach had to do something. So he decided to publish a monthly newsletter with a map in it. He figured it not only would provide directions but also create a sense of community for Scottsdale Airpark businesses. He was right on both counts.

Since then, the area has grown exponentially and now boasts the greatest concentration of industry in Scottsdale. *SAN* has grown with it. When it first appeared, the map showed seventy firms. Today, that figure has ballooned to twenty-five hundred.

SAN, which is owned by Scottsdale Publishing, is headquartered at 15855 North Greenway-Hayden Loop. For more information about *SAN*, call (480) 991-9057.

E.G. "Scotty" Scott's blacksmith, welding and machine shop was a popular place in downtown Scottsdale in the 1930s, 1940s and 1950s. Scotty's original shop was located on Scottsdale Road; he moved around the corner into this building in 1950 at the southeast corner of 1st Avenue and Scottsdale Road, where Ruth Mary Palmer posed circa 1950. In the year 2001, the building housed a Southwestern gift shop.

PHOTO COURTESY OF DEL JEANNE PALMER WEST

THE MARKETPLACE

Scottsdale's retail and commercial

establishments offer an impressive

variety of choices

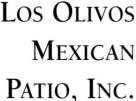

LOS OLIVOS MEXICAN PATIO, INC.

Above: A golden moment for Elena and Alvaro Corral when they celebrated their fiftieth wedding anniversary in 1998 at Our Lady of Perpetual Help Church. The Corrals have been operating Los Olivos since 1953.

Below: The one-story Los Olivos Mexican Patio restaurant on the edge of Scottsdale Civic Center Mall is an extension of the original sun-dried adobe structure built by the Corral family in 1927. The restaurant features the work of sculptor Jesus Corral including the Aztec figure on the roof.

When the Corral family first arrived in Scottsdale from Cananea, Sonora, Mexico on September 29, 1919, they pitched tents under the olive trees near the present Los Olivos Mexican Patio restaurant on Second Street in Old Town Scottsdale. The city's founder, Chaplain Winfield Scott, had planted the trees years earlier.

Town merchant, cotton farmer, and cattleman E. O. Brown sponsored Tomas Corral, Sr. and his wife, Cecilia, and brought them to Scottsdale to work the cotton fields. Alvaro Corral and his wife of fifty-two years, Elena, present owners of Los Olivos, credit Al's father with the foresight to save his money and buy the two corner lots at Second Street and Wells Fargo where the family first lived.

In 1927 the Corral sons—Emilio, Claudio, and Alvaro—built a 20 by 40-foot hall out of sun-baked adobe, which remains today as the main dining room of Los Olivos. The same original building was used for a billiard parlor, for Catholic Mass, a meeting place for agricultural leaders, a dance hall, a bakery, a corn grinding facility for making masa and as the family home. During World War II the building was divided into four rentals for G.I.s and after the war; it once again became home to Alvaro and his mother, Cecilia, before his marriage to Elena in 1948.

In 1946 Al, his two brothers, and nephew, Alfredo, started a beer and wine tavern. A local minister didn't think Scottsdale needed another drinking establishment and opposed its opening. The Corrals, however, proved the tavern was needed in the town's Mexican community since residents were not welcome at the other places. After two years, the brothers decided to add a small restaurant to the tavern. In 1950 the restaurant closed because Scottsdale, with a population of less than 2,000, couldn't support another dining spot.

Alvaro and Elena reopened the restaurant in 1953 and it has been operating successfully ever since. During the early years Alvaro took a job at Luke Air Force base until Los Olivos could support his family. By 1964 they branched out, starting Hacienda Corral on Scottsdale Road, which was sold in 1976 and presently is Avanti's. Los Olivos was remodeled in 1975-76 with a new kitchen, carpeting, restrooms, and office space. This began a trend to upgrade the colorful establishment every five years.

Their children—Ruby Corral-Peck, Alvaro R. Corral, John Corral, Maria Corral-Ramirez and Hector Corral—now operate the two Los Olivos restaurants, the original in Old Town and the new Los Olivos Norte off Frank Lloyd Wright Boulevard and Pima Road, Ruby, Maria, and sister-in-law Margarita, John's wife, operate the northern Los Olivos location, while Hector, John, and young Al run Los Olivos in Old Town.

The Corrals anticipate their legacy of excellent family recipe Mexican dishes and friendly service will be carried out by future generations of eighteen grandchildren and two great-grandchildren with more to come.

Alvaro Corral remembers the commitment his father, Tomas, made when settling in his newly adopted country—to work hard and put your best foot forward. "I believe," says Al, "that we have been able to measure up to what has been expected of us throughout the years."

When asked why Paul's Hardware has been so successful, Don Dauwalder doesn't go to the pie charts or burden the listener with a flurry of marketing jargon.

The answer is framed in a credo: "If we don't have it, we'll get it for you," says Dauwalder, owner and president of the firm: "We listen to what the customer wants, and we supply those wants."

The credo has held up for nearly a half century. During that time Paul's Hardware—named for founder Paul Dauwalder—has expanded from its original Scottsdale location to include thriving stores at Fountain Hills and Tempe. Several employees have been with the family-owned company for more than twenty years.

Paul's Hardware began as a modest facility at Scottsdale and Thomas Roads in 1956. It boasted two employees, including the owner. In those days Scottsdale Road had two lanes and no stoplights. Residents hunted quail where Railroad Park stands today.

But the timing was excellent. The Valley was in the midst of a postwar building boom. Former airmen who had trained at bases around the Valley were returning, now with wives and children, to start new lives in the Sun Belt. Paul Dauwalder understood. A husband and father of three sons, he also had moved to Scottsdale from the Midwest a decade earlier after military service.

Within two years, Paul's Hardware had to seek larger quarters. It was the first of three moves in coming decades to accommodate Scottsdale's growth. Eventually, the store would wind up where it had all started—Scottsdale and Thomas Roads.

In 1973 Paul—now partnered with son, Don—opened up a second Paul's Hardware in the budding community of Fountain Hills. When growth seized the area in the eighties, the store had to move to a former Bashas' Supermarket. In 1998 it moved to its present location in Bashas' Shopping Center on Palisades and LaMontana.

In 1990 a third Paul's Hardware opened in Tempe at 1153 West Broadway. A full-service lumberyard was eventually added that catered to both commercial and residential customers.

Needless to say, today's hardware industry is more demanding than ever before. "The technology has changed considerably," says Don, who is assisted by daughter and company vice president Julie Buchkowski. "We're much more sophisticated in how we buy and market." As a result, he adds, store employees receive more in-depth training.

"Behind the success, the most visible characteristic of Paul's Hardware is a genuine desire to help people. It is, in fact, a prerequisite for employment," Don says. "I think we're unique, because we have great people, and we provide great customer service."

PAUL'S SCOTTSDALE HARDWARE

✧

Above: Founder Paul Dauwalder and son Don take a photo break during the 1980s.

Below: Paul's Hardware at its Scottsdale location on Fourth Street during the 1970s.

Bottom: Paul's Hardware today, at the corner of Scottsdale and Thomas Roads.

SCOTTSDALE PLUMBING COMPANY

The family owned Scottsdale Plumbing Company has been serving Scottsdale's residential community for fifty-five years, one of the city's longest continuous businesses.

Started in 1946 by Art Bratzel, Scottsdale Plumbing, at 7501 East Osborn Road, now is operated by Art's three grandchildren—Linda Covington Barnett, president; Ed Covington, secretary; and Mike Covington, partner. When Bratzel started the business, he had but one 1940s vintage pickup truck. Today, the firm has 10 streamlined plumbing trucks, 19 full-time employees, including a crew of 7 plumbers, and 3 fourth-generation family members helping in the office.

Bratzel's wife, Mildred Kahle Bratzel, joined the firm in 1948 beginning a career that lasted twenty-five years. The couple lived in a two-bedroom apartment over the first plumbing store at 42 West Second Street where the Mountain Bell Service Center now stands. Mildred answered the phone, sold parts, and was the bookkeeper while Art serviced the plumbing needs of a growing community. His contribution to the city's growth was significant. Art installed nearly all of the sewers in the city. He also hooked up the residential homes to the new sewer system and installed and inspected plumbing in Scottsdale before the city had its own inspection department. He wrote, administered and graded tests in 1959

to the city's first building inspector and served twenty-five years on the city's Plumbing and Mechanical Advisory Board, with eleven of those years as its chairman.

As co-owner of Scottsdale Plumbing, Mildred took care of the business end and branched out into local politics. In 1958 she was elected to the Scottsdale City Council. That same year, the Scottsdale Business and Professional Women named Mildred "Woman of the Year." She also served as president of the Arizona Association of Plumbing Contractors Auxiliary; president of the Toastmistress Club; and was active in Red Cross and civil defense work. One of Scottsdale's pioneer women, Mildred was brought to Scottsdale at the age of two in 1910, the same year the Little Red School House was dedicated by Winfield Scott and Arizona was still a territory. She later rode her horse to class at the school and was in one of the earliest graduating classes at Scottsdale High School.

In 1956 Mildred's son, Mel Covington, a general contractor, joined the plumbing business. He helped run the family enterprise during the day and the Rusty Spur Tavern at night, which he owned for a time in the 1950s.

"My mom (Mary Covington) would get up early in the morning and bake pies for the Spur," recalls Linda, one of the first sixteen graduates of Scottsdale Community College in 1971. Linda currently serves on the Metro Phoenix Board of Plumbing, Heating and Cooling Contractors and is a member of the State Association of Plumbing Contractors Auxiliary, following in the footsteps of her grandmother, Mildred.

Mel Covington built the present 8,000-square-foot, two-story Bratzel Building at Osborn and Seventy-fifth Street in 1965. The Osborn headquarters features an official Kohler-registered showroom complete with Kohler Standing Body Spa, which recirculates forty-five gallons of water at eighty gallons a minute in waterfall action. Displayed throughout the showroom are pewter, porcelain, china, cast iron, and stainless steel sinks. Bathroom fixtures of chrome, polished and antique brass, platinum, satin nickel and baked enamel with brass, as well as twenty-four-karat gold, are also available. The showroom has been completely renovated with the latest kitchen, spa and bath displays.

"The new styles resemble artwork," Linda says. "Especially the pewter and spun glass vessel sinks. Children enjoy the Disney "Mickey and Minnie Mouse" sink and fixture sets. The Kohler hand-painted fly-fishing-themed sink and faucet set is for the fisherman who has everything." Scottsdale Plumbing also specializes in replacement parts for vintage and outdated fixtures. "We can order foreign and domestic parts from all over the world," Linda adds. "That's why a lot of people come here."

Volunteering their services in the community has always been a family tradition. The company has sponsored high school sports teams and in the past provided plumbing services for the Scottsdale Stadium and for projects of the Scottsdale Jaycees and the Scottsdale Boys & Girls Clubs. Fourth generation family members now helping with a variety of duties are Linda's two children, Nicole Barnett, twenty-three, a Scottsdale Community College honor student, and Steven Barnett, twenty, studying computer engineering at SCC. Ed's daughter, Emily Covington, nineteen, also works part-time in the office and showroom. The Scottsdale Plumbing name has stood for quality service for more than half a century. "We stand by our professional quality service and product warranty," says Linda, "which has been our signature since my grandparents established the business fifty-five years ago."

✧

A fourth generation family member, Steven Barnett, son of Scottsdale Plumbing's president, Linda Covington Barnett, shows this one-ton service vehicle that carries a line of replacement and service parts. The company has come a long way since Art Bratzel started with one 1940s pickup truck with which he called on customers.

PINNACLE PEAK PATIO

✧

Above: A Pinnacle Peak Patio steak cooked to perfection.

Top, right: The spread at Pinnacle Peak Patio.

Below: Visitors are greeted by a rough and tough hombre.

Pinnacle Peak Patio, located at the foot of Pinnacle Peak with a view of the McDowell Mountains, was founded in 1957. What began as a small store on a dusty trail, selling beer and bait to fishermen on their way to nearby lakes, has become the largest steak house of its kind in the world.

One weekend, with thoughts of expanding the small business, the original owner decided to experiment. He bought six thirty-two-ounce Porterhouse steaks, some lettuce and cowboy beans and held a western cookout using native mesquite wood. He discovered townspeople loved traveling out into the desert where the air was clean, the stars bright and they could get a great cowboy steak.

By 1959 the restaurant seated fifty diners. Today the multi-room Pinnacle Peak Patio seats more than 1,600 people inside and an additional 3,000 on the patios and at cookout sites. Since 1970 Pinnacle Peak Patio has been owned and operated by Southwest Restaurant Systems, Inc. under the direction of Scottsdale resident and president, Harvey McElhanon and members of his family.

In the beginning, the menu featured one steak with "fixins." Now, five are offered plus hickory smoked chicken and baby back ribs brushed with prickly pear/chipotle barbecue sauce. Since the beginning, Pinnacle Peak has served well over 11 million steaks. The cook, "Big Marv" Dickson has personally grilled

more than two million pounds of beef cut by the Peak's own butchers to assure the highest quality steaks.

"Besides starting with a great slab of meat, an important ingredient that adds to the flavor of our steaks is the mesquite wood we use for grilling," says Dickson. "Mesquite burns really hot and sears the meat to keep it juicy and the oils in the wood add a special flavor." Pinnacle Peak does not use mesquite chips, but actual logs of the wood to grill its steaks. One long-standing custom that stands firm is when a steak is ordered well done, the patron receives an old boot instead of prime beef on the dinner plate.

Another tradition that has survived the years is a strict "no tie" policy in keeping with the restaurant's casual setting. Years ago a local executive came to the Peak in a suit and tie. The owner gave the guest the option of removing his tie or having it cut off. The man ignored the warning and the owner promptly cut off the tie. Outraged at losing his tie and wanting to be recognized as a victim of the Peak's absurd policy, he demanded that his tie and business card be hung from the rafters. Over the years thousands of ties, adding up to more than a million, have been snipped by servers from the necks of unwary guests, including celebrities. One celebrity, who

never had a chance for his tie to be hung from the rafters was Jerry Lewis. As his tie was clipped, a customer jumped up, snatched the tie and ran off into the crowd.

Numerous celebrities have partaken of Pinnacle Peak's famous steaks. Celebrity watchers have been delighted at spotting such famous actors as Paul Newman, Tom Cruise, David Hasselhoff, Patrick Swayze, and Liza Minnelli seated at the next table. Paradise Valley resident Alice Cooper has celebrated his birthday at the Peak and old-timers such as Richard Boone, Joan Crawford, Amanda "Miss Kitty" Blake, Jane Russell, Tennessee Ernie Ford, and Ben Johnson, all frequented the steakhouse. Charley Pride, Glen Campbell, and Wayne Newton have sung with the band.

Sports celebrities also patronize the Peak. A baseball autographed by Yogi Berra is displayed in the showcase while a picture of Joe DiMaggio eating dinner hangs on the wall. Billy Martin, Bobby Knight, Bill Elliot, Richard Petty, and Mario and Michael Andretti have all visited the Peak.

Folks are invited to take a walk around the labyrinth of rooms and view the celebrity wall with collections of antique locks, bottle openers and horse bridles in the wait areas. Guests also can have an old-tyme western photo taken and browse in the gift shop while listening to live country western music in the background.

In 1998 the Peak opened its own microbrewery, which produces up to 250 kegs or nearly 4,000 gallons a month. The brewery features five standard and a variety of seasonal beers all of which are made with carefully selected ingredients. The Pinnacle Peak brand also is available at several Valley restaurants.

Although the steak house has grown over the years, the atmosphere, western hospitality and the promise of a "great steak" remains the same. With more than forty years of experience hosting groups, the Peak's capable staff plans the menu, books the band, gunfight or holdup for private or semi-private parties in rooms, patios or in cookout areas for groups of 30 to 3,000.

Be assured, the Peak sets the stage for a "rip roarin" western evening in the desert overlooking the Valley where the McElhanons' staff produce "steaks that are cooked to perfection every night out north at the Peak where the legend continues."

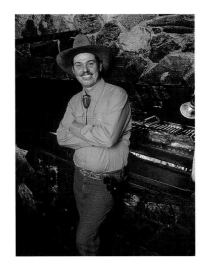

✧

Above: The staff of Pinnacle Peak Patio have cooked eleven million steaks and are still smiling.

Below: Anyone wearing a tie in the restaurant will find their tie hanging from the rafters as quick as the bite of a rattler.

SCOTTSDALE FASHION SQUARE

It would be hard to imagine Scottsdale without Scottsdale Fashion Square. From the moment it debuted in 1959, the elegant shopping center has set the standard for service and selection.

Today, Fashion Square boasts 220 retail outlets, nearly two million square feet of space and more than 9,000 parking spaces. It covers sixty-three acres and is home to Dillard's, Neiman Marcus, and Robinsons-May. In 1998 Fashion Square captured the "crown jewel" of fashion department stores when Nordstrom came aboard.

"Nordstrom is the most coveted fashion department store in the country," says John James, former general manager of Scottsdale Fashion Square. "They pick and choose where they go. It took a long period of negotiations to get them here."

In 1950 when the Scottsdale saga began, such sophistication would have seemed inconceivable. Scottsdale was an unincorporated crossroads with a handful of independent businesses. Most of its streets were unpaved and trailed off into the desert. Residents still rode horses into town and tied them up at hitching posts.

But there were stirrings. World War II had changed everything, including Arizona, which was no longer a stopover enroute to California. Attracted by the climate and freedom, former airmen who had trained at bases around the

Above: The Rain Curtain stairwell in Palm Court.

Below: The retail connection to the new expansion, which features Nordstrom.

Valley began trickling back in ever-increasing numbers, now with families. They brought their golf clubs and new ideas. They also brought a need for homes, schools, and places to shop.

That year, a small shopping center—the predecessor to Fashion Square—was built on the corner of Camelback and Scottsdale Roads. At the time there were only about a hundred shopping centers in the entire country. The new site featured a modest sampling of stores designed to accommodate the rapidly growing community. As new suburbs mushroomed, demand soon exceeded supply.

In 1959 Scottsdale Fashion Square opened for business as a single-level mall with forty stores. It was in the advance guard of more than 8,000 shopping centers that would be built nationwide over the next decade. Its first tenant was A. J. Bayless, followed two years later by Goldwater's department store. By 1974 Diamond's had come aboard.

As Scottsdale grew, so did Fashion Square, mirroring the once-sleepy village's transition to an upscale city offering unparalleled amenities. In 1983 Valley-based Westcor Partners, a fully integrated real estate development and management company, acquired Fashion Square and began a series of expansions that would transform the mall into the largest super-regional shopping destination in Arizona and one of the Southwest's premier retail locations.

When renovation started, Fashion Square comprised 377,000 square feet and 43 stores. By the time the first three expansions were completed in 1991, those figures had swelled to 897,000 square feet and 165 stores. The revitalized center featured retractable skylights, a multi-level rain curtain, fountains, and artistic sculpture. With the acquisition of adjacent Camelview Plaza in 1995, Westcor set the stage for Scottsdale Fashion Square's future growth.

"Our goal," James says, "was to bring in retailers who had not been here before, like Eddie Bauer, the Disney Store and Warner Brothers. We were able to entice eighty newcomers. Many have multiple locations now, but Fashion Square was the catalyst." Nevertheless, Fashion Square is the only shopping center in Arizona where shoppers can find a Nordstrom. Or a Tiffany. Or a Brooks Brothers or Dana Buchman. In all, Fashion Square lays exclusive claim to some sixty stores.

Scottsdale Fashion Square is more than just a place to shop; it is a place to socialize, enjoy a fine meal at one of several restaurants or take in a movie. Studies show that next to outdoor activities, notably golf, shopping is Scottsdale's favorite recreation. In a sense, Fashion Square serves as a glittering town square.

Shoppers needing assistance will find representatives at the concierge desk on lower-level Palm Court cheerfully dispensing information about Fashion Square, local activities and lodging. The desk also provides, in addition to other services, stroller rentals, wheelchairs, restaurant reservations, and Westcor gift certificates.

"It used to be that tourism accounted for about thirty percent of Fashion Square's clientele," James says, "but that has changed. As a result of the population surge in North Scottsdale, we are forming core patrons in substantial numbers. Tourism now accounts for about twenty-five percent."

"It is amazing how many patrons speak with European and Asian accents," James adds, alluding to the international flavor of Fashion Square. Mexican tourists, in particular, are prominent. "We do a lot of marketing in Mexico," he says. "If fact, we do more marketing in Mexico than anywhere else [outside the U.S.]."

While Scottsdale Fashion Square claims annual sales approaching $750 million, it gives back to the community not only through unparallel service but tax dollars and jobs. During the peak Christmas season, the mall employs more than 4,000 sales people. In summer, the figure is about 3,000.

Scottsdale Fashion Square would like to congratulate John James on his recent retirement and Bud Mason, Scottsdale Fashion Square's new general manager.

✧

Above: The Grand Rotunda, adjacent to the Bistecca Italian Steakhouse and Fog City Diner.

Below: The retractable skylight above the Palm Court.

HENRY & HORNE, P.L.C.
ADVISORS TO BUSINESS

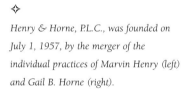

Henry & Horne, P.L.C., was founded on July 1, 1957, by the merger of the individual practices of Marvin Henry (left) and Gail B. Horne (right).

In 1957, when Marvin Henry and Gail Horne merged their practices and formed the partnership of Henry & Horne Certified Public Accountants, they began an accounting firm based on caring about the clientele they serve.

"Henry & Horne is truly a firm that cares," says Managing Director Wendell E. Jones, CPA. "We care about our clients, our staff and our community. We rejoice in their successes and we struggle with them through the difficulties. As an independently owned firm, we answer only to our clients and ourselves. We wouldn't have it any other way."

The firm's co-founder, the late Marvin Henry, was an Arizona native. He attended school in Gilbert; graduated from Arizona State University, and was an Air Force flight instructor in World War II before resigning and joining the Navy. While still in the Navy, he passed his CPA exam and started his own practice in 1946. Retiring from the firm in 1976, he passed away in 1984.

A member of an Arizona family that has lived in the Valley over one hundred years, Henry & Horne co-founder Gail Horne, was born and reared in Mesa. Also a WWII veteran, he served with the Army in Italy;

taught school at Mesa Union High School, and was an accounting instructor at ASU. Horne retired from the firm in 1988.

At the inception of Henry & Horne, there were three offices Phoenix, Mesa and Casa Grande—with a total of twelve employees. The firm's expansion began when the Scottsdale office opened its doors on January 1, 1958. At one point, the firm had 23 partners in 14 offices that were acquired by purchasing established existing practices around the state. Henry & Horne consolidated its locations and partners and now operates four main offices in Scottsdale, Tempe, Casa Grande, and Pinetop with thirteen directors (owners) and a professional and administrative staff of 127.

Mark Eberle, twenty-eight years with the firm, is director-in-charge of the Scottsdale office. Considered the largest single public accounting firm in the city, the twenty-thousand-square-foot, two-story Henry & Horne office building is located at 7098 East Cochise Road. The other directors in Scottsdale are Dean A. Young, Kathy E. Hostetler, Charles J. Inderieden, and Dana J. Krouth.

Forty years ago, as with most other accounting firms, Henry & Horne offered the basics—accounting, audit, and tax services. While these services are still offered, the firm today offers businesses and individuals a complete array of services for every financial need. These include: Merger and Acquisition, Business Valuation, Litigation Support, Estate Planning, Cost Segregation, Financial Planning, Investment Management, and a staffing service (ESP) to help clients find temporary and permanent personnel.

Henry & Horne also concentrates its efforts in several significant industry areas providing specialized teams for automotive dealers, not-for-profit organizations, international services and closely held businesses including professional service organizations and government and municipal entities.

It wouldn't be possible, however, to offer this multiplicity of services without advances in technology. In the beginning, accountants used adding machines and pencil and paper. It was not until Henry & Horne bought its first computer in the late 1970s—an Osborn with a screen that measured six-by-eight inches with no word processing capabilities—that modern day technology began to make a difference. By the mid-1980s, old computers were replaced with new Compaq desktop PCs with word processing and spreadsheet software that quickly changed the way the firm served its clients. An intra-office communication network now ties the offices together and the Henry & Horne internet website, *www.hhcpa.com*, gives clients and the public access to information about the firm and services offered.

In addition to maintaining a technologically advanced CPA firm, Henry & Horne takes pride in the community outreach volunteer activities of its employees. Its directors and staff are committed to non-profits to ensure that an organization's goals are achieved. The firm's Managing Director Wendell Jones, a past president of the Mesa Baseline Rotary Club, serves on several non-profit boards and is active with the Mesa United Way and the Mesa Chamber of Commerce. Scottsdale's director-in-charge, Mark Eberle, a past president of the Scottsdale Chamber of Commerce, remains involved in Chamber activities. He also is a past board member of the Valley of the Sun YMCA. Senior Director Dean Young, a member

of Scottsdale Rotary, is president of the Dorothy Garske Center. Director Kathy Hostetler, treasurer of the Scottsdale Education Foundation, voluntarily helps small organizations apply for non-profit status as well as develop their accounting systems. Director Chuck Inderieden, a member of the Arizona Cactus-Pine Girl Scout Council Finance Committee, also serves on the Boys & Girls Clubs of Phoenix Executive Council.

"As part of the Scottsdale community for forty-three years, we have had the pleasure of participating in the excitement of the Valley's growth," states Eberle. "As the largest Arizona based accounting firm, we take pride in not only what Scottsdale used to be and what it is today, but how Henry & Horne has grown with the community."

✧

Above: Henry & Horne's Scottsdale office on Camelback Road served the firm for twenty years.

Below: Henry & Horne's new Scottsdale office opened its doors in January 1999.

THE SCHUSTER CENTER FOR PROFESSIONAL DEVELOPMENT

❖

Above: Dr. Michael Schuster, founder and CEO of The Schuster Center for Professional Development.

Below: Doctors at the Learning Center of The Schuster Center for Professional Development.

As every professional knows, an overwhelming workload and long hours on the job do not guarantee success, fulfillment, and financial reward. In fact, they may have the opposite effect. This is particularly true in the profession of dentistry.

More often than not it is because dental schools have inadequately prepared their graduates to own and operate their own small business. Like many specialists, dentists are long on technical expertise and short on business savvy.

Dr. Michael Schuster discovered this disparity more than twenty years ago through his own experience as a young professional. Through years of owning and operating practices, combined with teaching other dentists in the technical arena, Schuster realized that a tremendous need existed for a professional and business model that dentists could apply in everyday practice settings. From his own success and years of applying his knowledge, he created a practice model for creating professional fulfillment and ethical economic success.

Schuster's lifelong desire was to develop a learning organization dedicated to teaching the professional model he has used his entire professional life. His model is based upon the timeless principles of quality and technical excellence, patient-centeredness, service, and profitability. In 1977 Schuster relocated from Iowa to Scottsdale, Arizona, to create The

Schuster Center for Professional Development. The Schuster Center was created to help dentists learn how to build a practice where the patient's needs are served at the highest level. The Schuster Center is dedicated to improving the quality of dental care offered in the United States.

Over the past twenty-one years The Schuster Center, located at 7272 East Indian School Road, has helped more than 3,000 dentists nationwide transform their practices into dynamic business enterprises. Their rewards have been financial and personal fulfillment and enhanced quality of life. A diversified faculty offers "real world" dental experience ranging from clinical management to marketing and human relations. Their academic degrees reflect a mosaic of expertise in dentistry and business.

The Schuster Model is a comprehensive approach to dental practice management that brings together the elements of experience, vision, management policies and systems, formal training curriculum and on-going support to help dentists shape their own unique interpretation of the high quality, low volume, patient-centered dental practice. It is a dynamic approach to understanding and managing all elements of the business. The model gives the dentist the tools that work through the formal curriculum, but the dentist must come prepared and motivated to learn and apply them.

"The curriculum requires discipline," says Brenda Penwell, senior vice president of The Schuster Center. "Dentists need to work on their practice, not just in it." Penwell says the dentists learn to see themselves not merely as highly trained technicians but managers and entrepreneurs. They become CEOs of their own practices.

As the entire dental team learns to take control of a wide range of day-to-day practice functions, important changes begin to occur; productivity and effectiveness increase, while the dentist has more time to spend one-on-one with patients due to a more smoothly run, less distracted environment. The elimination of unnecessary distractions gives the dentist time to establish and maintain patient relationships. This is a solid beginning to building the type of practice that may have attracted the doctor to dentistry in the first place: a dental practice that

is patient and health-centered, provides excellent quality care, allows the dentist to strike a balance between professional and personal life, and provides a rewarding financial return.

The Schuster Center curriculum is divided into two phases: the Management Program, which is a twelve-month program, and the Mastery Program, which takes two years to complete. Both require a "learn-by-doing" process that is individually tailored to the specific dentist and his or her practice.

The Management Program focuses on helping doctors achieve control over the dominant forces in their practice: time, money and energy or organization. The heart of the program is the doctor-patient relationship and all of the structures that are involved in patient care. All of the systems and structures in the practice are designed to optimize this relationship. Typical curriculum subjects include overhead control, time management, internal marketing, and team building. Through sound organization of the "business aspects" of the dental practice, dentists are free to direct their attention to the patients they serve.

The Mastery Program takes the practice of dentistry to a higher level, focusing on the development of the dentist as a leader to be seen by his patients as a model of health. The Mastery Program helps the dentist transition to a more health-centered approach to dentistry, where the patient's total health and well-being are considered to be an integral part of the dental care experience.

A hallmark of The Schuster Center's total management approach is that of student support facilitators—experts who develop a one-on-one relationship with dentists and their teams to help them transition through the needed changes in the practice. Support facilitators help doctors examine ineffective structures and assist them in creating unique practices. They are experienced dental professionals who have an understanding of necessary team skills and business management. The facilitator's role is to guide the doctor in adapting the Schuster Model to his or her professional vision through planning and refinement of systems to increase effectiveness, while keeping in mind that the doctor is the creator of the practice, and the practice is the reflection of the dentist.

Before dentists begin their program with The Schuster Center, a practice development analyst evaluates the practice to determine how the Management Program can best meet their needs. Information that will individualize the program is gathered and carefully assessed. The analyst appraises each dentist's circumstances, including all aspects of the dental practice: financial health, patient care, marketing, team development, the goals and objectives of the dentist, as well as the dentist's vision for the practice. The analyst strives to cultivate the partnering relationship, which is crucial to the relationship between the dentist and The Schuster Center team. Once the dentist makes a commitment to the process, he is directed to the first session of the Management Program curriculum.

In addition to the thorough practice analysis and monthly support, the dentist and team visit the Schuster Center three times a year for the intensive classroom training.

Throughout the year, The Schuster Center sponsors a host of additional continuing education events for dentists and their teams. They include one-day management courses by Dr. Schuster, two-day refresher courses for graduates of the program, and an annual Learning Conference, which is held in Scottsdale each year.

✧

Above: Schuster Center support facilitators work one-on-one with clients to achieve success.

Below: The Wellness Program facility, designed to help dentists improve physical health.

FRANCHISE FINANCE CORPORATION OF AMERICA

✧
Mort Fleischer inside the Fleischer Museum.

Mort Fleischer is fond of saying the capital may be in New York but many of the ideas are in the "hinterlands."

As proof, Fleischer can point to Franchise Finance Corporation of America (FFCA), which he began as a $100,000 Scottsdale startup twenty years ago and built into the nation's largest independent source of financing for single tenant real estate, such as restaurants and convenience stores.

At present FFCA claims $2.2 billion in market capitalization, 80,000 stockholders and 6,000 properties in fifty states. It offers leasing, mortgages, and interim financing for such culinary icons as Taco Bell, Burger King, and Arby's. In recent years FFCA has expanded its clientele base to include convenience stores.

Fleischer, who migrated to Arizona in the early 1960s after a hitch in the military, applauds the tradition of freedom and entrepreneurship that characterizes the state. He gives high marks to its work ethic. "People come here from the Midwest or the East, but they don't change this spirit," he said in a recent interview. "It changes them."

When Fleischer began FFCA, restaurants were considered risky ventures by most banks. This was especially true of "stand-alones" sitting at intersections or in parking lots. Most had mortgages, which tied up their operators' capital.

Fleischer's approach was to purchase stand-alones, then lease them back to their operators, who could then reinvest the sales proceeds into the business. But the stand-alones had to deliver. FFCA practically eliminated its margin for error in choosing properties by developing sophisticated credit techniques to measure economic viability.

As a result, FFCA rejects a substantial number of the proposals it receives. This professional approach to credit extension pays off when a tenant leaves and the property has to be rented out. "If you have a good 'square box' on a good corner, you can always re-rent it," says Fleischer. FFCA's tenant occupancy rate is in excess of ninety-nine percent.

FFCA headquarters are located at the Perimeter Center, a 260-acre commercial park developed by Fleischer as a model of innovative business environments. The center also is home to the Fleischer Museum, featuring an extensive collection of American Impressionist paintings. Fleischer's wife, Donna, is the museum's director.

When he isn't tending to business, Fleischer relaxes on his 200-acre ranch in North Scottsdale, where he breeds quarter horses. "I could ride all the way up to Canada if I wanted to," he quips, referring to the ranch's rustic environs.

Paul Messinger remembers getting up at 4:30 every morning as a boy to milk the cows on his family's farm in what is now downtown Scottsdale. "They ought to send city kids out to a farm," he quips. "On a farm you work hard, but you don't feel put upon. In fact, you're proud of the job you do."

Today, Messinger presides over Messinger Mortuary and Chapel, Inc., a major independent funeral and cemetery firm composed of four mortuaries, two cemeteries, and two crematory companies. Facilities are located in Scottsdale, Fountain Hills, and Payson. The work ethic Paul acquired from his parents has been passed on to his children, Ken and David, as well as grandson-in-law Bruce Schenkel. All are active in the organization.

"Our kids all put in their time [when they were young]," Paul says. "They mowed grass, washed cars, and performed other jobs, sometimes at night."

Paul and his wife, Cora opened their original mortuary on the corner of Indian School and Miller Roads in 1959, the former site of his parents' farm. Scottsdale, a fledgling community at the time, had no ambulance service. In a trade-off with the city, the Messingers agreed to provide a twenty-four-hour ambulance service in return for annexation to the one-square-mile municipality and rezoning of their property. The ambulance service grew with Scottsdale and

eventually included five vehicles before being sold in 1968.

In their first year, Paul and Cora, assisted by two employees, served 75 families. Today, assisted by 20 funeral directors and 30 staff people, they serve roughly 2,000 families annually. "I entered funeral service because I liked working with people," Paul says. "Funeral directors are like social workers; good ones have a deep concern for others."

Paul's concern also extends to the community-at-large, which he served as a three-term legislator in the Arizona House of Representatives. He also served five years as a Scottsdale city councilman and vice mayor.

In 1983 the family bought out their partners in North Scottsdale's Paradise Memorial Gardens to became the sole owners of the cemetery they had helped to start in 1973. As the Messinger staff grew and family members came aboard, it became necessary to expand the firm. "We had to provide opportunities for the young people to develop their funeral service practices," Paul says.

Paul and Cora are of one mind in describing their life: "Our family has been blessed with the opportunity to work with many wonderful families during a very special time in their lives. We have tried to care for each in the way they desired, to help each find personal closure and healing. We have tried over the years to always be sensitive to the special needs and concerns of each family."

MESSINGER MORTUARIES & PARADISE MEMORIAL GARDENS

✧

Above: Paul and Cora Messinger, founders of Messinger Mortuary & Chapel, Inc.

Below: The first mausoleum at Paradise Memorial Gardens, c. 1992.

PINK PONY RESTAURANT

Several years ago, *Sports Illustrated* ran a six-page article on Scottsdale's Pink Pony restaurant. As the saying goes: "You can't buy publicity like that."

Writer Ron Fimrite described the legendary restaurant as a sort of Toots Shore's West, with its roistering roster of spring training players, sportswriters, scouts and baseball executives. He even compared it to the Algonquin Table, Valhalla and the Mermaid Tavern, which, as everyone knows, were definitely big league.

Fimrite wasn't pitching wild. The Pink Pony has seen them all: Ty Cobb, Ted Williams, Mickey Mantle, Billy Martin, Ernie Banks, Gene Autry, Bill Rigney, Don Sutton, Roger Angell-the list goes on. "From late February to early April every year," Femrite wrote, "the Pony, as regulars call it, is beyond argument the most popular hangout for baseball people in the civilized world."

Of course, success depended on more than atmosphere. For fifty-one years, the Pink Pony has satisfied the diverse palates of clientele ranging from Hall of Famer Dizzy Dean (a big man at the plate as well as the mound) to Scottsdale's late Mayor Herb Drinkwater. It is famous for its stick-to-your-

Above: Gwen and Charlie Briley, proprietors of Scottsdale's Pink Pony.

Below: A sampling of the Pink Pony's renowned stick-to-your-ribs fare.

ribs steak and prime rib. For seafood lovers, there are savory entrees such as swordfish and Australian lobster tail.

The Pink Pony was a hit from the time Charley Briley acquired it in 1950. It appealed not only to hungry ball players but winter visitors and locals. At the time, Scottsdale was a dusty crossroads featuring a handful of businesses. Old Town did not exist and the city would not be incorporated for another year. It was so rural that the Pink Pony sported a hitching post, where patrons from nearby guest ranches would tie up their horses.

But the Valley was on the verge of the great postwar migration to the West, which-in addition to ex-GIs and their families-included spring training teams such as the [then] New York Giants. Following the Giants' example, other teams soon followed.

Briley, a transplanted Kentuckian who still owns the Pink Pony with his wife, Gwen, was a highly regarded bartender in those days. In fact, his friendship with developer and fellow baseball fan, Del Webb, resulted in his getting a job at the restaurant. Six months later he bought it, and the rest is Scottsdale history.

According to Gwen, word of mouth has always been the most effective form of advertising for the Pink Pony. During the fifties, when [then] Valley resident Dizzy Dean was color man on television's "Baseball Game of the Week," he often plugged the fledgling restaurant. With that kind of unsolicited support, it was bound to score. In no time at all, as old Diz might have said, the Pink Pony "slud into home."

MIDAS AUTO SERVICE EXPERTS

As the City of Scottsdale grew, so did the Robbins family business. Mike Robbins came to Scottsdale in 1947 at the age of twelve, attended Loloma Elementary School and Scottsdale High School. His parents moved to Scottsdale from Detroit and his father worked at the Phoenix Stockyards as a butcher. As Mike grew to adulthood, so did the city from a few hundred people to more than 6,000 by the time he became a Mobil Oil Corporation dealer in 1960. His first station was at Scottsdale Road and Second Street; then at Hayden and Indian School Roads and finally at Camelback and Miller Roads until 1976 when he became a Midas franchisee.

A self-taught mechanic, everybody knows and likes Robbins and respects his business practices. He served on the Scottsdale Board of Adjustment; is a member of the Scottsdale Chamber of Commerce, and active in the Scottsdale Charros for thirty years. Mike's son, Dennis, also served on the board of adjustment and went on to become a city councilman, serving from 1996 to 2000. In 1976 the Robbins family purchased the Midas Auto Service Experts franchise and now have 100 employees in seventeen retail locations throughout Arizona, that realize $11 million in annual revenue. They operate two each in Scottsdale and Tempe, four each in Mesa and Tucson, three in Phoenix and one each in Chandler and Flagstaff. The seventeenth Midas opened in October 2000 at Bell Road and Forty-third Street. Principals in the corporation, named "Dealer of the Year" in 1992, are Mike Robbins, president; his wife, Kitty, secretary, who maintains the accounts payable; their sons—Matt, vice president of operations, and his wife, Cindy, payroll; and Dennis, the company's general counsel, and his wife, Cheralee.

Nate Sherman of Macon, Georgia, offering the famous "As long as you own your car" guarantee, founded Midas International in 1956. Midas has added services over the years, including brake service in 1979, foreign car service in the mid-1970s, computerized suspension and alignment in 1990, and "Midas Cares" in 2000. Midas Cares stands for "Commitment, Attitude, Relationships, Execution, and Service" for a lifetime to customers. Midas shops offer full line of services, including brakes, shocks and struts, batteries, air conditioning, and, in some stores, tires.

"We really do it all now," Dennis adds. "We're in the automotive service business, but my Dad always reminds us we're in the people business. We fix cars but our focus is on solving people's problems."

✧

Above: One of the Midas Service Centers in Scottsdale on Scottsdale Road, south of Thomas Road.

Below: Mike Robbins, founder and president of Midas Auto Service Experts of Scottsdale, (center) with sons, Matt, vice president of operations, (left) and Dennis, general counsel (right). Together they operate seventeen Midas Auto Service Centers in Arizona. The senior Robbins has been in the automotive service business since 1960.

PRESTIGE CLEANERS, INC.

✧

Above: Prestige Cleaners Sonora Village location features a high roofed drive-thru and state-of-the-art unit that uses a new solvent not considered hazardous by the federal government.

COURTESY OF MARK BOISCLAIR PHOTOGRAPHY, INC., 1997.

Below: Prestige Cleaners executives Donn C. Frye (left) and his father, Don E. Frye, are recognized as leaders not only in the dry-cleaning industry but in the community of Scottsdale as well.

COURTESY OF SILVIO PHOTOGRAPHY.

In the Prestige Cleaners, Inc. headquarter's conference room at the Sahuaro plant walls are covered with congratulatory plaques attesting to the involvement of Don E. Frye and his son, Donn C. Frye, in civic and community service over the past thirty-five years.

Just as Scottsdale has grown the past three-plus decades, so has Prestige from its one location on Camelback Road to eight locations with more to come.

On June 1, 1964, Don E. Frye opened the Camelback Road store across from Scottsdale Fashion Square with four employees, two of which followed him from Ohio. In 1996, due to the city's redevelopment project, the Camelback operation was relocated to a state-of-the-art cleaning establishment at Goldwater Boulevard and Main Street.

Prestige now has eighty employees whose business is to greet customers with a cheerful smile and pleasant manner. "People, that's the secret of our success," says the elder Frye who was selected in 1980 as Arizona's Small Business Person of the Year. "The customers just know the nice people that wait on them."

The Fryes also keep their employees happy with company picnics, Christmas parties, and other holiday celebrations as well as incentive programs and employee recognition for loyal continuous service. "I've been told we were the first drycleaner in the state to have an employee benefits program," Don adds.

Although Don E. retired officially in 1981, he still can be found at the 7126 East Sahuaro Drive headquarters a few hours each day. Maintaining the title of chairman of the board, he turned the reigns over to son Donn, CEO and president, who began learning the business at age eleven.

Prestige is one of fourteen winners nationwide and the only Arizona firm to receive the "Model Cleaner Award." In 1999 the firm won for utilizing an environmentally safe dry-cleaning solution at its new locations and for a program that collects one million hangers annually for recycling. Additionally, in 1998, Prestige Cleaners was recognized by the State of Arizona for its environmental awareness and was awarded the Arizona Pollution Prevention Leadership Enhancement (APPLE) Award.

Community involvement has always been of extreme importance to both Fryes. Even before he opened his doors in 1964, Don joined the Scottsdale Chamber of Commerce and proceeded to work on "many, many committees" through the years. The two are the only father-son team to both serve on the Chamber board. Donn also followed his dad in joining Kiwanis International and became president of the McCormick Ranch Kiwanis Club. He is past president of the Scottsdale Foundation for the Handicapped; past president of Scottsdale/Paradise Valley YMCA; past chairman of the Scottsdale Mayors Committee on Employment of People with Disabilities and a member of the Boys & Girls Clubs of Scottsdale board of directors.

"Scottsdale is a real good place to live," says the elder Frye, who has logged fifty years in the business. "Donn and I have given back to the community because it's been good to us. We stress community involvement. That's our thing."

Prestige Cleaners, Inc. donates hundreds of drycleaning and laundry gift certificates each year to charitable causes. Prestige and its father-son team have come a long way since opening the first Prestige Cleaners store in 1964. The company plans to grow and give back to Scottsdale for another thirty-five years. You may visit Prestige Cleaners on the web at www.prestigecleaners.com.

THE CLOSET FACTORY

On what used to be Thunderbird Field II, a military airfield where pilots trained during World War II, now is home to Scottsdale Airpark, the city's most important light industrial center. One of the Airpark's most successful businesses is The Closet Factory, with a showroom and manufacturing plant located on the property. Established in 1991, making it the oldest closet company in Scottsdale, The Closet Factory is known for its custom designed closets, pantries, home offices, garages, and storage systems. The Closet Factory is ranked number one in its industry by the leading consumer magazine and promises "quality, service and dependability" to clients along with a lifetime guarantee.

"Our designers are expertly trained not only in design, but in how to solve storage dilemma's," says The Closet Factory President Daryl Zee. "We are truly custom," adds Allan Zee who is not just CEO, but also father of the president. "We can make anything to fit a customer's specific needs regardless of what they might be. We also offer a wide range of styles and finishes." The Closet Factory is unique in that it uses a floor-based system rather than wall hung systems. This means each unit is built from the ground up like fine furniture. The entire custom piece is finished with European hardware. Allan says, "It's the attention to detail and the extra special touches that make a house a home." The only regret Allan and Daryl have is that they are so busy installing closets for others throughout the Valley of the Sun, they haven't had time to customize their own.

✧

*Downtown Scottsdale offers a study
in contrasts: Western history and a
state-of-the-art medical campus. The
adobe building in the foreground of this
photo is the Cavalliere Blacksmith Shop,
built in 1920 to replace the original tin
shop opened in 1910. Still run by the
Cavalliere family in 2001, it is Scottsdale's
oldest, continuously-operating business.
In the background of the photo stands
one of the modern buildings of Scottsdale
Healthcare's (SHC) Osborn campus.
After a modest start in 1961 as City
Hospital of Scottsdale, SHC is now a
multi-campus health care provider that
is one of the largest employers in the city.*

PHOTO COURTESY OF JOAN FUDALA

MANUFACTURING, INDUSTRY & TECHNOLOGY

Companies producing and marketing

goods and services which contribute

to the economic growth

and vitality of Scottsdale

MOTOROLA, INC.

Motorola, Inc., and the City of Scottsdale have shared a half century of economic growth and community partnership. The company opened its facility at McDowell and Hayden Roads in 1957, just a few years after the city itself was incorporated. Over the years, Scottsdale's supportive business climate has helped Motorola fulfill its commitment to link people's dreams with technology's promise. A global leader in communication technologies and solutions, Motorola has continually demonstrated its leadership in the community through the involvement of employees and generous sharing of resources.

In 1930 the two-year-old, Chicago-based Galvin Manufacturing Corporation produced the first practical and affordable car radio, called the "Motorola." The name soon became synonymous with high-quality portable radio communications, and, eventually, Motorola became the company name. World War II provided a unique opportunity for the company to develop communications products for the military, a partnership that continues today. Dr. Dan Noble, who became Motorola's director of research in 1940, designed a high-frequency, two-way FM radio for front-line troops that was instrumental in winning the war effort. The backpack radio unit, which had a range of ten miles, was commonly known as the "walkie-talkie."

Before the war Motorola had been primarily an assembler of products from components purchased from outside suppliers. As a result of the war experience, Motorola transitioned to a developer and manufacturer of its own electronic components. The new research and development focus was an important evolution which would allow Motorola in the coming years to transform scientific discoveries into commercially viable technologies, products and solutions.

Motorola's Arizona presence, established in 1949 with a research facility on Central Avenue in Phoenix, was essential to the company's broader post-World War II direction. As the Cold War developed, the U.S. government urged manufacturers of defense equipment to locate their facilities in the Southwest and West, where many of the

wartime industries had been established. Phoenix was close to supply sources on the West Coast and was an air transportation hub; it was also familiar to Dr. Dan Noble, who had spent time in Arizona as a youth.

Noble had the foresight to understand that the development of semiconductors, a technology called solid state electronics, would be the wave of the future. The transistor, the simplest type of semiconductor, invented in 1948, would one day replace the vacuum tube, the primary component of electronics at the time. "Noble's Folly," as some skeptics called the new venture, grew steadily, and in 1957, Motorola opened a second facility in Scottsdale to develop transistors.

Motorola's venture into solid state electronics continued to expand in both government and commercial markets. The semiconductor business first turned a profit in 1958; by 1962, Motorola was the second largest semiconductor manufacturer in the country.

Following its equipment contract work during World War II, the company became a key partner in many important and highly visible U.S. government programs.

Much of today's solutions-driven advanced communications technology comes out of Scottsdale, where Motorola's Integrated Information Systems Group has the bulk of ts operations.

The Motorola facility in Scottsdale provided the National Aeronautics and Space Administration (NASA) with critical communications solutions for the *Explorer* satellite missions in 1958 and the *Mercury* missions that flew the first Americans into space beginning in 1961. Scottsdale engineers designed and built the communications equipment that enabled the world to hear Apollo astronaut Neil Armstrong say, "One small step for man, one giant leap for mankind," and watch him take his famous step onto the moon's surface in 1969.

Over the years, Motorola continued its visible presence in commercial ventures, as well, with state-of-the-art radios, televisions, automobile components and, later, cellular telephones. The development during the 1960s of integrated circuits—the equivalent of many individual semiconductors and

transistors embedded within one tiny silicon chip—had a profound impact on commercial and industrial markets, and Motorola expanded its customer base and operations overseas, encompassing a variety of new industries. In the second half of the century, Motorola sales grew from $117 million to well over $30 billion. Today Motorola employs more than 130,000 people worldwide.

Two events in the 1990s would affect Motorola's path to the future: the end of the Cold War and the Internet revolution. An increasing emphasis on communications and information technology has changed the way Motorola—and the rest of the world—does business.

✧

Above: From Scottsdale, Motorola designed and built the U.S. Army Common Ground Station, a communications solution that provided U.S. field commanders with a distinct advantage when first used during the Gulf War in 1991. The Common Ground Station provides the capability to quickly assess information through input from numerous sources on the battlefield.

Below: Motorola Integrated Information Systems Group provides advanced systems integration solutions for large enterprises in the commercial, defense, space, and government markets.

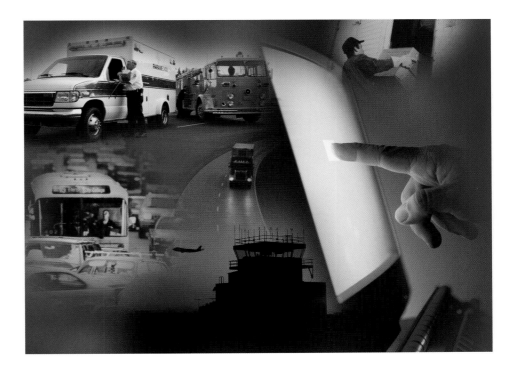

The fall of the Iron Curtain led to a tremendous decrease in the size and budget of the U.S. military, whose leaders realized that future battlefield advantages would depend on superior intelligence and information systems. Motorola began working with the government to deliver advanced solutions based on existing commercial technologies. This effort has produced combined technologies that seamlessly integrate information and communications systems, such as the Army's Tactical Operations Centers, a highly mobile and easily configured platform from which commanders can direct their mission-ready forces in the field.

The Internet has become an integral part of people's lives. Motorola's vision of the future is a "Web without wires," where people can access information anywhere anytime through embedded solutions and a new Internet Protocol-based communications architecture. This architecture is being developed through strategic alliances with other networking experts and will serve as the foundation for Motorola's end-to-end solutions "portfolio" of networks, access devices, content, applications, and services. Opportunities for Motorola's future growth will come, in part, through platforms like this, on which other companies can build and add value.

Motorola understands the commitment and responsibility inherent in being a good corporate citizen. From the beginning the company's employees have embraced the local community, including "adopting" needy families for the holidays, organizing blood drives and food bank donations, and sponsoring health and safety fairs and household hazardous waste collection days.

Over the years volunteer participation has grown along with the company, which is one of the largest private employers in Arizona. Motorola's employees have consistently, over the last two decades, conducted the largest employee United Way campaign in the Phoenix area, raising millions of dollars to support numerous health and human service organizations. Annually, Motorola supports the community, primarily in education and health and human services, with more than $4 million in grants, equipment, and other resources.

Education will help conquer the digital divide in the twenty-first century, and, to that end, Motorola has been a leading supporter of educational reform. More than 100,000 students, from kindergarten through college, have benefited from many Motorola-sponsored programs, while teachers and administrators have benefited from training opportunities.

Motorola maintains an enduring partnership with Arizona State University (ASU); the science and engineering library, which opened in 1983, was named for Motorola's Dr. Dan Noble. In 1997 Motorola pledged $11 million to the university to build a manufacturing institute and a teaching lab, along with neighborhood outreach and the

✧

Above: The Sectera™ Wireline Terminal provides high assurance security for both voice and data communications. The portable device easily snaps in between either a phone or computer and the telephone wall jack.

Below: When the Near Earth Asteroid Rendezvous (NEAR) spacecraft orbited the Eros asteroid early in 2000, Motorola's transponders, designed and built in Scottsdale, provided critical communications for the history-making mission.

establishment of a presidential professorship in neighborhood revitalization. A Motorola-ASU collaboration that benefits the entire educational system, kindergarten through college, is the Center for Environmental Studies, which trains educators, parents, and students in math and environmental sciences.

With 3,500 employees in Scottsdale, Motorola has a great impact locally. In addition to the Volunteer Program, which coordinates one-day projects like the "Christmas in April" home renovation, there are innumerable independent volunteer efforts. Motorola employees volunteer in schools, service clubs, senior centers, hospitals, and food banks. Scottsdale citizens volunteer with the Motorola/Scottsdale Community Liaison Council, a group of nearly forty concerned citizens who meet monthly to discuss issues and advise the company on its role in the Scottsdale community. The Council supports projects such as LINKS, the Scottsdale community collaborative; safe neighborhoods; book drives; and the Coronado High School mosaic restoration. Annually, the Council honors citizen volunteers through its Frances Young Community Heroes Awards, named for a long-time community leader.

Motorola's commitment to Scottsdale is apparent in more than half a million dollars of support and many years of services donated to the Boys & Girls Clubs of Scottsdale, Scottsdale Healthcare System, Scottsdale's Paiute Neighborhood Center, and Hayden Nature Park. Motorola was Paiute Neighborhood Center's first corporate sponsor when it opened in the mid-1990s.

Motorola was also instrumental in creating the Red Mountain Branch of the Boys & Girls Club, whose opening was celebrated with a showcase of student photography exhibited at the Heard Museum.

Motorola is committed to being the link between people's dreams and technology's promise. Through its involvement and support, Motorola is also the link to a better, more caring community. Motorola's half-century partnership with the City of Scottsdale is evidence that strong leadership and commitment to the community forges a solid connection that will endure for years to come.

❖

Above: For years, Motorola has focused volunteer time, equipment donations and funding into Arizona's educational system. An outreach team of Motorola employees provide hope and direction for the future, partnering with the educational system to educate students and teachers about the gap between the perception and the reality of the workplace, particularly the rapidly changing high technology industry.

Below: In partnership with the City of Scottsdale and Saguaro High School biology students, Motorola employees have preserved habitat in Hayden Nature Park.

STOCKETT TILE AND GRANITE

When Dave Stockett was growing up in Scottsdale, his parents never worried about how he was spending his spare time. From grade school on, he always had a job.

At one point, he was delivering the *Arizona Republic* in the morning and the *Scottsdale Progress* in the afternoon. As he got older, he parked cars, bussed dishes, anything that paid.

"I learned to appreciate an income," says the Saguaro High School alumnus. Along the way, he cultivated a solid work ethic and a desire to someday run his own business.

During the Seventies, Stockett attended Scottsdale Community College and developed an interest in environmentalism. Later, he became an independent subcontractor in the trades. "I was attracted to tile," he says, "because it is environmentally friendly."

Today, Stockett is president of Stockett Tile and Granite Company, which he founded in 1979. The company, located in Scottsdale Airpark, primarily serves the Valley but also does a brisk trade in outlying Arizona cities and key out-of-state locations. Stockett Tile and Granite Company are highly regarded for its service and craftsmanship.

An example of Stockett Tile and Granite Company craftsmanship can be found in the Desert Highlands Clubhouse.

Over the past three years, the company has undergone phenomenal growth, which is reflected in the increase of its workforce from 50 to more than 150 full-time employees. It boasts three divisions: ceramic and stone tile, slab marble and granite; and sealing and restoration. The growth is largely attributable to the soaring demand for natural stone.

"Five years ago," Stockett says, "Eighty percent of our work was in ceramic files and twenty percent in natural stone. Today, its ninety percent natural stone."

Stockett says several factors have contributed to the turnaround. Travel and the information explosion have created a greater awareness of natural stone. Also, technological developments in the industry and a corresponding increase in volume has made stone more affordable. Finally, consumers in today's economy are now in a position to take advantage of natural stone's value, beauty, and longevity.

Although North America still uses only about eight percent of the world's production of decorative stone—the rest goes to Europe, the Middle East, and the Far East—globalization is changing that. In fact, Stockett Tile and Granite has stayed on top of trends by ordering natural stone not only from North America but also worldwide.

"The majority of our customers are high-end homebuilders and designers," Stockett says. "But we do work for individual homeowners as well." A sampling of customers

✧

Above: This lustrous bathroom incorporates white marble into the countertops and floors.
COURTESY OF DINO TONN PHOTOGRAPHY.

Below: The countertops and sinks of this Scottsdale residence are fabricated using Galaxy black granite. Fabricating granite sinks requires highly skilled craftsmen.
COURTESY OF DINO TONN PHOTOGRAPHY.

reveals a sizeable proportion of professional athletes and Fortune 500 executives.

Two things that separate Stockett Tile and Granite Company from the competition are its practice of "growing" its own craftspeople and its ability to effect a fast turnaround without sacrificing quality. "We have a curriculum and on-the-job training in each department," Stockett says of the in-house training. "That way we keep standards high and turnover low." Regarding turnarounds, he says: "Our manufacturing facility has one of the shortest delivery times in the Valley."

The company also is skilled at making changes in the middle of a project. "We understand it is not always possible for buyers to visualize from a rendering exactly how a tile or stone feature will turn out," Stockett says. "If they need to make a change or addition, we're happy to help them." The ability to change orders midstream is greatly expedited by Stockett's automated estimating process, which provides pinpoint accuracy.

Finally, Stockett Tile and Granite Company are in the forefront of the new 'synergism' that exists among subcontractors, general con-tractors, architects, interior designers, and homeowners.

"The amenities that customers want today," Stockett says, "require more cooperation, tighter scheduling to eliminate overlapping costs and a marshaling of more resources to produce more in a shorter time frame. The result is better quality for the homeowner and lower costs."

Stockett Tile and Granite Company have received more than twenty-five awards for craftsmanship and excellence by state peers over the past decade. It has also won Contractor of the Year honors three times and is the recipient of several national awards.

LINTHICUM CONSTRUCTORS, INC.

Above: Scottsdale Stadium, located in the heart of downtown Scottsdale, has been described as a "masterpiece" by Al Rosen, former San Francisco Giants president and Cleveland Indians slugger. The stadium was designed by Hellmuth, Obata & Kassabaum, Kansas City, Missouri.

Below: This dynamic North Scottsdale home reflects innovation, imagination and vitality. It received the prestigious Gold Nugget Grand Award for the Best of the West. Designed by H&S International, Scottsdale.

COURTESY OF MARK BOISCLAIR.

The search for new ideas and solutions by Linthicum Constructors, Inc., is never more obvious than at its headquarters in North Scottsdale's Perimeter Center.

A spectacular concrete entry wall welcomes visitors, clearly demonstrating the company's appreciation and use of natural materials. Inside, concrete floors, stained and buffed to a bright patina resembling fine leather, complement a custom-designed table with a rebar base in the conference room. Curved walls and irregular spaces throughout the building heighten the effect.

"This building is who we are," says Gary Linthicum, founder and president of Linthicum Constructors.

Building one-of-a-kind structures, as well as exquisite custom homes, is the business of Linthicum, a full-services-contracting firm serving the Southwest since 1984. The building roots of the Linthicum family run deep. From three Welsh carpenters who landed on the shores of Maryland in 1654 to the accomplished contractor responsible for many of Arizona's landmarks, the Linthicum name represents the essence of the truly professional builder.

Similarly, Linthicum headquarters represents the essence of the firm's philosophy of providing clients with projects that enhance their business, serve their communities and respect the delicate environment within and surrounding their structure. While it may take extra time and care to protect a stately saguaro or a small, fragile prickly pear cactus during construction, Linthicum considers it a priority.

As recognition for these efforts, the Valley Forward Association awarded the company its coveted Crescordia Award for environmental excellence. Linthicum is proud of this honor, which recognizes sensitivity to growth as well as professional accomplishment.

The company's craftsmanship and uncompromising dedication to quality and integrity can be seen in gathering places throughout Scottsdale. They include Scottsdale Baseball Stadium, Arizona School of Real Estate and

Business, Discover the World Marketing Headquarters, USF Bestway Corporate Headquarters and Scottsdale Hampton Inn. In addition, Linthicum's imaginative expansion and renovation of the Scottsdale Civic Center Library more than doubled its size.

Linthicum prides itself on its association with world-class golf clubhouse facilities such as Desert Mountain's Apache and Chiricahua Clubhouses, Troon North Country Club, and Legend Trail Clubhouse. Spectacular custom homes built in prestigious communities throughout Scottsdale and the Valley also bear the Linthicum signature of quality.

Linthicum's dedication to sharing construction expertise with the community can be seen in the award-winning Webster Auditorium Historic Restoration and the Desert House, an energy-efficient residence. Both are on the grounds of the Desert Botanical Garden.

As Linthicum Constructors looks to the future, the firm remains committed to its well-defined business plan. "It's tempting to take on as much as possible, but our focus is not merely on growth," Linthicum says. Meeting and exceeding the unique needs of each client remains our ultimate mission."

✧

Above: Troon North Country Club meant building around boulders, giant saguaros and other native vegetation. Designed by Swaback Partners, Scottsdale.
COURTESY OF MARK BOISCLAIR.

Below: With its pallet of warm colors and natural materials, the Apache Clubhouse blends into the surrounding desert environment. Designed by H&S International, Scottsdale.
COURTESY OF MARK BOISCLAIR.

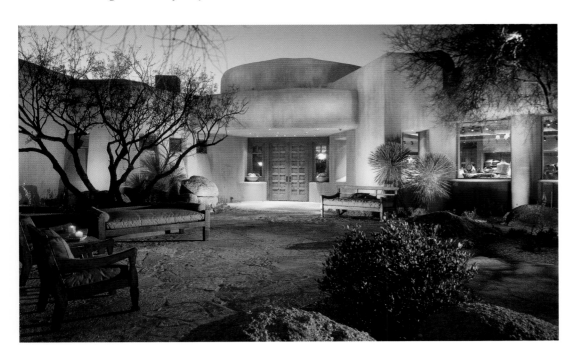

CORNELIS HOLLANDER DESIGNS, INC.

✧

Cornelis Hollander, president of Cornelis Hollander Designs, Inc.

When Cornelis Hollander gets the urge to sketch, he sketches. It doesn't matter whether he is on a plane, in front of the TV or sitting in a restaurant. Anywhere will do.

But unlike doodlers who put aside their drawings when finished, Hollander converts his into beautiful jewelry.

"I design all the time," says Hollander, president of Cornelis Hollander Designs, Inc. "I can design different collections all day long."

In the world of jewelry, Hollander has compiled an enviable record. He has captured the DeBeers Diamond of Distinction award three times, the AGTA's Spectrum Award eight times, the International Platinum Design of the Year Award three times and Japan's International Pearl Design Contest nine times.

Since founding his business in 1984, Hollander has seen his trend-setting designs embraced by upscale jewelry stores throughout the world. His forte is one-of-a-kind creations, which are crafted by a staff of sixteen skilled artisans and international craftsmen.

In addition to custom-designed jewelry, Cornelis Hollander Designs, Inc., offers an array of jewelry services, including an unsurpassed selection of fine diamonds and gemstones, remounts, expert repairs, and appraisals.

The firm prides itself on superior service and customer relations. Hollander learned early that "little things" count in more ways than one.

As a youth, he studied art and jewelry design at the Vrije Academie in Den Haag, Holland, where he earned his masters degree as a goldsmith. "I wanted to be a sculptor," says Hollander, a native of The Netherlands. "I did large sculptures, then smaller and smaller ones. One day I made a ring and cast it. I found I enjoyed working in miniatures."

Hollander's father was so impressed by one of his son's designs that he urged him to seek an apprenticeship at Hattan Garden, London's renowned jewelry district and Mecca for those seeking exquisite work in platinum.

After honing his skills for two years at Hattan Garden, Hollander left for South Africa, the diamond capital of the world, where he continued to "soak up design and creative innovation." Johannesburg was an adventure for the young designer. "It is definitely a country of gold and diamonds," he says. "Jewelry is a big industry."

While there, Hollander met his future wife, Christa, who had moved to South Africa from Switzerland. Together, they spent their leisure time horseback riding and exploring the wilderness and coastal areas of the country.

Before long, Hollander's work began attracting international attention. In 1979 he received job offers from New York, Chicago, and Los Angeles. At the time, South Africa was experiencing deep social and political unrest.

CORNELIS HOLLANDER

Uncertain about the future, Hollander and his wife decided to visit the United States.

While checking out opportunities in Los Angeles, the couple drove to Phoenix for a brief visit with Dutch friends. They were delighted by the similarity of Phoenix's relaxed lifestyle and good weather to those of Johannesburg. In addition, Paul Johnson jewelers offered Hollander a job on the strength of his impressive credentials, as well as sponsorship should he choose to immigrate. They opted to stay.

In 1982 Hollander, now a designer at Grunewald and Adams, was urged to enter the "Gold 82" competition, the biggest jewelry design contest in the country. Hollander had only three days until deadline. He quickly created a ring for the store and one for himself (done in his garage). Hollander's ring won the grand prize, while the Grunewald and Adams entry won first prize.

The success inspired him to step up his design activities and, two years later, go into business for himself. At first, he worked out of his home. Christa helped financially by working at administrative positions. She rendered a similar service at home, freeing her husband to focus on creative matters. Soon, his innovative designs employing unusually cut gemstones marked him as a trendsetter.

As Hollander's business grew, so did his family. Between 1984 and 1991, two girls and a boy were born. The business moved to new quarters twice and accrued a half dozen employees. Although ninety-five percent of his business was wholesale—upscale jewelry stores and department stores coveted his work from the start—Hollander still managed to service a few local clients who admired his work.

After a 1987 trade show in Basel, Switzerland, the company began getting orders from around the world, especially Japan. In 1993 Hollander hired Nobuko Okuni, a recent graduate of Western International University in Phoenix, as his marketing director for a trade show in Japan. Since then, Okuni has increased business with Japan tenfold.

In 1998 Cornelis Hollander Designs, Inc. opened its first retail store in Scottsdale's art district. It was largely an outgrowth of Hollander's desire for more "one-on-one" contact with his customers. A year later, the company

CORNELIS HOLLANDER

CORNELIS HOLLANDER

annexed the gallery next door, providing ample space for both retail and wholesale operations.

Today, Hollander continues to follow his muse with such inspired creations as the Archi-tech and Gem Directions collections. His children are engaged in extracurricular activities such as cheerleading, hockey and dance. He and his wife enjoy hiking the Phoenix Mountain Preserve with their two dogs and taking "exciting vacations." In short, they are living the American Dream.

NKK
SWITCHES OF
AMERICA, INC.

When NKK Switches of America Inc. opened its doors in Scottsdale nineteen years ago, it had a single rented office suite with four employees and a cross-cultural product catalogue featuring awkward English and the metric system of weights and measures.

It was a modest start for the Japanese-owned company. Today, NKK Switches is a leader in the switch industry, boasting one of the three top market shares in the country. It continues to expand its reach globally by accommodating today's changing business practices. NKK Switches now owns a 45,000-square-foot facility and occupies 30,000 square feet for its operations in the Scottsdale Airpark location. It numbers forty-eight employees.

How did it happen? NKK Switches President Kiyoko Toyama attributes it to parent company Nihon Kaiheiki Industries Co., Ltd., of Kawasaki, which took the unusual approach of allowing the firm to develop independently. "There is nobody from Japan here," says Toyama, a thirty-five-year resident and a citizen of the U.S. who has been with the company from the start. "All the employees are from the Valley. We are a U.S. corporation."

Early on, NKK Switches set about building itself as an American company. Its first task was to establish a sales network throughout North America with well-respected representative firms and distributors, a move that has paid handsome dividends and established lasting professional relationships.

In 1987 the company discarded the old, hard-to-decipher catalogue and created a new one titled *Design Guide*. It was clear, comprehensive and geared to American customers. Unlike the previous catalogue, it featured both American and Metric units. The new guide boosted company credibility as well as sales.

"After that," Toyama says, "things took off with an extended period of dynamic growth." The period from 1989 to 1991, in particular, saw explosive growth in product development and the introduction of such popular items as super-subminiature toggles, pushbuttons and a multitude of illuminated pushbuttons. During this period, the company newsletter, *Switching Times*, also was launched.

In 1993 another milestone occurred with the installation of the computerized Order Administration System (OAS), which processes orders and manages backlogs. In the past, only NKK Switches' inventory had been computerized. The customized OAS, Toyama says, "greatly expedited business processes."

According to Toyama, who replaced founder Glenn Hoelz as president in 1999, NKK Switches of America chose Scottsdale as its headquarters not only for its "business-friendly" atmosphere but the quality of its life and workforce.

"NKK has made tremendous strides in modernizing operational processes, as well as securing a strong web presence and developing the architecture necessary for B2B transactions," Toyama says. In fact, she adds, *Design Guide* catalogue will be completely E-accessible by mid-2001."

✧

Above: President Kiyoko Toyama (right) has been with NKK since its inception and served as its vice president until the retirement of the company's founder and original president in 1999. Todd E. Harris, vice president, joined the company shortly after it began its operations in the Scottsdale Airpark.

Below: NKK's product array includes power switches large enough to fill your soup mug all the way down to miniatures smaller than half the nail on your little finger. These products are used in industrial settings; communications and network equipment; medical diagnostic devices; and much more.

When his company was in its infancy, PLP Digital Systems President Michael Addison logged 1,600 miles a week on the job. And that was just the commute.

"I would leave San Francisco on a Monday," recalls Addison, who co-founded the Scottsdale company in 1989 with partner Chris Morrison, "and come back home Friday."

It was a prudent approach, all things considered. "I financed the company to start," says Addison. "We didn't go for venture capital. Chris wrote the software; I went out and sold it." By 1992 PLP Digital Systems clearly was on fast-forward, and Addison decided to move his family to Scottsdale.

Today, PLP Digital Systems grosses more than $5 million annually and boasts thirty-five full-time employees. It features an international clientele ranging from small service bureaus to giant corporations such as Mercedes Benz.

PLP Digital Systems was one of the first software companies to enter the emerging field of digital reprographics. "We have been instrumental in guiding the world away from blueprints and toward paper," says Addison, referring to the company's cutting-edge expertise in creation, storage, retrieval, and high-speed printing of large-format technical documents.

Using PLP Digital Systems' PlotWorks and DCRS (Document Control and Reprographics System), businesses are able to dramatically enhance their reprographics operations.

PlotWorks is a production tool that provides high-speed copying, scanning and printing. It enables users to control selected combinations of printers and scanners independently or simultaneously at each device's highest-rated speed. Its modular, open-architecture design permits easy customizing. PlotWorks is installed at some 400 sites in more than 30 countries.

DCRS is a sophisticated management tool that weds scanning, printing and document control. Its configurable indexing and tracking techniques, combined with a virtual database, allows users to access technical drawings and documents from multiple servers in multiple locations and print them from one desktop. Like PlotWorks, DCRS can be adapted to existing business processes.

To assist clients in developing solutions tailored to their needs, PLP offers an experienced cadre of design engineers, technicians, and programmers. These experts are available worldwide.

In 1933 builder and architect R.T. Evans opened the Jokake School for Girls on the southern slopes of Camelback Mountain, adjacent to the Jokake Inn. As part of the school's horseback riding program, students would make weekend trips to the Jokake Mountain Camp in the McDowell Mountains, as shown in this 1930s photo. According to the Jokake School brochure, "the camp is comfortably furnished and equipped with bathrooms, showers and good bunks with the best of springs and mattresses." The brochure also stated that "there is probably no more beautiful desert country to be found in the southwest."

PHOTO COURTESY OF LABEULA STEINER MOWRY

Quality of Life

Healthcare companies, educational institutions

and recreational facilities

contribute to Scottsdale's quality of life

TOURNAMENT PLAYERS CLUB OF SCOTTSDALE

Holes No. 12-15.

Fourteen years ago desert land in northern Scottsdale was turned into the Tournament Players Club of Scottsdale, a thirty-six-hole Tom Weiskopf and Jay Morrish-designed championship golf course. The TPC, a resort/daily fee facility, offers both the Stadium and Desert courses and serves both resort guests and local residents. Operated by the PGA Tour Golf Course Properties, Inc., the facility sits on land owned by the Federal Bureau of Reclamation and leased by the City of Scottsdale. An agreement with the Five Diamond Fairmont Scottsdale Princess Resort aligns the TPC course with the Princess, which is renowned for providing luxury accommodations and service. As the PGA Tour stop with the largest crowds of any golf event in the world, the Phoenix Open Tournament brings international attention and respect to the Stadium Course. A highlight, which has gone down in golfing history, is Tiger Wood's hole-in-one on No. 16 during the 1997 Phoenix Open. In 2000, the Phoenix Open, sponsored by the Phoenix Thunderbirds, raised over $3 million for local youth charities, bringing their total charitable donations to more than $18 million over the years.

"The Stadium Course's signature hole No. 15 is an outstanding par 5 for either a high or low handicapper," said TPC General Manager, Bill Grove. "For the high handicapper, two reasonable shots puts the player in a great chance to get a third shot to a well-bunkered green that has some very interesting pin placements. The water that surrounds the entire green multiplies all of this. For the low handicapper, a well-struck drive will give the player an opportunity to try and reach the green in two shots for a possible eagle. While a poorly struck shot will result in a definite penalty due to the water challenge. Playability and aesthetics of No. 15 are excellent for all players."

Additionally, the last four holes—15, 16, 17, and 18—are considered the most exciting finishing holes on the PGA Tour. The award-winning Stadium Course Golf Shop, recognized for twelve consecutive years as a "Top 100 Golf

Shop" by *Golf Shop Operations*, was remodeled in 1996. The TPC of Scottsdale courses have won numerous top awards including being recognized as one of *Golf Digest's* "Top 25 Best Courses in Arizona;" one of the top ten public courses in Arizona; one of Conde Naste's "Top 40 Golf Resort Destinations;" and as one of the top one hundred golf resorts in the world. The property also has been recognized for environmental excellence as a certified Audubon Cooperative Sanctuary for the fifth consecutive year. The courses have continually undergone improvements in keeping with high TPC and PGA Tour standards. In 1997 all eighteen greens of the Stadium Course were completely rebuilt resulting in outstanding playing surfaces praised by Phoenix Open participants who compared them to U.S. Open quality. In addition, all seventy-two bunkers were renovated, several championship tees were lengthened, and the Clubhouse, Grill Restaurant, and locker rooms underwent substantial remodeling.

The summer of 1998 brought additional enhancement to the Stadium Course with 13,000 plants and 100 mature desert trees planted to reflect the Sonoran Desert's beauty and add new challenge to the course. In the summer of 2000 the Stadium Course bulkhead project was completed with the replacement of all wooden railroad ties and pylons with inlaid rock formations on all water holes and at many tee boxes. One project was the replacement of the wooden bridge on signature hole No. 15 with a rock bridge.

In 1999 the Desert Course and Grill Restaurant underwent improvements. All greens were completely rebuilt and resurfaced using Bermuda grass upgrading playability to match the Stadium greens. The TPC of Scottsdale recently partnered with the Nicklaus/Flick Private Tee Program to provide guests with an individualized instructional program designed to maximize their golfing potential. This simple goal served Jack Nicklaus during thirty years of competitive golf and is the same goal TPC instructors have for each of their students. At the Scottsdale course, golfers receive instruction from some of the game's most respected and talented personnel who use the most innovative technology and learning tools to help individuals become the best golfer possible. With rounds of golf on both courses in excess of 120,000, the Tournament Players Club of Scottsdale is clearly an operation well managed by the PGA Tour. "As one of the flagship courses of the TPC network of clubs nationwide," Grove states, "the TPC of Scottsdale continues to provide a great golf experience with our goal being to exceed the expectation of each guest with a quality product and unsurpassed customer service."

✧

Hole No. 12.

COURTESY OF KEIICHI SATO.

Scottsdale Cardiovascular Center

Driving past the Scottsdale Cardiovascular Center at the intersection of Civic Center Plaza and Earll Drive, the handsome edifice with the patina copper roof often attracts the attention of people. It stands out among the buildings in the area.

That is the way Dr. Fuad Ibrahim, founder and president of Scottsdale Cardiovascular Center, intended it.

"I didn't want just a building," Ibrahim reflects. "I wanted a beautiful building that people would notice, a building easily described when directing new patients to the practice. It was the first building in Scottsdale with a copper roof. Copper lasts forever."

That quest for longevity is a hallmark of Ibrahim's specialty of cardiology. Since establishing his office practice in Scottsdale in 1977 Ibrahim has been a moving force in increasing longevity and improving the quality of life of Valley residents.

In the early 1980s Ibrahim, supported by fellow cardiologists, worked with the administration of Scottsdale Memorial Hospital (now Scottsdale Healthcare-Osborn) to add a Section of Cardiology to the hospital's Department of Internal Medicine. His energetic and thorough approach to organizing cardiology services at the hospital was appreciated by his fellow cardiologists who elected him as the first chairman of the Cardiology Section. At that time, Ibrahim recalls, Scottsdale Memorial Hospital on Osborn Road was the only major hospital in Scottsdale.

During the same period, Ibrahim's long-standing interest in non-invasive vascular

studies again brought him in close contact with the hospital administration. Through his initiative, the hospital added equipment and staff to provide non-invasive vascular procedures. This vascular service was then and is still supervised by Dr. Ibrahim.

Later, in conjunction with his colleagues, Ibrahim spearheaded the establishment of a cardiovascular rehabilitation program under the auspices of Scottsdale Memorial Hospital for patients who are recovering from heart attacks or those who had undergone bypass surgery. This program has proven to be highly popular among heart patients, and Ibrahim coordinates the program—now at both Scottsdale Healthcare hospitals—as its medical director to this day.

Above: Dr. Fuad Ibrahim, founder and president of Scottsdale Cardiovascular Center.

Right: The Scottsdale Cardiovascular Center at the intersection of Civic Center Plaza and Earll Drive.

In 1981 ground was broken for the construction of Scottsdale Cardiovascular Center. Its designer was the architect Kamal Amin, a disciple of the legendary architect Frank Lloyd Wright. Ibrahim worked closely with Amin to ensure that the Center would reflect his aesthetic as well as his professional vision. It had to be "unique, tasteful, readily recognizable and, of course, specially adapted for the practice of cardiology in an ambulatory setting."

Ibrahim's goal was to establish a state-of-the-art center of cardiologic excellence that would include all subspecialties in the field of cardiology. With the opening of Scottsdale Cardiovascular Center in 1983, this goal became reality. Shortly before the opening of Scottsdale Cardiovascular Center, Ibrahim was joined by Dr. W. Scott Robertson, an invasive cardiologist with special training in stress echocardiography, and the first of three partners to follow. Dr. Barbara Prian joined the partnership a few years later as an invasive cardiologist who also was responsible for pacemaker implantations. As the boundaries of cardiology widened and new modalities of treatment became available, Dr. Andrew Jacob, an interventional cardiologist skilled in angioplasty, became the fourth partner.

Through the periodic addition of partners and associates with special skills, Ibrahim and his colleagues made Scottsdale Cardiovascular Center a full-service cardiovascular practice which focuses on consultation, cardiovascular testing and non-invasive vascular evaluations in the ambulatory setting, and on conservative inpatient treatment as well as cutting-edge interventional procedures in the areas of cardiac catheterization, angioplasty, stenting and electrophysiologic procedures, all carried out in the inpatient environment of the two Scottsdale Healthcare hospitals.

"I was the first cardiologist in Scottsdale to use the team approach," Ibrahim says, adding, "and that approach has proved to be the quintessential ingredient of the Center's success. Over the years, we at the Center have kept up with technology and the latest techniques by adding physicians skilled in the most recent advances in cardiology to the Center's team."

"Our staff of cardiologists and paramedical personnel stay abreast of the changes and advances in cardiology through attendance at meetings and conferences, but keeping up with the constantly changing, bureaucratic managed-care environment is one of the most vexing and taxing aspects of practicing cardiology—or for that matter medicine—in today's healthcare setting."

"The true rewards in this time of escalating costs and diminishing compensation," says Ibrahim, "lie in the fact that our efforts, day after day and night after night, have contributed significantly to longer lives and, especially, the quality of the lives of our patients. I still love to practice cardiology. I think that says it all!"

✧

Above: Dr. Fuad Ibrahim (right) and Dr. W. Scott Robertson, Scottsdale Cardiovascular Center.

Below: Scottsdale Cardiovascular Center physicians (from left to right): Andrew Jacob, M. D.; Barbara Prian, M.D.; W. Scott Robertson, M.D.; Fuad Ibrahim, M.D.

SCOTTSDALE HEALTHCARE

As the City of Scottsdale grew following its 1951 incorporation, residents seeking convenient, quality health services began discussing the need for a hospital. Their dreams were realized in 1962 when City Hospital, now known as Scottsdale Healthcare Osborn, opened with a staff of 55 physicians and 200 employees.

The forerunner to Scottsdale Healthcare, a not-for-profit community-based health system, City Hospital enjoyed a special relationship with Scottsdale residents. As the city thrived, so did the hospital as it responded to the community's health needs. Over the next decade, intensive care and critical care units were opened, and additional departments were established. Licensed bed capacity was increased through the addition of new patient towers. And when a medical staff library was needed, physicians' wives established a volunteer-based facility—an early indication of the high level of community involvement that would shape Scottsdale Healthcare's future.

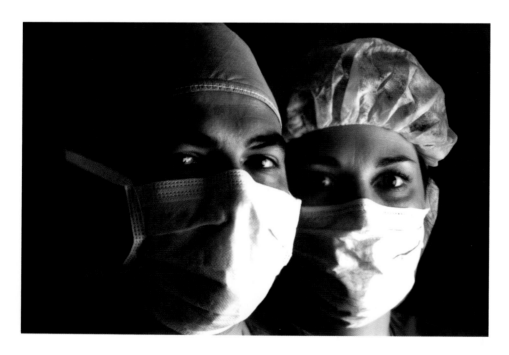

✧
Skilled clinical staff provide cancer treatment and research at the Virginia G. Piper Cancer Center at Scottsdale Healthcare.

Following a brief change in ownership soon after its opening, the hospital was re-established as a not-for-profit community hospital in 1971 and the name changed to Scottsdale Memorial Hospital. The community-owned facility flourished during the 1970s, opening the first hospital-affiliated freestanding outpatient surgical center in the U.S. and establishing a family practice residency program.

To better represent its diversification beyond the scope of a single hospital, in 1981, the company was incorporated into a not-for-profit community health system and the Scottsdale Healthcare Foundation was formed as its philanthropic arm.

During the early 1980s forward-thinking community and hospital leaders began planning for a second hospital near Shea Boulevard and Pima Road. The system's second hospital, Scottsdale Healthcare Shea, opened its doors as Scottsdale Memorial Hospital-North in 1984.

Scottsdale Healthcare took a leading role in developing partnerships with other health providers and community organizations, creating a dynamic, multi-faceted system of programs and services designed to increase longevity, improve quality of life, and meet the special needs of underserved areas of the community and individuals most at risk for lifestyle-related illness and injury.

"Meeting our community's healthcare needs has always been the top priority for Scottsdale Healthcare," says Tom Sadvary, senior vice president and chief operating officer. "Throughout its history, Scottsdale Healthcare has continued adding services not previously available to residents of greater Scottsdale, while maintaining cost-effective, high quality care."

Led by a community-based board of directors, Scottsdale Healthcare is renowned today for its emphasis on patient care, a commitment to superior quality, and an awareness that the community is its sole reason for being. It is the city's largest employer with more than 4,000 staff members, 1,200 volunteers and an active medical staff numbering over 1,300 physicians.

Scottsdale Healthcare Osborn, the original hospital facility at 7400 East Osborn Road, is home to the Valley's busiest Level I Trauma Center, cardiovascular, oncology, neurosciences and orthopedic services, a kidney transplant program, inpatient rehabilitation and women's services. Adding services to meet the needs of south Scottsdale and surrounding areas, a new Greenbaum Outpatient Surgery Center and additional physician offices are being planned.

Scottsdale Healthcare Shea, at 9003 East Shea Boulevard, features a Level II Emergency Department along with comprehensive cardio-vascular, oncology, neurosciences, orthopedic, reproductive medicine and obstetrics services. An affiliation with Phoenix Children's Hospital offers pediatric patients access to specialists closer to home. In 2001, the newly-expanded hospital completed a dedicated Women's Center and birthing unit, along with a five-story patient tower for the future addition of up to eighty-four inpatient beds.

The state's newest major cancer center, the Virginia G. Piper Cancer Center at Scottsdale Healthcare, opens on the Shea campus in November 2001. Comprehensive treatment services and support programs will provide a unique environment including medical, spiri-tual, psychological and practical elements of cancer treatment and access to research not previously available in the Valley.

"This is not just a place to treat cancer. It is a center that provides diagnosis, treatment, research and support for the individual who has cancer," says Susan Brown-Wagner, RN, director of Oncology Services for Scottsdale Healthcare.

An exciting aspect of the Virginia G. Piper Cancer Center is the fact that it is home of the Arizona Cancer Center, Greater Phoenix Area. Scottsdale Healthcare's partnership with the University of Arizona's Arizona Cancer Center includes clinical trials, cancer prevention trials and laboratory research involving development of new anti-cancer drugs. The proximity of researchers and clinicians to one another will help speed research findings into treatment, notes Brown-Wagner.

Scottsdale Healthcare is an acknowledged leader in wellness and prevention, offering programs that make a positive, measurable impact on residents' health and wellness. Its Community Health Education and Outreach Services extend into the neighborhoods of greater Scottsdale. School-based health clinics are staffed by nurse practitioners, volunteers conduct vision and hearing screenings annual-ly for elementary schools, and speakers, health fairs and screenings are provided in neighbor-hoods and master-planned communities through the Northeast Valley, to name just a few of Scottsdale Healthcare's outreach efforts.

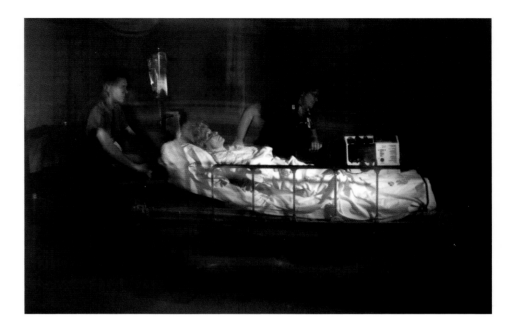

Looking ahead to serve our growing community, a third medical campus is now open near the intersection of Scottsdale Road and Thompson Peak Parkway. The Scottsdale Healthcare Thompson Peak campus currently includes medical offices and will add services in the future according to area residents' needs.

Trees in the desert survive by putting down deep roots. They thrive when they adapt to their unique, challenging environment. Like those trees in the desert, Scottsdale Healthcare has thrived by meeting the changing healthcare needs of the community it serves and will continue to do so for generations to come.

✧

Above: The Level I Trauma Center at Scottsdale Healthcare Osborn is consistently the Valley's busiest.

Below: Surgeons provide advanced care for cardiology patients in Scottsdale Healthcare's busy operating rooms.

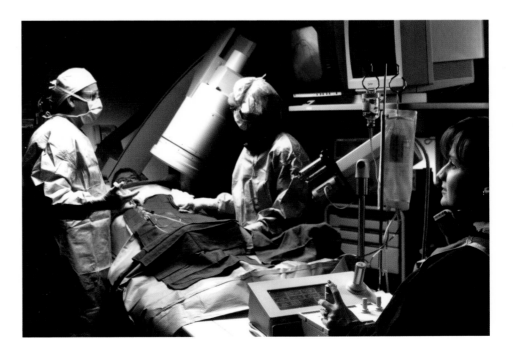

QUALITY OF LIFE

PCS HEALTH SYSTEMS, INC.

In 1969 a group of Valley executives in the fields of employee benefits, insurance, pharmacy operation, and system analysis originated the prescription benefit management industry when they founded PCS Health Systems, Inc.

Today the Scottsdale company has combined with another firm to become the nation's largest pharmacy benefit manager, serving 75 million people and managing 450 million prescriptions annually.

The innovators created a prescription card to make it easy to fill prescriptions and process claims, solving many problems for insurers that were just beginning to expand drug benefit coverage thirty years ago. For employees, the card greatly simplified their benefit. For employers, the system was superior to the labor intensive and costly direct reimbursement method.

Innovation continued to be instrumental to PCS' success. Using high-end mainframe computers, PCS developed systems to administer and process its rapidly increasing claim volume. The company drove development of the universal claim form and national standardization of pharmacy claim procedures. Then came RECAP, the first online, electronic pharmaceutical claims processing system. Perhaps the most significant milestone in PCS history, RECAP was welcomed by payers, pharmacists and patients as the new standard for handling claims. RECAP has processed billions of pharmacy transactions while greatly reducing costs and claims rejections.

PCS broadly expanded its business and enhanced its services by creating such programs as disease management, therapeutic interchange and mail order pharmaceuticals, which have provided added value to all participants in the healthcare process. By concentrating on innovative information systems and pharmaceutical care management, PCS has linked medical knowledge and research, health information management systems, and patient education to lower healthcare costs and improve the health of patients.

In 1983 PCS moved from Phoenix to new headquarters in Scottsdale, where it is one of the city's leading employers with more than 2,000 people. The company demonstrates its strong belief in corporate citizenship through financial contributions and special event sponsorship. PCS employees are active in civic and cultural organizations and their volunteerism benefits many non-profit groups.

As the twenty-first century begins, PCS is entering a new era with a new identity through its acquisition by Texas-based Advance Paradigm, Inc., another pharmacy benefits management company.

"Preserving desert wildlife through community education and participation."

The Center for Native and Urban Wildlife (CNUW), born January 2000, is an innovative project designed to promote and maintain Sonoran Desert habitat and native wildlife. CNUW provides educational opportunities for students and community members to participate in restoring damaged Sonoran Desert habitats, and aid in the preservation of Sonoran Desert ecosystems for the benefit of all desert species, including humankind.

CNUW is the result of Scottsdale Community College Biology Professor Roy Barnes' vision and dedication to Sonoran Desert wildlife. The organization was initially funded by a Nina Mason Pulliam Charitable Trust grant in partnership with the McDowell Sonoran Land Trust. Other partnerships of CNUW, which share a common vision of desert wildlife preservation include Arizona Game and Fish Department, Liberty Wildlife Foundation, the City of Scottsdale, Salt River Project, and Desert Botanical Garden.

The grant provides for new facilities including a Greenhouse/Vivarium, an Outdoor Plant Propagation Center and a Learning Center, as well as enhancement to the existing Wildlife Demonstration Garden. These facilities aid in the successful completion of CNUW's goals, which include desert habitat restoration projects; rearing of endangered amphibians and fishes; elementary and high school outreach programs; a web page and database; and a community outreach process designed to educate citizens of the value of desert wildlife.

"Our vision, as a real community service and outreach program, is to change the hearts and minds of the community so all will understand and value desert wildlife. There is a need to assess the impact of growth on native desert species and

CENTER FOR NATIVE AND URBAN WILDLIFE AT SCOTTSDALE COMMUNITY COLLEGE

to educate citizens about the means to reduce the detrimental effects on native plants and animals," states CNUW Director Virginia Korte.

Perhaps there is no better setting than Scottsdale Community College for just such efforts. There is much to appreciate and protect in the McDowell Sonoran Preserve, located just a few miles north of the college. This fifty-seven square-mile ecosystem of desert floor, mountains, hills, and arroyos is home to the well-known native saguaro cactus, the cactus wren—and so many little-known varieties of flora and fauna that will become the source of much learning.

SCC President Art DeCabooter has led the charge up the preservation hill as chair of the McDowell Sonoran Preserve Commission, which has successfully expanded the preserve and limited homebuilding. "My motivation was for future generations to be able to enjoy the mountains of the Sonoran Desert," says DeCabooter.

"The value of CNUW's programs and direct participation by students will impact their education for the rest of their lives. There is no better way to learn about and appreciate the Sonoran Desert and its inhabitants than through 'hands-on' experience in the conservation of these ecosystems," adds Barnes.

To learn more about CNUW contact Virginia Korte, director, at (480) 423-6730, or at virginia.korte@sccmail.maricopa.edu.

✧

Above: Roy Barnes and CNUW students surveying a habitat restoration site with Greg Woodall of McDowell Sonoran Land Trust.

Bottom, left: CNUW students working on creating a wash in the Wildlife Demonstration Garden on Scottsdale Community College campus.

Crescent Moon Ranch
SCOTTSDALE, ARIZONA

✧

Innovative home builder George Ellis designed and built Crescent Moon Ranch in the remote but beautiful Pinnacle Peak area north of Scottsdale in 1948. Mrs. Lois K. Maury used the ranch as her residence, where she hosted holiday parties for area children each year. There were also guest cottages on the 127-acre property that she rented out to seasonal visitors. The adobe and redwood main house was torn down in the 1990s to make way for the Four Seasons Resort, which named one of its restaurants in honor of Crescent Moon.

PHOTO COURTESY OF THE ELLIS FAMILY

SCOTTSDALE LIVING

Scottsdale's resorts, hotels, and professional services provide an environment which balances the natural beauty of the land and the need for living space for visitors and residents

PINNACLE PARADISE, INC.

In 1969 developer Jerry Nelson could stand in the middle of Pinnacle Peak Road and see nothing but rolling Sonoran Desert. The handful of rustic dwellings nearby was submerged in palo verde, ironwood, and cactus.

"It was thought of as a place to hunt quail or eat at Pinnacle Peak Patio," Nelson says. "It had a cowboy image."

In fact, just seventeen years previously, a cattle drive—the last of its kind—had churned up dust along Scottsdale Road as it made its way from the Tempe railhead to a nearby ranch. Cattle still grazed amid creosote bushes.

Today, North Scottsdale is quilted with spacious planned communities, golf courses and commercial centers. The transformation owes much to the trailblazing Nelson, whose upscale Pinnacle Peak Village and Troon developments set the standard for what followed. At Troon Village, for example, the Tom Weiskopf and Jay Morrish-designed eighteen-hole golf course was touted by *Golf Digest* as the nation's best private golf course. *Golf Magazine* called the PGA-rated links "one of the 100 greatest courses in the world."

Over thirty years, Nelson has developed more than 9,000 acres and 8,000 home sites in North Scottsdale. He has overseen the construction of golf courses, commercial centers, parks and a botanical garden, where his wife, Florence, devoted twenty years to helping educate an estimated six thousand school children annually through her Desert Center programs. Yet the desert still thrives amid all the change. Thanks to Nelson's environmental leadership lush Sonoran vegetation runs through and around low-slung neighborhoods and clings to the pristine upper slopes of mountains. Nature trails and preserves abound. By his directive, Troon North Golf Club donates $2 per round to the McDowell Sonoran Land Trust.

Saving the desert was not a serious concern when Nelson, then a newcomer, bought a 160-acre parcel on the northwest corner of Pima and Pinnacle Peak Roads in 1969. Most developers considered desert terrain unattractive and a nuisance. Preserving it as natural landscaping, they said, would be expensive and cut into profits. It was easier to "blade" everything down with a caterpillar tractor and replace it with grass and gravel. As a result, thousands of indigenous plants and centuries-old Saguaro cacti were destroyed.

The public held largely similar views; especially out-of-state transplants partial to the grassy lawns and shrubbery of "back home." Nelson, on the other hand, loved the desert's austere beauty and spiny mountains. He believed a natural landscape would enhance the attractiveness of low-density neighborhoods and increase their value. It would be

expensive to remove the vegetation, store it, then replant it after construction, but Nelson believed buyers would be willing to pay the difference. He believed setting aside recreation areas and exempting hillsides from development was a must.

Before he could put his theory to work, Nelson had major obstacles to overcome. He needed money, water, roads, and telephone service. In 1969 the northern border of Scottsdale stopped at Gold Dust, except for a finger of land poking Shea Boulevard a few blocks north. From that point, it was as if the twentieth century stopped. Everything beyond was unincorporated—a blank canvas in terms of amenities.

It was a tall order for the Hollywood, California native who wanted to transform the desert into the "Bel Aire of Phoenix." But Nelson was an adventuresome sort who had been, by turns, a student at UCLA and Georgetown, a paint salesman, assembly line worker, merchant seaman and congressional assistant. He relished the challenge. Moreover, he had spent the past five years as the owner of a construction company in Michigan's frigid Upper Peninsula, where "cold weather" is writ large.

"When we first came out here in October 1968, Michigan already was having snow flurries." Nelson recalls. "Arizona was having perfect weather. We were not looking forward to another winter. We decided then and there that we wanted to live here." Soon after, Nelson closed his Michigan operations and moved to Arizona with Florence and infant son Nicolas. Two more sons, Thomas and J. P., would arrive within four years.

His peers met plans for Nelson's proposed Pinnacle Peak Village with skepticism—not entirely, he says, without reason. The only access to Pinnacle Peak from the south was Scottsdale Road. It was thirteen miles to groceries. If Nelson needed a phone or gas, he had to drive ten miles to Scottsdale Road and Shea Boulevard. Because of the distance, suppliers charged extra to deliver lumber and concrete. Even Valley National Bank [now Bank One] balked at giving him a loan. "They said nobody would live north of Bell Road [Frank Lloyd Wright Boulevard] until 2000," Nelson says. "So I got partners and financed it in bits and pieces by myself."

With the help of a hydrologist from Arizona State University, Nelson began drilling for water around Pinnacle Peak. At 560 feet—110 feet deeper than originally estimated—he struck a huge aquifer. It was the first of eight wells sunk over the years by Nelson's Pinnacle Paradise Water Company. When Scottsdale incorporated the thirty-six-square mile area north of Bell Road in the 1980s, providing municipal services, the city assumed ownership of the wells.

Nelson's Pinnacle Peak Land Company set up "base camp" at the defunct Rancho Vista Bonita guest ranch, just across the road from Pinnacle

✧

Top: One of the first wells to provide water for the yet-to-be-built Pinnacle Peak Village.

Above: The beautiful Arizona landscape provides a natural backdrop to Pinnacle Peak Plaza.

Above: Dr. Charles Redman, an Arizona State University archeologist, gives Jerry Nelson (center) and Scottsdale Mayor Herb Drinkwater (right) a briefing on the Hohokam Indian ruins unearthed in 1988 during the construction of Troon Village. The Archeological Conservancy now owns the Hohokam site.

Below: Scottsdale Mayor Sam Campana (right) thanks Nelson (left) for a donation he has just made in cooperation with the Troon Golf Corporation to the McDowell Sonoran Land Trust. Ellen Carr, then chairperson of the Trust, listens in.

Paradise, the first phase of his proposed Pinnacle Peak Village master plan. Nelson and his family lived in the main house while workers occupied the twelve guest cabins. To save time and off-site travel, Florence prepared lunch for the work crews. During this period, Nelson received a financial jump-start when the Nichimen Trading Company of Japan joined Pinnacle Peak Land Company as a partner. Between 1970 and 1974, six residential suburbs were built, and Pinnacle Peak Realty was established to handle sales.

"Nichimen was the first major Japanese investor here," Nelson says. "Its presence encouraged other Japanese investors." In 1997

Nelson was honored with Scottsdale's first History Maker Award for his role in pioneering foreign investment in the area.

Pinnacle Peak Village created a template for North Scottsdale communities. Most notably, it imposed restrictions aimed at preserving the desert ambiance. Air conditioners, for example, could not be placed on roofs. Full lawns and non-indigenous vegetation were prohibited. The restrictions also provided for hillside protection. "They rankled some people at first," Nelson says. "But we won them over."

Nelson insisted that power lines be underground. When told by the utility company that it would cost three times as much as stringing them up on conventional poles, he made an offer: his company would dig the trenches and cover them back up if the utility company would lay the lines. Today, there are no telephone poles to mar the scenery of Pinnacle Peak Village neighborhoods.

The Pinnacle Peak Village experience lit a fire under a nascent environmental movement that resulted in city ordinances and state legislation. Over the years, Nelson has lent his expertise to several government advisory committees concerned with land use and the environment.

In 1974 the guest ranch was torn down to make room for Pinnacle Peak Plaza, a Spanish colonial-style commercial center with a general store, post office, shops and gas station. The plaza was inspired by an off-the-cuff idea Nelson and Florence had sketched on shelf paper during their honeymoon. When the store opened in 1975, it provided much-needed basic food items and served as a stopover for sightseers enroute to Pinnacle Peak Patio restaurant and Reata Pass Steakhouse.

Nelson recruited Steve Simonson, a twenty-four-year-old Californian and family friend, to run the general store. At first, the young manager did everything: he made sandwiches, pumped gas, sorted letters, and other sundry chores. In those early years, Nelson fondly recalls, it was a tradition to hang Christmas stockings on the store's fireplace for every child in the village. Since then, the store has expanded four times, with retail shops, haute cuisine restaurants, and businesses filling in around the brick courtyard with its bell tower and fountains. Simonson now oversees more than thirty employees.

In 1976 Pinnacle Peak Country Club opened up for private membership. The exclusive development, wrapped snugly around the plaza, featured an eighteen-hole golf course ringed with luxury home sites. Within five years the country club sold out, a solid testimonial to Nelson's conviction that discriminating buyers would flock to developments with desert landscaping. By 1980, nine more subdivisions had opened.

A few years later, Nelson built Troon Village, a 2,655-acre community anchored by Troon Golf and Country Club and the acclaimed Weiskopf-Morrish golf course. The 48,000-square-foot clubhouse received the Grand Award for Architectural Design at the 1987 Pacific Coast Builders Gold Nugget Awards. According to Nelson, it cost his company $1 million to remove cactus from the golf course site, keep it alive and re-plant it after construction. Additional expense was incurred when the remains of an ancient Hohokam Indian Village were unearthed, and Nelson halted construction while Arizona State University archeologists explored the site.

In 1989 Nelson broke ground for Troon North, which straddles Dynamite Road between Pima and Alma School Parkway. Troon North is a self-contained community offering parks, schools and shopping. It also features two Weiskopf-Morrish golf courses, a resort and several types of living quarters. The scenic community adjoins a 19,000-acre state preserve open to hiking and bicycling. With an average elevation of 2,700 feet, residents are guaranteed cooler summers.

At seventy-one, Nelson shows no signs of slowing down. His latest North Scottsdale venture is Stonehaven, a 732-home development featuring a Greg Norman golf course. Asked why he feels so strongly about desert preservation, Nelson answers: "I never wanted my kids to look back and say: 'Dad, you ruined the desert.'"

✧

Above: Florence and Jerry Nelson today, still leading the way in support of the community they love.

Below: Development and preservation coexist, thanks to Jerry Nelson's vision and generosity.

DC RANCH

Even before the small colony of Scottsdale gained notoriety for its dry, healthy air, soft water, and fertile soil, Dr. W. B. Crosby, registered the DC Ranch cattle brand at the hour of 11:30 a.m. on June 1, 1885, with the Maricopa County Recorder's office.

It is believed that DC stood for "Doc Crosby." In December 1919, when Scottsdale merchant Edwin Orpheus Brown obtained the brand, the initials took on a new meaning—"Desert Camp"—by which it is known today. The original DC working cattle ranch, located in far northern Scottsdale, is now the city's largest master-planned community covering 8,281 acres. The development extends from low-desert terrain to mountain peaks nearly 4,000 feet above sea level. Within the property are 3,700 acres of developable land that offer views of the McDowell Mountains, Pinnacle Peak, and a panoramic scene of the valley below. DC Ranch developers have pledged to preserve the most sensitive land forms as community open space while at the same time creating a built environment inspired by the beauty and character of the land.

In the early 1900s, E. O. Brown came from Wisconsin and became the town's general storekeeper, postmaster, and later, operator of the community's cotton gin and a school district trustee. He extended credit to area homesteaders and as severe drought drove settlers back to the cities and towns, they paid their debts at E. O. Brown's General Store with waterless range land. Over the years, Brown's family and partners accumulated 43,000 acres, which included the only continuous running spring in the McDowells', as well as the Silver Leaf mining claim. The spring water was piped to tanks throughout the ranch and today still produces a steady three gallons a minute within the DC Ranch Community.

By the end of World War II, cattle ranching had changed drastically. Brahmas and Herefords grazed on the Indian Wheat and filigree grasses where the Mexican Longhorns had in E. O. Brown's day. His son, E. E. "Big Brownie" Brown now ran a vast herd of 4,000; contracts replaced

❖

Above: Ranch headquarters surrounded by corrals. Merchant E. O. Brown began acquiring DC Ranch land in the early 1900s, which grew to 43,000 acres in Scottsdale's northern district.

Below: DC Ranch beef cattle being driven to market in Phoenix by the Browns and wranglers. The Ranch was home to the first purebred Brahmas in Arizona. The DC brand was used until the mid-1990s.

handshakes, and a new, sophisticated way of doing business was introduced.

Today, residents and homes have replaced previous inhabitants. Life at DC Ranch is a celebration of family, friends, and community. While home and neighborhood design play an important role, there is no greater showcase for the DC Ranch lifestyle than "Desert Camp," a nine-acre community recreation center that offers swimming, tennis, basketball, and fitness facilities. Residents of all ages gather here to take advantage of a number of civic, social, cultural, and entertainment opportunities, utilize on-site computers or consult with the on-site Scottsdale Healthcare concierge.

DC Ranch neighborhoods are connected with miles of paths and trails that give residents easy access to existing and proposed amenities as well as nearby wilderness areas. As a result, residents are able to go anywhere in the community without having to cross a major roadway.

Technology also plays an important role in connecting the community. DC Ranch has partnered with Qwest® to offer digital cable television, Internet access, and telephone service. On-line connections to schools, businesses and medical facilities as well as the community intranet, RanchNet®, allow people of all ages to get involved in specific areas of interest and take part in community life.

In addition to being recognized nationally with a Gold Nugget Award for the "best master planned community in the West," membership is also available at The Country Club at DC Ranch. This exclusively private club features an eighteen-hole, par 71 Scott Miller-designed golf course, tennis, swimming, fitness facilities and fine and casual dining.

In the future, DC Ranch will meet virtually every resident's need at Market Street, a thirty-acre mixed-use development, featuring a retail and commercial facility that offers shopping, dining and entertainment venues. Plans also call for a second golf course designed by Tom Weiskopf and a mixed-use Town Center.

DC Ranch youngsters will attend Copper Ridge School, which is being built by the Scottsdale Unified School District and is scheduled to open in the Fall of 2001.

As DC Ranch grows, a comprehensive vision guides the community to put in place facilities of all kinds, including a local police and fire station and places of worship. This is a vision that DMB President Drew Brown believes is both timeless and dynamic. "We began with the goal of creating a real community that will endure, that betters the lives of the people who live here," he states. "I am proud to say that we are well on our way to achieving that dream."

❖

Above: Neighborhoods are connected with miles of paths and trails, which give residents easy access to amenities and nearby wilderness areas.

Below: Residents enjoy added convenience, quality and communication options thanks to pioneering alliances with Qwest® and Scottsdale Healthcare.

DESERT MOUNTAIN

As the Rolls Royce of golf communities, Desert Mountain has won international recognition and more awards for excellence than any other Arizona development. "To live there," said one industry observer, "means you have arrived."

It is a fitting accolade for the private 8,000-acre community in North Scottsdale, which features five award-winning Jack Nicklaus Signature golf courses. Elevated tees drop to gently rolling fairways, while dramatic canyons shelter manicured greens. Deep washes and

boulder outcroppings form natural hazards not found anywhere else.

The dramatic sweep of the landscape so impressed officials of the Senior PGA Tour that in 1989 they chose Desert Mountain's 7,019-yard Cochise course to host The Countrywide Tradition, one of four majors on the Senior PGA circuit. Since then, the annual event has drawn capacity crowds eager to glimpse not only golf legends like Nicklaus, but the beautiful scenery as well.

Bounded on the west by Pima Road and on the south by Cave Creek Road, Desert Mountain ascends northward from an elevation of 2,500 feet to more than 4,500 feet, where it touches Tonto National Forest and Continental Mountain. Summer temperatures are typically five to ten degrees cooler than the Valley floor. The high desert terrain is studded with majestic saguaro and yucca cactuses, as well as paloverde, mesquite, and juniper trees—perfect habitat for quail, coyotes, mule deer, and other wildlife.

From selected points residents can see Four Peaks and Weaver's Needle in the distant Superstition Mountains, as well as Pinnacle Peak and the nearby McDowells. Inspired by such views, Desert Mountain founder Lyle Anderson set out in 1985 to create a world-class golf community with unparalleled amenities, while simultaneously preserving the integrity of the natural surroundings.

For starters, Anderson chose Taliesin Associated Architects, founded by Frank Lloyd Wright, to create the original master plan. True to Wright's principles, the plan called for homes, golf courses, and clubhouses to be of, rather than on, the land. They had to blend architecturally with the desert. Furthermore, native vegetation could be removed only from spaces earmarked for construction. Later, it would be replanted.

The wisdom of this painstaking approach can be seen today in 2,500 acres of permanent natural open space and more than five miles of walking, jogging, and biking paths. Four clubhouses, designed to complement the rolling desert, feature distinctive dining opportunities as well as numerous recreational options.

Located in the heart of the community is the Sonoran Clubhouse, with tennis (hard surface, clay and grass), two swimming pools, a state-of-the-art fitness center with personal

trainers, aerobics classes, and a wide range of cardiovascular and strength-training equipment, and spa services including facials and massages. The Desert Mountain Club's amenities are available only to members and their guests.

Setting the tone for this vital and varied lifestyle is the Cochise/Geronimo Clubhouse. Its floor-to-ceiling glass-enclosed dining room offers contemporary American cuisine, with panoramic views of verdant fairways, mountains and the Valley below. It also boasts a highly regarded art collection. The Apache Clubhouse, which opened in April 2000, features an elegant steakhouse and piano bar overlooking lush greens and Apache Peak. The Chiricahua Clubhouse (scheduled to open late 2002) will feature an authentic northern Italian restaurant designed to evoke the character of an Old World estate.

The Chiricahua course, which followed the Renegade, Cochise, Geronimo, and Apache links, debuted in 1998. Nicklaus, who was frequently on-site during its construction, has referred to it as the "Pine Valley of the desert." Chiracahua winds its way over 900 feet of dramatic elevation changes and is surrounded by The Saguaro Forest, an exclusive village of custom home sites and one of Desert Mountain's final stages of development.

Although Desert Mountain is home to a number of retirees, the majority of residents still pursue full-time careers. About one-third are from Arizona and California, with the rest hailing mostly from the Midwest. The average age is fifty-five.

As part of dynamic North Scottsdale, Desert Mountain is in close proximity to a growing number of quality retail and business centers. The town of Carefree, only three miles away, features upscale shopping, restaurants, and medical facilities. Nearby freeways put residents within minutes of the area's outstanding physicians and health services, including Mayo Clinic and its hospital, as well as providing speedy access to educational, cultural, and business destinations in downtown Scottsdale and Phoenix.

Police and fire protection are equally accessible. Rural/Metro Corporation recently unveiled a 1,000-square-foot fire station, the first of three such facilities planned for North Scottsdale. Meanwhile, the Scottsdale Police Department has moved into a fully staffed $3.5 million station along north Pima Road, with plans for another facility on the northern edge of the city.

Desert Mountain offers prospective residents a choice of custom home sites, with no deadline to build. They may also choose from a small selection of remaining developer luxury homes. The long-term master plan calls for fewer than 2,700 residential units on 8,000 acres, with more than 2,000 already sold.

Lyle Anderson's company in partnership with Crescent Real Estate Equity, Inc owns Desert Mountain.

THE FORUM PUEBLO NORTE

❖

Above: The entrance area to one of the lovely residential villas at The Forum Pueblo Norte.

Below: The Healthcare Center entrance at Pueblo Norte.

In 1927, when J. W. Marriott opened his first root beer stand in Washington, D.C., it was with high hopes and great expectations. Although it took a number of cold root beers before the Marriott dream was realized, satisfied customers responded to the young entrepreneur's devotion to hospitality and service. That same hospitality, service, and commitment continues today in more than 150 Marriott Senior Living Communities such as The Forum Pueblo Norte.

The Scottsdale community, located at 7090 East Mescal Street, was established seventeen years ago as one of the city's first retirement communities to include independent living, assisted living and a healthcare center. The Forum, with its Southwestern style architecture, meticulously manicured gardens and lawns, sprawls over twenty acres in a park-like setting. The Retirement Community has 167 apartments and villas ranging in size from a studio of 400 square feet to deluxe apartments of 1,336 square feet. In Assisted Living, there are thirty-three suites for seniors who need some assistance with daily activities such as bathing, dressing and medication. While in the Health Care Center, more than ninety residents receive twenty-four-hour skilled nursing, post-surgical, or restorative care.

Amenities for village residents include an Olympic-sized heated pool where water aerobics classes are well-attended; a Jacuzzi; an exercise room; a beauty and barber shop; a billiards room and shuffleboard court; a putting green; a snack shop; and a private memorial chapel. Residents dine in a comfortably furnished upscale dining room at linen-covered tables and enjoy a wide variety of appetizing entrees. While in the Assisted Living Center and Health Care Center special emphasis is placed on dietary needs. A library with the latest book titles and numerous popular magazines bring residents in for quiet time reading as well as for card games, group discussions, and monthly socials in the adjacent lounge. An arts and crafts studio and media center with a giant television

screen are available to residents, as are shopping trips, planned outings to the theater, the circus, stage plays, the symphony, or to nearby casinos. Residents are well informed and enriched by quality activities.

"You can tell a great deal about a senior living community by the quality of the activities its residents enjoy," says Joy Ricci, director of sales and marketing for Senior Living Services. "At The Forum we're proud to offer a diverse selection of life enriching activities which are designed to lift the spirits, challenge the mind and tone the body." An example of cultural events during Music Month at The Forum found residents taking five trips to Phoenix Symphony Hall to see presentations as varied as *Swan Lake* to "An Evening at the Pops" with Doc Severinsen to a Forum-sponsored on-site piano recital for budding Van Cliburns. As well as a popular Golden Oldies program narrated by Julian Reveles in the Forum Auditorium.

Seniors leave their worries behind when they move into a Marriott senior community.

"When you move here, you become a part of a large and loving family who cares about you and you quickly learn to care about them," says Dr. Robert Beers, a retired internal medicine physician and Pueblo Norte resident. "The residents who live here are sharp, well educated and never cease to amaze me. One quickly learns that chronological age has very little to do with mental acuity and that using the brain is necessary to keep it sharp."

Others residents agree that living at The Forum gives them a secure feeling. Shirley Kranicz, twenty-seven years with the Salt River Project and a seventh generation Arizonan, finds the community "friendly and congenial." While Patty Clifford, says "it's a happy life and a warm, caring community." Clifford and her friend, Louise Schellenberg, Smith College classmates years ago, now enjoy one another's company as elder citizens. Schellenberg likes the secure feeling of having her own furnishings and says, "I think they do an excellent job for us." Mary Moreland-Kostelnik, retired after twenty-seven years in banking adds "I think this is the best."

The Forum Pueblo Norte residents are experiencing the same traditions of quality and integrity today that were so important to J. W. Marriott when he first sold root beer seven decades ago.

❖

Above: A perfect place to spend a relaxing afternoon.

Below: An overview of the pool area at Marriott's Pueblo Norte.

CHAPARRAL SUITES HOTEL AND CONFERENCE CENTER

✧

Above: The Chaparral Suites Hotel courtyard, pool and fountain where guests relax in the Arizona sun when not golfing, playing tennis, sightseeing, or shopping.

Below: Hoteliers Ray, Carole, and Tom Silverman operate the family owned 311-room Chaparral Suites Hotel and Conference Center, which started forty-seven years ago as a small guest ranch.

The Ray Silverman family of hoteliers may not be native Arizonians, but they are considered an institution in Scottsdale. Owners and operators of the Chaparral Suites Hotel and Conference Center located at 5001 North Scottsdale Road, the Silvermans, came to Scottsdale nearly a half-century ago to escape the harsh Midwest winters. The senior Silverman purchased the twelve-unit Paradise Valley Guest Ranch in 1953 as it was nearing completion and has since developed the property into an upscale 311-room suite hotel and conference center.

Scottsdale had but 2,000 residents; Scottsdale Road was still two-lanes and the twenty-acres of prime desert land was still in Maricopa County when Silverman moved his wife, Lee, and children—Carole, Tom, and Richard—from rural Iowa where they were living at the time. The family previously resided in Chicago when Ray was comptroller for fifteen years with Match Corporation of America.

"We were way out in the country when we came here forty-seven years ago," noted the eighty-seven-year-old president of the family owned Chaparral Associates, Inc. "The city

limits only went to Camelback. When we started, we had 12 units, one maid, one gardener, and the season didn't start until February and lasted through March."

Within a short time, a dozen more units were built and, by 1956, thirteen more cottages were added for a total of thirty-seven. "Scottsdale had started to grow," he said. "Each cottage had its own carport and guests could walk out their front door and pick grapefruit from the trees."

On this same acreage today, Tom Silverman, vice president general manager of the enterprise; his sister, Carole Silverman, secretary of the corporation and food and beverage director; and their father, operate the very successful Chaparral Suites and Conference Center which attracts more than 100,000 guests each year. By comparison, the guest ranch in its twenty-five years of operation, hosted 100,000 people. Tom Silverman recalls pitching in at age eleven and working the guest ranch switchboard. He also filled in as night maintenance man and helped guests with problem TV sets or to light wall heaters.

Through the years, the resort has been known as the Granada Royale Hometel and the Embassy Suites. In 1999 the Silvermans became independent hoteliers, renaming their facility the Chaparral Suites Hotel. The new 11,200-square-foot, high-tech Chaparral Convention Center and Grand Ballroom is considered one of the best conference facilities in the state.

The Silvermans have always given back to the community. In 1978, twelve of the guest cottages were given to the Salt River Pima-Maricopa Indian Community and are still used as offices. In 1984, when Ray and Lee Silverman's twenty-five-year-old family home faced demolition, it was given to the city and today provides offices at WestWorld. They also made it possible to open up Chaparral Road to the east by dedicating one-quarter mile of their property to the city.

Inducted into the Scottsdale History Hall of Fame in 1994, Ray Silverman also gives generously through the Silverman Family Foundation. Scottsdale City Councilman Tom Silverman has followed in his father's footsteps serving on numerous community and state boards, including serving as president of the Scottsdale Chamber of Commerce.

Amidst flowering flora, waterfalls, and lighted pools, stand stately palm trees and a manicured golf course. Hyatt Regency Scottsdale Resort at Gainey Ranch sits on land that once was a working Arabian Ranch of the Daniel E. Gainey Estate. With a spectacular view of the entire McDowell Mountains, the 27-acre, 493-room destination resort opened in December 1986 as part of the 560-acre Gainey Ranch.

Recreational amenities at the Hyatt Regency Scottsdale include a two-and-a-half-acre water playground with 10 pools; a sand beach with a three-story waterslide; 27 holes of championship golf at the Gainey Ranch Golf Club, the Sonwai Spa, world-class tennis, and bicycle and jogging trails. In addition the resort offers four award-winning restaurants, Venetian-style gondola rides on the lake, and Camp Hyatt Kachina offering programs for children ages three to five and six to twelve. Unique to the Hyatt Regency Scottsdale is the Hopi Learning Center where visitors can obtain a better understanding of the Hopi history, culture, and teachings from interpreters.

"This is a vanishing story," notes Bill Eider-Orley, vice president and managing director of the resort. "If we don't preserve this important part of our American Southwest, we lose the very thing we want to experience and share with future generations."

The Old West also is brought to life through character re-enactments such as "The Arizona Cowboy," telling of ranch life in the Arizona Territory, the law of the Old West and the legend of the Lost Dutchman Mine as well as Native American artisan demonstrations and "Family Fun Sing-a-Longs" with a singing cowboy and Native Dancers 'round the campfire. An international art collection featuring a variety of art is displayed throughout the property. The collection is a selection of cast bronzes, wooden sculpture, stone carvings, oil paintings, cast paper and watercolors.

The casual elegance of the award-winning Golden Swan Restaurant features an outdoor pavilion-style gazebo surrounded by a lagoon. On Sunday, the Chef's Brunch invites guests into the kitchen "marketplace" for a backstage view and fun interaction with the chefs.

The resort has received major recognition and awards for its environmental program of reducing air and water pollution, recycling and reduction in energy and water consumption and landscape ecology. Management and its 900 employees volunteer in many charitable organizations. Over the years, being a good civic neighbor has brought much-deserved acclaim to the Hyatt. Residents also consider it the most architecturally pleasing of "Scottsdale Places" to visit and to take guests.

"The character we've created at the resort," adds Eider-Orley, "is an enhancement of what our visitors expect when they come to this part of the Southwest."

❖

Above: Hyatt Regency Scottsdale's Fountain Court is known for its elegant, yet tranquil setting with the majestic McDowell Mountains in the background.

Left: The Gahn Dancer sculpture by Apache artist Craig Dan Goseyun is on display in the lobby of Hyatt Regency Scottsdale.

RAMADA VALLEY HO RESORT

Guests at the Ramada Valley Ho Resort could be forgiven if they sometimes hear, late at night, the ghostly tinkle of a piano and a raspy voice singing "Inka Dinka Do."

Legend has it that when the late Jimmy Durante stayed at the resort, he sometimes got restless and wandered down to the piano in the airy Frank Lloyd Wright-designed lobby. There, he would belt out song after song as delighted guests looked on.

Durante is gone, along with the other celebrities—Bing Crosby, Jimmy Cagney and Natalie Wood—who graced the premises during the '50s and '60s. But the Ramada Valley Ho Resort is still, as the Schnozz would say, "gettin' inta the act."

Chalk it up to the resort's center stage location in Old Town Scottsdale, superb amenities and seasoned service.

From the Ramada Valley Ho, guests can walk to art galleries, craft shops and restaurants. They are a stone's throw from cultural events at Scottsdale Civic Center, world-class shopping at Scottsdale Fashion Square and spring training games at Scottsdale Stadium. Ditto for the Desert Botanical Gardens and Camelback Mountain, with its hiking trails.

"In March," says Ramada Valley Ho General Manager Mike Doherty, "probably 40

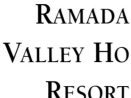

to 50 percent of our guests are here to watch spring training."

Guests wanting to take in regular season basketball or baseball games are just twenty minutes away from Bank One Ballpark and America West Arena. It takes half again as long to reach college football at Arizona State University's Sun Devil Stadium.

The Ramada Valley Ho Resort sits amid fourteen acres of manicured lawns, palm trees, and flowers. It features 292 rooms, including 52 mini-suites, four parlor suites, and two spacious two-bedroom suites. All rooms have private balconies or patios.

When they aren't sightseeing, guests can unwind on the tennis court, shuffleboard court or at poolside. At day's end, they can enjoy a hearty American-style meal and their favorite beverage at Summerfield's Restaurant and Lounge.

Arizona hoteliers Evelyn and Robert Foehl founded the Ramada Valley Ho Resort, the first year-round resort in Scottsdale, in 1956. In 1957 teen idols Robert Wagner and Natalie Wood were married at the resort, making it a trendy destination in those early years for show business celebrities and baseball types, such as Ted Williams, Bob Feller, and Leo Duroscher.

As the Ramada Valley Ho Resort starts a new century, it continues to stay ahead of the curve in meeting the needs of its guests. Yet it still retains the old-fashioned values of prompt and friendly service.

Above: The Valley Ho attracted a sizeable number of baseball types in the '50s and '60s, as evidenced in this shot of Founder Robert Foehl (left) with "The Splendid Splinter" Ted Williams (center) and pitching great Bob Feller.

Below: In the early years, the Valley Ho Resort was a magnet for Hollywood celebrities. Here, Valley Ho Resort Founders Evelyn and Robert Foehl (second and fourth from left) take time out for a photo with Tony Curtis and Janet Leigh.

Steeped in Southwestern tradition, The SunBurst Resort in the heart of Scottsdale traces its lineage to the city's founder, Chaplain Winfield Scott. The locally designed, five-acre boutique style resort is proud of its heritage for it anchors the northernmost edge of the founder's original 640-acre section of land homesteaded in 1888.

The fifty-one-year-old Army chaplain intended to turn the land bounded by Scottsdale, Indian School, Hayden and Chaparral Roads into irrigated citrus orchards. Expenses mounted, however, and Scott was forced to sell off some of his land. One piece, returned to the federal government, was the forty acres northwest of the Arizona Canal, which included the present site of The SunBurst Resort. The land had not been irrigated which was a requirement of the Desert Land Act of 1877.

Even today water continues to play a significant role in The SunBurst Resort's amenities. One main attraction of the property is its water features. These include a Pacific blue crushed marble sand beach pool with sixteen-foot waterslide; a tropical torch-lighted main pool and a Mediterranean lagoon linked by waterfalls and footbridges. The resort's interior award-winning public spaces continue with a "fire, water, and air" theme in the Southwestern-style lobby. The comfortable guest "Living Room" features a custom handcrafted stone fireplace that rises to the twenty-eight-foot-high lobby ceiling, oversized leather and brocade-like upholstered sofas and armchairs, and Native American rugs.

The SunBurst began as the Executive House in the 1960s, opening a few years after the Safari and the Ramada Valley Ho Resorts within one square-mile of each other, which started Scottsdale's growth as a tourist destination.

The resort today is one of the only full-service resorts in the central Scottsdale corridor. The 210-room resort is located conveniently within walking distance of Scottsdale Fashion Square, art galleries, cultural venues, and historical attractions. Rooms are furnished with natural wood furniture and Southwestern accents with each room opening through French doors onto a private terrace.

The award-winning Rancho Saguaro Restaurant, with indoor-outdoor seating, reflects the area's ranching heritage featuring hand

painted "antique" adobe walls, trompe l'oeil accents, and cattle and sheep brands. Elements of the region's Hohokam, Mexican, and Old West cultures also are incorporated in the SunBurst's 14,300 square feet of banquet and conference facilities. Management specializes in accommodating groups of 200 or less.

The SunBurst's reputation of friendly, courteous service the past forty years has made it one of the city's most popular establishments. Just as in the past, the staff continues to make guests feel welcome with a handshake and a friendly, "Hello!"

✧

Above: The SunBurst Resort guest "Living Room" features a Southwestern style with handcrafted stone fireplace and comfortable upholstered sofas and armchairs in conversational seating areas.

Below: A tropical torch-lighted main pool is one of the water amenities that attract visitors to Scottsdale's SunBurst in the city's central corridor.

PEARSON & COMPANY

Through the ornamental gates of Pearson & Company in Scottsdale's West Main Street Gallery District is an extraordinary garden courtyard canopied with paloverde and filled with exotic pots of all sizes and shapes from all over the world.

Nine years ago owner Craig Pearson purchased the 1926 two-story cottage from Gregg and Gloria Hauser. He turned it into an up-scale decorating center filled with oversize plants to ornament the Valley's country clubs and high-ceilinged large-scale homes. The young entrepreneur, who has been in the plantscape business sixteen years, grew up in a small town in northeast Nebraska and moved to the Valley in 1979 to attend college and decided to stay. He feels a real kinship to the area since his grandparents began coming here as snowbirds in the 1950s.

The cottage, one of Scottsdale's oldest frame homes, has been used through the years, first as a home, then as a Mexican curio and sandwich shop, as a design studio for Gloria Hauser and finally as Pearson & Company. Architects advised Craig to tear the house down but he chose to restore it by adding a tin-roofed greenhouse wing with fourteen-foot ceilings.

In the Pearson greenhouse are exotic varieties of dracaena, euphorbia, and palm. Also bromehad and orchid plants in full flower just waiting to take up residence in niches and entry halls of homes with twenty-foot ceilings or in

commercial office buildings, hotels and resorts. They will be placed in unusual containers imported from Mexico, South America, Asia, Africa, India, China, and Europe as well as contemporary pottery crafted by local artisans.

"Our accessories and artifacts come from all over the world," Craig says pointing to old wooden bowls from Indonesia, a carved African crocodile bench, grass thrasher from Spain, and huge silver-plated copper pots from India.

"We're known for doing things to proper scale," he adds. "Making one large statement rather than a bunch of little ones. We go into a home, look at the space and light, while taking into account the preferences of the customer and then we propose a plantscape. We have a big market here because outside is the desert and inside the people want something rush and green," he continues. "After we install plants, we offer a maintenance plan where the customer doesn't have to do anything but enjoy the plantings. We take one hundred percent responsibility for the plants."

Seventy percent of the business is residential and thirty percent commercial. Pearson plantscapes can be found accentuating such dining establishments as RoxSand's, the Tempe Mission Palms Hotel, the FINOVA lobby as well as Compass and Johnson Banks and House of Representatives desks at the state capitol.

Craig, president and owner, is assisted in the business by his two sisters, Christi LaDeaux and Cyndi Pearson, both corporate officers; Kate Favreau, an artist and floral designer who creates colorful collages and dried floral arrangements; Colin Floyd and Jim Baker, both plantscape designers; Mike Noecker, director of plant maintenance in charge of more than four hundred accounts and Craig's nephew, Patrick Pearson.

Above: Huge pots of all kinds and shapes, garden sculptures and artifacts from the world over can be found at Craig Pearson's East Main Street garden design shop.

Below: Patrons feel a cooling effect as they enter the courtyard of Pearson & Company with its water treatment and canopied trees.

HEYLCORP, INC.

At Lost Canyon, residents take pleasure in watching javelina and quail drink from the solar garden spring, where the azimuths of each solstice and equinox are marked out. Recently, a couple of baby bobcats were spotted scampering about the 233-acre community and its thirty-five homesites.

Those are typical scenes at Lost Canyon, which, nestled in the foothills of the McDowell Mountains, was created with an eye to preserve not only the desert, but its habitat as well. It is a tribute to HeylCorp, Inc., the Scottsdale-based company that planned and developed Lost Canyon.

During construction, for example, workers were directed to remove only as much desert vegetation as needed, then replant it later. That, in addition to thirty-five homesites averaging more than six acres, has resulted in Lost Canyon conserving eighty percent of the natural terrain.

HeylCorp, Inc., a real estate investment and development firm founded in 1993 by Kent Heyl, is known for its environmentally-sensitive projects. Before moving to Arizona in 1992, Heyl spent twenty years working in all phases of California real estate. He was founder and president of HeylCorp, a California firm specializing in land investment. In 1974, prior to HeylCorp, he was a co-founder of Coast Equities, Inc., a Southern California real estate marketing and sales firm.

Ross Smith, formerly long-range planning manager for the City of Scottsdale, is vice president of HeylCorp. Smith also served as urban and commercial development director for the Arizona State Land Department.

HeylCorp, Inc. of Arizona has been involved in various capacities with several other Valley projects, usually as the managing member of limited liability companies. The most recent include Raintree Office Center, comprised of two office buildings totaling 111,000 square feet at the Raintree-Loop 101 Interchange, and the development of industrial buildings at Glendale Airpark.

HeylCorp, Inc. also played a role in the birth of Desert Village shopping center in north Scottsdale, Homestead Village hotel in downtown Scottsdale and the Downside Risk Restaurant at Scottsdale Airpark. Future plans are to develop office, industrial, apartment, and self-storage properties for its own portfolio. HeylCorp, Inc. also will continue to assist homebuilders and commercial development clients in acquiring state land through its SLAQ division.

✧

Above: Lost Canyon.

Below: Raintree Office Center.

SWABACK PARTNERS
ARCHITECTURE & PLANNING

Before Scottsdale had reached a population of 5,000 people, Vernon D. Swaback left his home in the heart of Chicago to live in a tent at the base of the McDowell Mountains, where he served as Frank Lloyd Wright's youngest apprentice. He remained with the Wright organization for twenty-two years before founding an independent practice which has grown into multiple organizations including the work of architects, planners, and an interior design firm known as Studio V.

When Camelback Road was mainly an empty street, Swaback planned the 1,000 acres that are now Arizona Biltmore Estates. He is a strong advocate for turning the built environment into our greatest works of art. He is a frequent speaker on design issues, including serving as moderator for a series of television shows concerning both large and small communities. He is the author of *Production Dwellings*, published by the Wisconsin Department of Natural Resources, and *Desert Excellence, A Guide to Natural*

Landscaping. His comprehensive book on community planning, *Designing the Future*, was published by Arizona State University's Herberger Center for Design Excellence and became the Center's all time best seller.

The Swaback firm, including the work of partners John Sather and Jon Bernhard, have been responsible for the restoration and additions to the Arizona Biltmore Hotel, the 8,000-acre DC Ranch, Paradise Valley Country Club, the Citadel at Pinnacle Peak, Troon North Golf Clubhouse, Ancala Country Club, Cactus Park Aquatics and Fitness Center, the master plan and restoration of the Webster Auditorium for the Desert Botanical Garden, the Stone House Pavilion at the Phoenix Zoo, the Ullman Center for the art of Philip C. Curtis at the Phoenix Art Museum, the Scottsdale Water Campus, Kartchner Caverns Discovery Center for Arizona State Parks, and a variety of custom residences, hotels, and corporate office buildings. The firm's work has been widely published and has consistently received honors and awards for projects in environmentally sensitive areas.

Vernon Swaback has served on the Scottsdale Cultural Council's Art Collections Advisory Board, he was the director of Scottsdale Visioning, the vice chair of the city's Desert Preservation Task Force, and a member of the Scottsdale Redevelopment Board. He is a member of the American Institute of Architects, the American Institute of Certified Planners, and is a registered architect in fourteen states.

Nancy Kitchell once told an interviewer she regarded herself as more of a "tailor and collagist reflecting the lives of interesting people" than an interior designer.

It mirrors not only her strong belief in the collaborative effort but a genuine affinity for clients. As a result, Kitchell Interior Design Associates has earned a reputation for excellence in high-end residential and commercial design.

"New construction, remodels—we do it all," says Kitchell, who started her Scottsdale business twenty years ago with the late Brad Newlon, a noted interior designer. Typically, Kitchell is involved with a project from its earliest stages, which often includes consultations with the architect. "We do as much or as little as the client desires," she says.

While Kitchell Interior Design Associates has custom-tailored scores of Valley homes and businesses, it also counts clientele in such out-of-state locales as Los Angeles, Chicago, Carmel, La Jolla, Jackson Hole, Aspen, and Montecito. Notable local commercial projects include the 8700 Restaurant in north Scottsdale, the Thea Swengel Shoe Store at the Borgata, and Founders Bank of Scottsdale.

Kitchell has a flexible approach to design, but is noted for her thematic use of local and regional art, particularly that which is primitive or folk-based. Moreover, she delights in textiles—or, as she says, "all manner of woven things."

To glean an insight into Kitchell's work, one need only visit the main room of her contemporary Southwestern home in Scottsdale. The house itself is an elemental rectangular "box" built of cement blocks and gray stucco. After entering through a sculpted five-inch-thick door of brushed aluminum, visitors find themselves in a capacious room containing two fireplaces along the same wall. The room serves not only as the living area but the dining and entertainment area as well. White walls counterpoint eclectic furnishings bathed in earth tones. It is, as Kitchell says, "casual, comfortable, and interesting."

Although Kitchell is, in her own words, "not one to seek awards," she has garnered honors from the National Association of the Remodeling Industry, the National Trust for Historic Preservation, and the American Association of Architects. She also has earned kudos from *House Beautiful* magazine and its design book, *Great Style*. For the past two years, *House Beautiful* has chosen Kitchell for its annual listing of "America's Top 100 Designers."

Kitchell is a longtime patron of the arts, having served on boards and committees of the Desert Botanical Garden, Contemporary Art Forum, Arts in Parks, Phoenix Art Museum, and the Scottsdale Arts Council. She also participated in the compilation of *An Illustrated Catalog of the Work of Phillip C. Curtis*, concerning the famed Scottsdale artist.

✧

Above: An inviting Kitchell corner in a residence at The Boulders.

Below: A perfectly appointed Kitchell interior in Paradise Valley exudes spacious comfort.

MERV GRIFFIN'S HILTON SCOTTSDALE RESORT & VILLAS

On the land where early day resident George Ellis farmed cotton, alfalfa, cantaloupe, and maize from the 1930s through the 1950s today stands one of Scottsdale's finest luxury resorts—Merv Griffin's Hilton Scottsdale Resort & Villas.

The farmland along Scottsdale Road, which was a two-lane macadam surface that ended at Lincoln Drive where it became gravel and dirt, became property too valuable to farm by the 1960s. When Robert H. Karatz came to Scottsdale from Minneapolis in 1970, he recognized the city's need for an upscale hotel to provide more hotel rooms for Scottsdale's increasing tourism industry. Hilton Scottsdale opened in 1973 and was considered "the nicest high-class resort hotel" in the area as well as the first Hilton in Arizona. The resort's first convention twenty-eight years ago was International Harvester and it has been welcoming international visitors and business travelers ever since. Recently undergoing an $18 million renovation of convention facilities and amenities, the resort has taken on a more Southwestern theme with the use of native copper and slate in the elegant porte cochere, landmark tower, and throughout the high-ceilinged, comfortable hotel lobby. Surrounding the resort's three-and-a-half-acre, seventy-foot long, free form swimming pool, are 185 elegantly appointed guest rooms and luxury suites with the latest in communication technology.

Also featured is a 10,000-square-foot Grand Ballroom with an additional 6,000 square feet of meeting space and world-class dining at Griff's just off the main lobby. Guests can dine in quiet serenity surrounded by a mural of the Grand Canyon with puffy clouds overhead. In addition, gourmet dining is available at Fleming's Prime Steak House & Wine Bar—one of the city's most popular dining establishments. Recent additions include a kosher kitchen, outdoor bar, beauty salon, bi-level fitness center, and car rental desk and business center in order to offer complete services to guests.

Through the years, the Hilton Scottsdale has been known for its intimate setting and central location whether for business or pleasure including tennis and golf vacations. On the trolley line to Old Town Scottsdale, the Arts District and Fifth Avenue as well as Scottsdale Fashion Square, the resort is close to golf courses, parks, recreational venues, and over 100 boutiques and restaurants. Since the twenty-acre resort opened in January 1973, it has had three owners: Karatz, Trammel Crow, and entertainer, entrepreneur, and humanitarian Merv Griffin, who added the Hilton Scottsdale to his portfolio in 1994. The Griffin lodgings include the Beverly Hilton, Miami Beach's Blue Moon Hotel, the Givenchy Resort and Spa in Palm Springs, and the St. Clerans Manor House in County Galway, Ireland, once owned by film director, John Huston. Griffin's portfolio also included the Wickenburg Inn & Dude Ranch until November 2000 when he generously donated the 192-acre ranch to the Scottsdale-based Childhelp USA. The $10 million property has become a residential treatment center serving severely abused children. In honor of its donor the center has been named Childhelp's Merv Griffin Village.

Just as his predecessor, Robert Karatz, who had the vision to build the first Scottsdale Hilton and who has devoted the past thirty years to serving his adopted city, Merv Griffin will be remembered not only for updating the world-class hotel, but for making life more meaningful for Arizona's abused and neglected children.

Above: A jewel in Scottsdale's resort scene, the Hilton Scottsdale's recent facelift featuring native copper and slate gives a Southwestern sophisticated look to the porte cochere and landmark tower.

Below: A lush green oasis in the desert is offered at Merv Griffin's Hilton Scottsdale Resort around this free form swimming pool and terraced patio.

At Grayhawk, residents have the freedom to customize their lives in a location many consider to be one of the finest in the nation. Located three miles north of Frank Lloyd Wright Boulevard between Scottsdale and Pima Roads, Grayhawk is in the hub of the prestigious north Scottsdale corridor, providing countless lifestyle advantages within its 1,600 acres.

"At Grayhawk, we feel like we're living in a small town with all the benefits of a close-knit neighborhood," said Roger Mann, a Grayhawk resident for four years. "My wife and I have enjoyed the sanctuary Grayhawk's community provides with the added convenience of being just minutes away from the city."

Nestled between its two award-winning daily-fee golf courses, the Grayhawk community contains several of the Valley's finest homebuilders specializing in single-family homes, town homes, condominiums and custom home sites.

Providing more than simply a place to live, Grayhawk also works to build a sense of community. The nearby Grayhawk clubhouse provides an ideal location for community get-togethers with its exceptional amenities and services, including its two outstanding restaurants—Phil's Grill and the Quill Creek Café—located within the clubhouse.

Putting residents in touch with each other and their surroundings is the focus of life at Grayhawk. With the inception of its partnership with Cox Communications and CyberSmart, Grayhawk takes this concept a step further by becoming one of Scottsdale's first master-planned "cyber communities." The three companies have teamed up to provide sophisticated technology that opens the door to a whole new way of connecting with family, friends, and the community.

Grayhawk residents also benefit from other community features, such as thirty miles of hiking, biking, and jogging trails; barbecue pavilions; tennis courts; and neighborhood swimming pools. The community's two distinct, yet interconnected neighborhoods, The Park and The Retreat, offer a fifteen-acre park, playgrounds, schools, volleyball and basketball courts, multi-use fields, a future medical campus and a proposed future resort complex.

Additionally, every Grayhawk resident has access to the resident program director, who maintains a yearly calendar of sporting events, social functions and cultural activities designed to help residents get to know one another and customize their lives while taking advantage of all Grayhawk has to offer. You may visit Grayhawk on the web at www.grayhawk.com or call at (480) 502-1547.

SUMMERFIELD SUITES BY WYNDHAM

Sharon Karel isn't your usual guest at Scottsdale's Summerfield Suites by Wyndham. She isn't a winter visitor or a business traveler. Nor is she part of a vacationing family.

Karel is a full-time resident at the hotel, which gives her a 360-degree perspective, so to speak.

"It's one of the nicest places for people like myself or people who want an extended stay," says Karel, who has lived there two years. "You are treated with special care."

"Everyone is attentive. When you come in at night you get a 'Hello.' When you're not there, they worry about you. No task is too great or small for the staff; they keep working until the job is done. Also, you can call the guys in maintenance in the middle of the night—they're on beepers—and they will come."

What makes Karel happy, of course, is likely to make other guests happy as well. In addition to its unexcelled service, Summerfield Suites by Wyndham also offers superb amenities, guest suites, business facilities, and dining options. Moreover, it is centrally located on Drinkwater Boulevard in Old Town, a stone's throw from world class dining and shopping.

"You can practically walk to Fashion Square," Karel says, referring to the famed mall just west of the hotel. Fashion Square features 220 retail outlets, including 60 stores not found anywhere else in Arizona, including Nordstrom, Brooks Brothers, Tiffany's, and Dana Buchman.

Summerfield Suites by Wyndham also is close to the Scottsdale Center for the Arts and Scottsdale Stadium, the site of popular spring training games. Nearby Main Street and Marshall Way offers an array of arts and crafts galleries, while fine restaurants abound throughout the city.

Guests are entitled to complimentary van service (based on availability) within a five-mile radius of the hotel. Those with other transportation needs will find ready assistance from special hotel representatives.

Valley-wide attractions include Biltmore Fashion Park, the Phoenix Zoo, Desert Botanical Gardens and the western theme town of Rawhide. Sports fans are only minutes away from the Phoenix Suns and Phoenix Coyotes at America West Arena, or the Arizona Diamondbacks at Bank One Ball Park.

Karel, who finds the "homey" ambiance of Summerfield Suites by Wyndham "conducive to the lifestyle I prefer" calls her one-bedroom/one-bath suite "a mini-apartment with maid service. I have televisions in the living room and the bedroom, and a fully equipped kitchen. It's comfortable."

Summerfield Suites by Wyndham also offers a two-bedroom/two-bath suite. Each of its 163 guest suites features a full-size desk with data port and voice mail, plus an iron

and ironing board. All kitchens include a refrigerator, microwave and coffee maker.

Business professionals, who comprise a growing number of hotel guests, or vacationers plugged into the information age, have access to:

- A meeting room for sixty
- Audio/video equipment
- Phone line with speaker/conference capability
- Overhead projectors and flip charts
- Fax transmissions and photocopying
- Catered gatherings
- An in-house meeting consultant
- A complimentary breakfast buffet for meetings, plus special menu requests
- Extension cords with power strips

Whether guests face a hectic business day or eighteen holes on the links, Summerfield Suites by Wyndham offers a healthy and delicious complimentary breakfast buffet. The menu includes cereal, fruit, homemade muffins, breads, juices, and coffee. At day's end, guests can relax at a complimentary social hour featuring beer, wine, sodas, and light appetizers, such as veggies. Delivery service is available from local area restaurants.

For ardent golfers who like to plan ahead, Summerfield Suites by Wyndham can reserve tee times up to 120 days in advance. This applies to such premier courses as Grayhawk, Legend Trail, Troon North, Sunridge Canyon, Eagle Mountain and Estrella Mountain Ranch.

Other guest perks include an exercise room with stationary bikes and treadmills, a swimming pool/whirlpool, a twenty-four-hour on-site convenience store featuring snacks and beverages, and on-site video rentals. Guests also receive a complimentary grocery shopping service, as well as complimentary daily newspapers and satellite television.

Summerfield Suites by Wyndham began its history as the Residence Inn Hotel in Wichita, Kansas, in 1975. By the mid-'80s, it had evolved into the Summerfield Hotel Corporation. In 1998 Summerfield and Sierra Suites merged with Patriot American/Wyndham International.

Opposite, top: For a refreshing dip or some cardiovascular laps, the pool is just what the trainer ordered.

Opposite, bottom: A guest gets in a little homework as he relaxes in one of the well-appointed suites.

Above: Informal get-togethers are easy on the patio at Scottsdale's Summerfield Suites by Wyndham.

Below: Getting the day off to a good start is a given at the healthy and delicious breakfast buffet.

HOMESTEAD SCOTTSDALE

Whether a Fortune 500 business traveler or an extended stay winter visitor, Homestead in Scottsdale offers a home away from home atmosphere within walking distance of excellent restaurants, shopping areas, movie theaters, and walking paths.

Homestead's Scottsdale property on Goldwater Boulevard and Marshall Way is one of five Homestead properties in the Valley. Others are located in Tempe, Mesa, Northwest Valley, and Deer Valley. Headquartered in Atlanta, Georgia, Homestead is one of the leading owners and operators of moderately priced, extended stay lodging properties with 136 studio style hotels in 28 states.

"Recent industry studies show that extended stay is the fastest growing segment of the lodging and hospitality market," says Homestead Area Sales Manager Al Balizado. "Currently less than one-quarter of that demand is being met."

Guests are provided with all the amenities needed whether for a few days, a week, a month, or longer. Comfortable studios include a fully equipped kitchen with full-size refrigerator, stovetop, microwave, coffeemaker, toaster, and cooking and dining utensils; a king or queen-size bed; an easy chair or sofa; an iron with full-size ironing board; a remote control television, and a twenty-four-hour on-site guest laundry.

Business travelers are catered to with personalized voice mail, a computer dataport, and a separate work area. Local calls are complimentary and copy service is available on premise. In addition, all messages, mail, faxes, and overnight packages are delivered to each guest at the end of the business day.

A personable staff looks forward to making each visitor's stay a pleasant one, adds Balizado. "Our staff prides itself in getting to know guests on a first name basis," he says adding that managers and staff consider themselves "a family whose desire is to exceed a guest's expectations."

The Scottsdale property is within walking distance or a short drive to many attractions including Old Town Scottsdale, the Main Street Galleries, Scottsdale Fashion Square, which includes Neiman Marcus and Nordstrom among its 175 retailers, and such dining establishments as P. F. Chang's China Bistro, Bandera's, Mailee's on Main, and Baby Kay's Cajun Kitchen. Guests can get a taste of the Old West by driving to northern Scottsdale to take in Rawhide's Steakhouse, located in an 1880s western town complete with cowboys, live country-western music, and stagecoach rides.

Visitors to the Scottsdale property also will find they are not far from the Scottsdale Stadium where the San Francisco Giants play their spring training games and within driving distance of 100 world-class traditional and desert golf courses. Professional football and college games as well as stage and musical productions at Arizona State University's Grady Gammage Theater are within minutes of Tempe's Homestead site. Mesa's Homestead is near the Fiesta Mall; the Northwest Valley Homestead is on West Dunlap in close proximity to downtown Phoenix where professional basketball and baseball are played and the northern most Homestead is in Deer Valley, close to Arrowhead Mall and Metro Center.

Founded in 1992, the corporation, headed by James C. Potts, president and chief operating officer, realizes annual revenue of more than $250 million. Potts served previously as managing director of Homestead; as co-chair and chief investment officer for Security Capital Atlantic, Inc.; and as a past managing director and trustee of Archstone Communities, which are apartment complexes owned by Homestead. The current managing director of

the Atlanta-based firm is Gary A. DeLapp. He is responsible for overseeing the company's operating portfolio of 136 properties and its more than 1,000 employees.

"Our Scottsdale property is situated on Goldwater and Marshall Way where early day pioneers grew sweet potatoes and alfalfa crops," notes Balizado, a member of the Scottsdale Chamber of Commerce. "We are proud to be a part of Scottsdale's tradition and history as we enter the twenty-first century."

✧

Above: Scottsdale's home away from home is one of five Homestead properties in the Valley of the Sun meeting the needs of extended stay visitors.

Below: To meet everyday needs of travelers, Homestead studios feature a fully-equipped kitchen, dataports and separate work areas.

HOMEWOOD SUITES BY HILTON

In today's global economy, it is not uncommon for professionals to spend weeks or months away from home. The old phrase about "living out of a suitcase" has taken on new emphasis.

The Valley, in particular, with its strong economy and thriving high-tech industry, has fueled a demand for extended-stay lodging, which is not likely to diminish in the foreseeable future. Not surprisingly, guests who spend a good part of their lives on the road are becoming increasingly more selective about where they stay.

Scottsdale's Homewood Suites by Hilton, an upscale business-class hotel located at 9880 North Scottsdale Road, is proving that extended stays can be both productive and enjoyable. Service is the key. "Our guests like the home-away-from-home atmosphere," says Homewood Suites by Hilton City Manager Keith Buck. "Everything they need is here."

Andy Morrell, a computer consultant who spent a year at Homewood Suites by Hilton, says: "The staff made me feel like I was a guest in somebody's house. They were the most sincere bunch of people I've come across in a long time."

During his stay, Morrell made friends with many guests. "I still talk on the phone to a couple of people from California," he says. "The hotel atmosphere is conducive to meeting people. There is no way you can go to the social hour and not meet anyone."

Buck agrees: "You meet people who are here for weeks, even months. They become part of your family. My wife and I lived here before we got our house, and she became particularly close to some winter visitors. She still e-mails about fifteen of them."

Morrell says there are two primary types of clientele. "In the winter, you get a lot of winter visitors. The rest of the time it's business people. I noticed a lot of insurance and computer professionals. Just before I arrived, there had been a group of about twenty postal managers."

Cherrie Bertsch opted for Homewood Suites by Hilton because it provided shuttle service to the Mayo Clinic, where she was receiving therapy. The Mayo Hospital is also located near the hotel. She liked the centralized location and amen-ities, which enabled her to be "self-sufficient without going to an apartment." The staff especially impressed Bertsch, who spent several months at the hotel. "If they didn't see me for a couple of days," she says, "They would call

up and ask how I was doing. They are geared beyond [conventional] hotel service."

"Home-away-from-home" is a phrase Homewood Suites by Hilton hospitality associates work hard to make a reality. Homewood Suites begins with courtesy and a desire to put guests at ease. It is reflected in prompt, friendly service and accommodations that leave them wanting for nothing.

For example, each suite features a fully equipped kitchen, separate living room and bedroom, a pullout sofa and hair dryer, plus a full-size iron and board. In addition, there are two televisions, a videocassette player, on-command movies and cable television. Those wishing to work "at home" are provided with data ports, two-line phones with voicemail and Internet access. Guests can do their own laundry using coin-operated machines at the hotel or send it out through a valet service.

The business center at Homewood Suites by Hilton is equipped with a computer featuring Excel and Word, plus a printer and data ports for laptops. "I used the center a lot," Morrell says. Copies can be made and faxes sent (the first four fax pages are free) at the front desk. "Mayo Clinic would fax me things to save trips," Bertsch says. "If I didn't feel well, staff would bring the fax up to my room." Homewood Suites by Hilton also features two meeting rooms, the Hopi and Navajo, which can seat up to twenty people each, or they can be converted to one large room. Each room has a wet bar and white board.

The hotel shuttle service, which transports guests to destinations within a five-mile radius of the hotel, operates from 6 a.m. to 10 p.m. but is most active in the morning and late afternoon. During the day, Buck states that most guests are out. Aside from ferrying people to business meetings, the shuttle also makes stops at The Borgada shopping center, Fashion Square Mall, the Mayo Clinic, and nearby locations such as Gainey Ranch.

"We get a lot of people from Mexico who are going to the Mayo Clinic," Buck says. "They use the van not only for the clinic but to go shopping." Although the Mayo Clinic is outside the five-mile-radius, Homewood Suites of Hilton makes the exception. Bilingual staffers at the front desk strive to make Hispanic visitors feel at home.

"Sometimes, when I left the clinic after therapy, I would be exhausted," says Berstch. "But the people driving the vans were so upbeat, it turned out to be a pleasant ride. Once, when I was returning a tray after social hour, a young van driver passing me in the hall—he was very polite—took it out of my hand and returned it himself."

Homewood Suites by Hilton offers a complimentary breakfast that includes fresh bagels and fruit, scrambled eggs, coffee and tea, danish pastries, hot and cold cereals, muffins, waffles, french toast, yogurt and fruit juices. A managers reception, held Monday through Thursday from 5 to 7 p.m., features soda, wine, beer, and light meals such as

✧

Above: The Homewood Suites by Hilton pool is an excellent place to catch some Arizona sunshine, take a dip or have a cookout.

Below: A typical business center at Homewood Suites by Hilton. With Internet-accessible computers, printers, copiers and data ports, guests are guaranteed to be online.

tacos, fish and chips, spaghetti, soup, and tossed salad. Guests are given monthly calendars with a bill of fare so they can plan ahead.

The hotel also offers a twenty-four-hour convenience store—Bertsch fondly calls "the world's smallest Circle K"—that offers frozen entrees, such as Lean Cuisine, and burritos, plus a variety of snacks and sodas.

When guests staying at the hotel are unable to shop for their own groceries, Homewood Suites by Hilton does it for them. "There are days when we buy groceries for three or four rooms," Buck says. "They leave a list, and we go to the store for them. We don't charge for the service. Most guests using it are business people with a very tight schedule."

"I had limited use of my hands and wrists," says Bertsch. "So the staff did my shopping. I usually sent them to two stores, depending on what I needed. One time, when I was out, they put the perishables in my fridge. They tacked it onto the bill, so I didn't have to worry about cash."

Fitness buffs will find an exercise room equipped with treadmills, stationary bicycles and a stair-climbing machine–everything needed for a rigorous cardiovascular workout. There is also a sports court with basketball backboard and net. Those interested in pumping iron are eligible for complimentary passes to the nearby YMCA. Others may prefer a leisurely swim or just lounging around the pool, where a barbecue is provided for those wanting to grill a burger, chicken, or steak.

Homewood Suites by Hilton is also a participant of the Hilton Honors Program. The Hilton Hotel Corporation holdings include more than 1,700 hotels.

Jean Schaller likes to think of the Renaissance Scottsdale Resort as a "hideaway" because of its understated location next to The Borgata and the private elegance of its accommodations.

"We have guests who come back year after year," says Schaller, a concierge who has worked at the resort since it opened in 1980. "They say it feels like they're coming home."

Over the years, the Renaissance Scottsdale Resort has hosted thousands of leisure visitors and business professionals, along with occasional celebrities such as Sean Connery, Mark McGwire, Tea Leoni, Ernie Banks, and Morley Safer.

The resort's southwestern architecture and casita-style suites, with their beamed ceilings and spaciousness, exert a powerful attraction for those wanting to "get away from it all." The fully appointed 171 guest rooms boast 34 luxury suites and 72 one-bedroom suites. All rooms feature mini-bars and private patios, while 106 suites have hot tubs. Luxury suites have fireplaces and kitchens.

In addition, the Renaissance Scottsdale Resort is just across the street from The Borgata and its European-themed shops. There are more than ten restaurants within walking distance; among them the resort's own Moriah, acclaimed for its Mediterranean cuisine.

Less than two miles away, guests can experience world-class shopping at internationally known Scottsdale Fashion Square. Another half mile brings them to Scottsdale's Old Town, with its eclectic mix of art galleries, craft shops, restaurants and cultural venues. Those venturing farther a field will discover, all within ten miles, America West Arena, Bank One Ballpark, Arizona State University, the Heard Museum, Rawhide, and the Phoenix Zoo. Sky Harbor Airport is twenty minutes away.

Business professionals, who comprise a healthy portion of the resort's guests, will find dataports in every room and a business center equipped with the latest office machines and computers. In addition, there are nearly eight thousand square feet of meeting space equipped with technology sophisticated enough to handle the most demanding conferences and seminars.

Many guests are content to stick close to the resort and get in a couple of sets of tennis on one of four courts (two lighted). Some spend time honing their skills on the putting green or

getting a cardiovascular workout on the Parcourse jogging trail. Others play croquet or swim laps in one of two pools. For nature lovers, there are day trips to Sedona and the Grand Canyon, as well as river rafting trips, balloon rides, and Jeep tours of the desert.

"Many guests walk over to the Kerr Center," Schaller says, alluding to the nearby cultural center owned by Arizona State University. "They have free morning coffee there a couple of times a week. Sometimes students provide music."

With twenty-five acres of serene desert landscaping and Camelback Mountain as a backdrop, Renaissance Scottsdale Resort is immediately invigorating and restful. It is a civilized experience. "We've managed to keep our wonderful relaxed atmosphere," Schaller says. "Guests say that staying here really does feel like a vacation."

RENAISSANCE SCOTTSDALE RESORT

✧

Above: A couple enjoys a luxury suite at Renaissance Scottsdale Resort.

Below: A place for soaking up the Arizona sun.

ACKNOWLEDGMENTS

Researching and compiling this most recent history of Scottsdale has been a journey of discovery that I hope will continue for all involved. A host of enthusiastic collaborators helped me assemble photos and artwork that, for the most part, have never before been published. Many of the pictures are treasured family heirlooms or seldom-seen pieces in public and private collections. So many people—all sharing a love for Scottsdale—contributed time, talent and treasures that I fear I cannot thank them adequately...but I want to try to single out a few for their extraordinary contributions.

First, heartfelt appreciation to the McDowell Sonoran Land Trust for having the vision and patience to take on this complex project. Most particularly I want to thank the Land Trust's heart, soul, and executive director, Carla, who gave countless hours toward making this book a success. The Land Trust's board member emeritus, Carol Schatt, also spent untold hours encouraging, enabling, and editing the text for *Historic Scottsdale*.

For sharing their technical expertise, I thank Greg Woodall, archaeologist; Professor Ed Stump, geologist; and JoAnn Handley, curator of the Scottsdale Historical Society. Judy Register, Leigh Conrad, and the staff of the Southwest Research Room of the Scottsdale Public Library were all exceptionally helpful in providing me research materials, as were the staff of the Luhrs Reading Room at Arizona State University's Hayden Library, the Arizona Historical Foundation, the Arizona Historical Society library in Tucson, and the Arizona Department of Libraries, Archives and Public Records.

Nearly every department of the City of Scottsdale assisted in my research, from the Airport, to Records, to Community Planning, to Preservation, to Water, to Communications and Public Affairs, to the Clerk's Office, and more. The Scottsdale Chamber of Commerce was quite helpful as well.

The most enjoyable part of researching this book was visiting with dozens of Scottsdale area residents and businesses that invited me into their homes and offices to share photos, artwork, mementos, and memories. Among those who were extraordinarily helpful were Virgie Lutes Brown, E.O. Brown, and Jeryl Brown Varsolona (all descendents of Scottsdale pioneer E.O. Brown); Kax Herberger, Paul Messinger, Dr. Joe Carson Smith, Rachel and Janie Ellis, Del Jeanne Palmer West, and Ileen Snoddy (SRP archivist).

Authors usually recognize their spouses, and I won't be the exception...for an unusual reason. One month before the book was due, I broke my ankle and was basically housebound. My husband Gene took time off from his busy career as a pilot to pick up photos, drive me to appointments, and do the myriad of errands required to finish the book.

To the staff at Historical Publishing Network, my thanks for combining your many talents to ensure that *Historic Scottsdale: A Life from the Land* was a beautifully designed and executed book.

My final thanks go to the past, present, and future citizens of Scottsdale—for making and keeping our city such an interesting subject, and for preserving the bits and pieces that make up our rich heritage. I hope future generations will appreciate what we've saved, and continue to preserve our history.

Joan Fudala

BIBLIOGRAPHY

Geology of Arizona, Dale Nations and Ed Stump, 1983

Personal interview, Professor Edmund Stump, PhD, Department of Geological Sciences, Arizona State University

Brad Archer, curator, Arizona State University Geology Museum

Personal interview, Greg Woodall, McDowell Sonoran Land Trust, Scottsdale

"Geologic Highlights of the Phoenix Region," by Stephen J. Reynolds/Arizona Geological Survey, Fieldnotes, Fall 1987

"North Scottsdale Reconnaissance Survey," prepared for the City of Scottsdale by RECON Regional Environmental Consultants, September 21, 1987

"Scottsdale Seeks Sustainability 2000 Report," City of Scottsdale Department of Environmental Planning, 2000

Guidebook to the Geology of Central Arizona, edited by Donald M. Burt and Troy L. Pewe, Special Paper No. 2, State of Arizona Bureau of Geology & Mineral Technology, reprinted 1987

A Natural History of the Sonoran Desert, edited by Steven J. Phillips and Patricia Wentworth Comus, Arizona-Sonora Desert Museum Press and University of California Press, 2000

Roadside Geology of Arizona, Halka Chronic, Mountain Press Publishing Company, 1983

Dr. Liz Slauson, Desert Botanical Garden

Personal interview, Virginia Korte, Director, Center for Native and Urban Wildlife, Scottsdale Community College

Arizona Fish and Game Department pamphlets

Parrot fact sheet, The Phoenix Zoo

"Wildlife Through Arizona's Ages," Arizona Highways, Carroll Lane Fenton, March 1960

"Urban Raptors," Guy Webster, Tribune Newspapers, March 18, 2000

Arizona Wildlife Viewing Guide, John H. Carr, Falcon Press, 1992

Camelback : Sacred Mountain of Phoenix, Gary Driggs, Arizona Historical Foundation, Arizona State University, 1998

Western Region Climate Center Web site, (November 2000)

Those Who Came Before - Southwestern Archaeology in the National Park System, Robert H. Lister and Florence C. Lister, Southwest Parks and Monuments Association, 1983

Exploring the Hohokam : Prehistoric Desert Peoples of the American Southwest, edited by George J. Gumerman, University of New Mexico Press, 1991

McDowell Mountains Archaeological Symposium, edited by K.J. Schroeder, City of Scottsdale, 1999

Archaeological Investigation of Parcel M at Troon Village, K.J. Schroeder, Roadrunner Publications, 1994

Scottsdale millennium series: yesterday, today & tomorrow: Prehistoric Arizona, videocassette, City of Scottsdale, 2000

Winfield Scott - A Biography of Scottsdale's Founder, by Dick Lynch, published by the City of Scottsdale, 1978

Studies in Arizona History, Julie A. Campbell, Arizona Historical Society, 1998

Salt River Pima-Maricopa Indian Community Web site, (November 2000)

"History and Geology of the McDowell Mountain Regional Park Area," McDowell Park Association, 1999

Vanished Arizona: Recollections of the Army Life of a New England Woman, Martha Summerhayes, 1960

"Photographs, Written Historical and Descriptive Data, Reduced Copies of Drawings, Arizona Canal, HAER Report No. AZ-19," Shelly C. Dudley, Salt River Project Research Archives, 1991

SRP Pamphlet, "SRP Canals," 2-97

The Taming of the Salt, Salt River Project, 1979

Portrait of a Heritage : A Photographic Study of the Pima and Maricopa Indians from 1870 to 1970, Valley National Bank of Arizona, 1970

A Pima Past, Anna Moore Shaw, The University of Arizona Press, 1974

The Papago Indians of Arizona and their Relatives the Pima, Ruth Underhill, PhD, Department of the Interior, 1979

Verde Valley Lore, Bob Mason, L.J. Schuster Company, 1997

The Last Bugle Call: A History of Fort McDowell, Bill Reed, McLain Printing Company, 1977

Carefree Cave Creek Foothills: Life in the Sonoran Sun, Foothills Community Foundation, 1990

Phoenix: The History of a Southwestern Metropolis, Bradford Luckingham, University of Arizona Press, 1989

Arizona, A Cavalcade of History, Marshall Trimble, Treasure Chest Publications, 1989

An Arizona Chronology, Douglas DeVeny Martin, University of Arizona Press, 1963-1966

Arizona, Historic Land, Bert M. Fireman, with a foreword by Lawrence Clark Powell, Knopf, 1982

Personal interview, E.O. Brown, grandson of Scottsdale pioneer E.O. Brown; son of E.E. Brown

Personal interview, Jean Thomas Scott, granddaughter of Sarah Ellen Coldwell Thomas, daughter of George Thomas, Sr.

Personal interview, Dr. Joe Carson Smith, grandson of Charles and Clara Coldwell; son of Jackie and Nora Smith

The History of the Scottsdale School System at Scottsdale, Arizona 1896-1944 by Wilburn W. Dick, Arizona State Teachers College, 1944

The Authentic History of Scottsdale, Arizona since 1891. Byrd H. Granger, Scottsdale Convention and News Bureau, 1956

The Story of Scottsdale, David S. Matthews, 1965

Jewel of the Desert, Patricia Seitters Myers, Windsor Publications, 1984

Arizona Republican, June 1898

Arizona: Its People and Resources, Jack Lee Cross, University of Arizona Press, 1960

Personal interview, Virgie Lutes Brown, widow of Alvin "Cotton" Brown and daughter of Carlton and Lucy Lutes

Personal interview, Dorothy Cavalliere Ketchum Roberts

Personal interview, Thelma Holveck

Personal interview, Paul Messinger

Personal interviews, Rachel & Janie Ellis

Personal interview, Del Jeanne Palmer West, daughter of K.T. Palmer

Personal interview, Chester Chatham

Scottsdale Photo Album: Yesterday and Today, Scottsdale, Arizona, 1989

For Land's Sake: The Autobiography of a Dynamic Arizonan, Kenyon T. Palmer, 1971

Caro Amigo, the Autobiography of Jesus C. Corral, Jesus Corral, Westernlore Press, 1984

Reflections on Early Scottsdale, the way it was, Bill Kimsey, 1987

Road to Scottsdale, Albert J. Lieber, foreword by Kurt Vonnegut, A.J. Lieber, 1999

The New Deal in Arizona, William S. Collins, Arizona State Parks Board, 1999

The Faust-Ball Tunnel, John Hammond Moore, Random House, 1978

An Economic, Political and Social Survey of Phoenix and the Valley of the Sun,
    Arthur G. Horton, Southside Progress, 1941

Various editions of the Southside Progress, Tempe, Arizona, 1937-38

Various files, Scottsdale Historical Society

Arizona Highways, Arizona Department of Transportation, various issues

Personal interview, Bill Arthur

Personal interview, The Honorable William P. Schrader

Personal interview, Pat Thompson, The Sketch Book

Personal interview, Wesley Segner

Personal interview, The Honorable Bill Jenkins

Personal interview, Katherine "Kax" Herberger

Personal interview, Roberta Pilcher

The Bob Herberger Story, Jim Smith, privately published, 1990

"Roman Report, a chronology of the Scottsdale Airport/Airpark,"
    Roman & Associates,1986

Scottsdale Progress and Scottsdale Tribune various issues, 1948-2000

The Arizonian, various issues, 1953-1969

Various files, Arizona Historical Society, Central Arizona and
    Southern Arizona archives

Various files, State of Arizona, Department of Libraries, Archives and Public
    Records – Arizona Collection

Various files, Luhrs Reading Room, Arizona Collection, Arizona State University,
    Hayden Library

Various files, including The Krause Collection, Arizona Historical Foundation

Personal scrapbooks, the Ed Tweed family, BruSally Ranch

The Central Arizona Project, 1918-1968, Rich Johnson,
    The University of Arizona Press, 1977

Information provided by City of Scottsdale Water Resources Department,
    Dave Mansfield and Bob Berlese

City of Scottsdale annual reports

Personal interview, Dick Bowers, former Scottsdale City Manager

Personal interview, The Honorable Sam K. Campana

The Arizona Republic/The Phoenix Gazette, various issues, 1970-2000

"Exploring Scottsdale's Northern Border," Judith Smith, Scottsdale Scene, August 1986

"Indian Bend Wash," City of Scottsdale Communications and Public Affairs
    pamphlet, 1985

City of Scottsdale Web site, (November 2000)

"Scottsdale/Paradise Valley Lodging Statistics, Part I," City of Scottsdale, January 2000

Vertical files, Southwest Research Room, Scottsdale Public Library

"Scottsdale Visioning Report," City of Scottsdale, 1992

City of Scottsdale Hillside Ordinances, 1977, 1978, 1979

City of Scottsdale Environmentally Sensitive Land Ordinance, 1991

City of Scottsdale McDowell Sonoran Preserve fact sheets and newsletters

Personal interview, Robert J. Cafarella, City of Scottsdale Preservation Director

Personal interview, Jane Rau, co-founder, McDowell Sonoran Land Trust (MSLT)

Carla (her full legal name), Executive Director, MSLT

Arizona Department of Water Resources Web site (September 2000)

RESOURCES FOR SCOTTSDALE HISTORICAL INFORMATION AND EXPERIENCES:

If your interest is piqued, here are additional ways to learn more about Scottsdale and Arizona history (or to research your family history in Arizona):

Southwest Room, Scottsdale Civic Center Library, 3839 N. Drinkwater Blvd., (480) 312-2693. Public access archives, books, directories, yearbooks, and periodicals.

Scottsdale Historical Society Museum, 7333 Scottsdale Mall, (480)945-4499. Call for hours to see Scottsdale's original Little Red Schoolhouse, built in 1909, now a museum of Scottsdale history.

Arizona Collection – Luhrs Reading Room, Arizona State University, 4th Floor, Hayden Library, (480) 965-4932. Books, periodicals, documents, photos, manuscripts, databases, reference services.

Arizona Historical Foundation, 4th Floor, Hayden Library, Arizona State University, (480) 965-3283. Founded in 1959 by the late Sen. Barry Goldwater, it is a full range, regionally specific historical repository that collects every means of storing information: books, manuscripts, videos, films, photos, newspapers, personal papers, collections, etc.

Arizona Historical Society, Central Arizona Division Museum, 1300 N. College Avenue in Papago Park, (480) 929-0292. Changing exhibits, Historymakers display, library, and archives. Also has museums and archives in Tucson and Flagstaff. Tucson archives contain good Scottsdale information, photos, and documents.

State Research Library, Arizona Department of Libraries, Archives and Public Records, State Capitol Mall, 1700 W. Washington Avenue, Phoenix, AZ 85007, (602) 542-3701. Arizona Collection, Photo Archives, Arizona Newspaper Project, genealogy research room, maps collection, state and federal agency publications

Local, private archives or museums that have information and/or photos on Scottsdale include: **Taliesin West/Frank Lloyd Wright Foundation**, **Salt River Project**, **Arizona Military Museum library**, **ASU Geology Museum**.

The Government Documents Section of Arizona State University's **Hayden Library** also contains numerous documents, reports, studies and publications of/about the City of Scottsdale since incorporation in 1951.

Scottsdale's **CityCable 11** airs programs on Scottsdale history; pick up a schedule at any Scottsdale public library, citizen service center or City Hall.

(INFORMATION CURRENT AS OF NOVEMBER 2000)

INDEX

SPONSORS